How to Read Hegel Now

HOW TO READ HEGEL NOW

Shannon Hoff

The University of Chicago Press   Chicago and London

The University of Chicago Press, Chicago 60637
The University of Chicago Press, Ltd., London
© 2026 by The University of Chicago
All rights reserved. No part of this book may be used or reproduced in any manner whatsoever without written permission, except in the case of brief quotations in critical articles and reviews. For more information, contact the University of Chicago Press, 1427 E. 60th St., Chicago, IL 60637.
Published 2026
Printed and bound by CPI Group (UK) Ltd, Croydon, CR0 4YY

35 34 33 32 31 30 29 28 27 26   1 2 3 4 5

ISBN-13: 978-0-226-84707-8 (cloth)
ISBN-13: 978-0-226-84708-5 (paper)
ISBN-13: 978-0-226-84709-2 (ebook)
DOI: https://doi.org/10.7208/chicago/9780226847092.001.0001

Library of Congress Cataloging-in-Publication Data

Names: Hoff, Shannon author
Title: How to read Hegel now / Shannon Hoff.
Description: Chicago : The University of Chicago Press, 2026. | Includes bibliographical references and index.
Identifiers: LCCN 2025032543 | ISBN 9780226847078 cloth | ISBN 9780226847085 paperback | ISBN 9780226847092 ebook
Subjects: LCSH: Hegel, Georg Wilhelm Friedrich, 1770–1831 | Liberty
Classification: LCC B2948 .H544 2026
LC record available at https://lccn.loc.gov/2025032543

♾ This paper meets the requirements of ANSI/NISO Z39.48-1992 (Permanence of Paper).

Authorized Representative for EU General Product Safety Regulation (GPSR) queries: **Easy Access System Europe**—Mustamäe tee 50, 10621 Tallinn, Estonia, gpsr.requests@easproject.com
Any other queries: https://press.uchicago.edu/press/contact.html

*This book is for all the curious and generative readers
of philosophy with whom I imagined myself speaking in writing it*

She would not say ... I am this, I am that.

VIRGINIA WOOLF, *Mrs. Dalloway*

CONTENTS

INTRODUCTION 1
Reading a Tradition 1
The Ideas and the Interlocutors 9

CHAPTER ONE: HOW "WE" LIVE NOW 19
Revolutionary Existence 22
Hegel's Alternative 24

CHAPTER TWO: RECOGNITION 27
The Struggle to the Death 27
Mastery and Servitude 33
Fanon and Racist Perception 42
Benjamin on the Mother-Other 56
Coda: Hegel on Gender 67

CHAPTER THREE: ETHICAL LIFE 74
Greek Ethical Life 80
Ethical Life and Philosophy 87
Coulthard, la paperson, and Settler Colonialism 119
Mahmood, Abu-Lughod, and Colonial Feminism 129

CHAPTER FOUR: CONSCIENCE 141
The Determinacies and Relations of Conscience 143
Fanon, Merleau-Ponty, and Liberalism 151
Absolute Spirit 164

CHAPTER FIVE: OBJECTIVE SPIRIT 174
The Dimensions of Materiality 175
Canguilhem, Garland-Thomson, and Ableism 189
Hegel on Civil Society, State, Constitution, and Government 197

CONCLUSION 223

Acknowledgments 225
Notes 229
References 239
Index 249

INTRODUCTION

Reading a Tradition

The content of the philosophical tradition can sometimes seem indifferent to or incompatible with liberatory concerns and projects. Those moved by issues of justice can find themselves recoiling both from the words of traditional philosophical texts as well as from those engaged with them, and go elsewhere for the pursuit of their commitments. Others remain, but suspiciously: Are the goods offered by philosophy fundamentally contaminated by the exclusion of those who have been perceived as idiosyncratic from the point of view of prevailing norms?[1] Meanwhile, rifts emerge in philosophical communities, between those who cannot imagine ignoring such questions and those who cannot imagine being unswayed by traditional sources.

This is complicated and contentious terrain, made more challenging by the fact that we are always already inside the traditions we query, and so the resources by which we answer to our concerns tend to draw on the philosophy in question. If we are trained in philosophy, we are trained in and through these traditions; they have shaped our sense of the nature of philosophy and what we think when we do it. Consideration of the possibly gendered nature of reason or the racist and colonial assumptions of social and political philosophy, for instance, seems to call for contemplation of the nature of reason and social life, in which case it often finds itself scurrying down the same rabbit holes traversed by, say, Locke, Plato, and Kant. Further, to decide whether any given philosophical account is thoroughly "contaminated," we would have to be inducted into said philosophy; this takes time, the effort of digesting its implicit projection of indifference or hostility toward oneself if one is not counted by it, and also its meaningful incorporation into our perspective, which means that getting to the standpoint from which we could meaningfully assess whether philosophy is ultimately contaminated would seem to paradoxically require one to expose oneself to that contamination. Those who would invest such time and effort find their loyalties divided and their task doubled: It takes time to be inducted, and it takes time to elaborate one's concerns about exclusion and about the complicity in exclusion of that into which one would be inducted.

This project is essentially a result of these divided loyalties and this doubled task, and hopes to work through some of these challenges. It is a small attempt to reconcile, through the figure of Hegel, an appreciation of the philosophical tradition with a commitment to emancipatory politics, and to center the purposes of emancipatory politics in interaction with the philosophical tradition. I began to study Hegel many years ago for probably two reasons: First, I thought that at least I would learn a lot just by doing the work it would take to understand it; but second, and more importantly, I was taken by the subtle ways in which he managed to juggle truths that seemed important and yet in tension with each other. At that time (and still now), I was interested in these two truths—that we are individuals, and that those who built the world we inherit and those with whom we now share it can "get inside of us" in debilitating ways. It was important to me, politically, that this vulnerability to others be recognized; my experience growing up in a religious community with some influential conservative adherents had made me allergic to the view that "hard knocks" were simply a matter of individual responsibility and not an effect of disempowering relations. For better or worse, this book exists because of that twenty-one-year-old's dismay about the harsh attitudes circulating in her own social context, and her (uninformed) sense that Hegel provided the best philosophical building blocks by which to speak to the problems of exclusion and injustice relevant there. This sense opened the path of the dual task—to study and articulate, first, Hegel's philosophy, and, second, contemporary diagnoses of the problems of social life.

In fact, one of the central points of Hegel's philosophy is that thinking is inspired by its own concrete world; that it happens in situ, in history, never separate from the determinate "attentions and utensils" (Merleau-Ponty 1964, 112) of its time and space, linked to the no-longer-present others who have thought through the issues of their own time and to the materiality that has carried their ideas into our present. This happens to thinking in ways it can never fully comprehend, since what seems to demand consideration resonates for the thinking being because of the specificity of its own irretrievable history. What is to be thought makes a claim upon us for reasons that are entangled with who we already are and with our history, and we attend to it not as generic thinkers but as these specific, historical beings who have cause to notice specific kinds of things in specific ways. While thinking works to consider reality beyond the confines of its own situation, it carries with it this "from"—its "body," its "place," and the meanings that moved it to consider the objects it considered. The appearance of what appears is shaped by where the thinker stands in the world and how the thinker's attention has been cultivated, the specific character of which recedes into the darkness of non-awareness.

Hegel's sensitivity to the historical determinacy of thinking supports a critical orientation to traditional sources such as his own work: These sources will be, predictably and inevitably, both complicit *and* transformative, part and parcel of systems of domination in the process of congealing, with or without their knowledge, while bringing powerful and potentially world-transforming insight to expression. Thinkers can disavow their own position, the work of their own attention, and the strings that keep them attached to their own embodied, determinate, worldly situations; they can fail to notice the way that their attention centers the preoccupations of their own world and the way the world brings certain realities to their attention while concealing others. But this is the context from which thinking unfolds and, as Hegel does, we must think through the historical determinacies by which our thinking is led and think through their hold upon us. Further, if we know that this is where thinking begins, then we can be careful about the possibility that it sees only the familiar when it is trying to look for the true.

We should notice here that a similar rootedness, a similar embeddedness in a time, or a similarly unthought inhabitation supports contemporary thinkers in seeing contemporary social problems as problems. This is what *our reality* gives us to think; in other words, our thinking is hardly the unprecedented capacity to think beyond the habits of our time. It may not be our "superior intelligence" that leads us to perceive the world's problems, but rather our enactment of the largely unreflective habits of our own time, such that moral outrage at the apparent ignorance of those who come before us can be in disavowal of the relevance of others and of history to what appear to it to be its own moral insight.[2]

Nevertheless, thinking is both rooted and aspiring, determinate and transcending. Particularly because of Hegel's sense of the importance of the "where and when" of thinking, he does not simply pursue the preoccupations of his own time but excavates the thought of other determinate worlds. In his work we see a more or less unprecedented historical and intercultural sensitivity coming to life in so-called Western philosophy and demanding the name "philosophy." The aspiring and transcending capacity of his own thought, its capacity to illuminate the one-sidedness of his own time, is aided by this historical mindset, by the experience of bringing to life the thought of other times and peoples alongside his own. Further, his work goes beyond its own embeddedness in feeding future thought: When a text opens us up to the experience of the ongoing unfolding of meaning and is fed by our own investment, our own cultivation as readers, and our own situations as much as by its own content, then it continues to be alive and fertile, to foster thought. The thinking of the text is thus never "over"—and so we use the present tense when citing the words of dead authors. Thinking is expansive; it proliferates; it becomes something new in relation to new forms of determinacy.

My sense—having experienced the expansiveness of Hegel's philosophy and the urgent demands presented by pervasive practices of injustice—is that this philosophy has tremendous resources for addressing political problems to which it may not have been particularly alive, and that its power in this regard should not be jettisoned. Stephen Houlgate captures it well when he says, in an interview, that we might not in fact have "got to Hegel yet": "there is such a lot of Hegel and of our world that hasn't been explored yet in the way that Hegel would do or we as Hegelians would do" (2024). Houlgate identifies particularly Hegel's critique of the liberalism that makes the individual into the primary unit and ontological foundation for social organization, and the import, grounded in mutual recognition, of forming associations with each other. I too find profound fertility in Hegel's work in relation to contemporary social issues, and I want to illuminate the answers that keep pulling me back, as they help me make sense of issues with which they may not have explicitly conversed. This engagement is possible most basically because Hegel is a thinker of relations, cultures, contexts, structures, and history, and these are relational, contextual, structural, cultural, and historical problems. If these ideas admit of becoming powerful means for confronting forms of domination to which they were not particularly alive, I believe it is important to mobilize them for that purpose and to undermine their possible use in opposed or indifferent projects.

This work is mobilized, then, by the conviction that it can be of significant value to feminist, anticolonial, antiracist, anti-ableist, and anticapitalist projects to read and deploy Hegel and to channel the trajectory of Hegel scholarship and philosophy as such in those directions. It is mobilized also by the conviction that the value of this scholarship depends on our use, on people bringing it to life inside of their determinate situations, and that it is of significant value to Hegel's philosophy as such to approach it through the lens of such concerns, since they in turn expand or reveal the sense it has; their concreteness lends itself to its expansion and clarification. Other ways of thinking, that is, can enliven Hegel's text in new ways, as he would be the first to affirm, given the concrete and historical thinker he is. Thus I intend this project both to give readers better insight into Hegel's philosophy, as well as to show what it means in interaction with contemporary political thinkers who are preoccupied with issues beyond those that seemed to have concerned him. To invoke Gayle Rubin's similar orientation to Freud, this "is not for the sake of [Hegel's] good name" (1975, 184). Rather, this project is intended to mobilize several of his most profound ideas because resistance to oppression is a cause that calls for the best resources we can muster.

I take this to be one strategy among many, part of a family of different kinds of efforts, not as the only mode of *rapprochement* with the history of philosophy. My project here is to help make it philosophically mainstream to draw on figures from the Western philosophical tradition (which is the tradition in which I have found myself) for critique of what is also their heritage: racist, capitalist, sexist, ableist, and colonial domination. This particular strategy is not without risks, particularly that of the ongoing privileging of "Western" interests and traditions and the neglect of that of others, and thus it is enacted in the belief that there are other vital strategies as well. The project also brings in other thinkers and traditions to do the work of diagnosing and addressing the social problems that Hegel is used to address. It aims at what Linda Martín Alcoff has called "internal Western critique": first, I would say, by exposing a tradition's own critical orientation to the temptations and shortcomings of its world, many of which continue to operate today; second, by wresting elements of that tradition from their original contexts and appropriating them for the needs of our time; and third, by showing through dialogue with those who are othered by that tradition its "simplification and repudiation of non-Western thought" (Alcoff 2007, 91).

Before introducing the specific ideas in Hegel's philosophy that seem particularly productive for engagement with contemporary political discourse, I want to address the more basic question of why we would use Hegel to address problems such as racism, sexism, colonialism, ableism, and capitalism when he does not seem significantly alive to these problems and when we might think that there are better options. Readers might have in mind the following: (a) He characterizes the women of ancient Greek ethical life as "the eternal irony of the community" in the *Phenomenology of Spirit* (PS §474/PG 259) and sequesters them in the domestic arena in the *Philosophy of Right* (PR/GPR §166); (b) his writing on race and colonialism seems at times to be racist and colonialist, and student notes register that in lectures Hegel spoke of American Indigenous people, Indians, Asians, and Africans in ways that could be interpreted to recommend or justify colonialism (see "The New World" and "The Old World" in *LPWH* 162–94/*VPW* 198–241); (c) with the exception of a discussion of mental illness or "derangement" (*die Verrücktheit*) in the *Encyclopaedia*'s "Anthropology" (*PM/E* §408), he does not speak of issues of ableism and disability; and (d) he does not seem to directly target capitalism, and the equation of the actual with the rational in his political-economic writing, as well as his presentation of a civil society that prioritizes freedom in individual enterprise and engenders poverty, seems possibly consistent with capitalist exploitation. The answer to why we would go to such a source cannot come in one sentence, however, because it depends on the work of presenting these ideas and showing how they interact with existing arguments and modes of opposition against domination, which is the overall project of the book. Here, however, I will briefly outline a proposal for a dual strategy that I believe is called for by our very existence in a scholarly tradition: first, scholarly engagement; and second, a critical pairing that would carry the powerful ideas of the past into the present and future.

Philosophy is done by a community of philosophers, however at odds or disjointed it might be, and how we do philosophy and what we choose to talk about has an effect on those who also inhabit the world of philosophy. Philosophy is not just a move we make in the domain of truth, but a move we make in this interpersonal domain, in ways that support or undermine its health and ongoing activity. This domain is characterized by concrete people: singular beings with singular lives, but also people whose particularities are taken by their social worlds to be defining in specific ways. Namely, they are swept up in racial, economic, sexual, gendered, material, religious, and cultural systems of meaning; or, they are people of color and they are white; they are working class, poor, middle class, and wealthy; they are oriented to specific kinds of sexual intimacy with others; they appear in gendered terms to gendered perception; they are disabled and nondisabled; they have relations to religious traditions; they inhabit different cultural worlds and historical trajectories. Many of these concrete readers, scholars, and students of philosophy find that philosophy excludes or degrades them, and it can be hard to encounter and work through these texts without first doing some kind of personal reckoning: namely, grappling with the effect of being excluded, by virtue of one's particularities, from the very thing one is learning to care about. Results of that reckoning are various and can have significant impact on the discipline of philosophy:

We turn away from the offending texts; we critique them; we work to digest the harm; we build ourselves up in communities of like-minded people and engage with philosophy motivated by the concerns of that community; we work through or suppress the challenges of that initial encounter; we project what the philosophy would be like had it had the good sense to actually "count" us. When readers of philosophy do not do this reckoning, or do not feel or acknowledge the need for it, this has an effect on the way the philosophical community feels to those who do. In this vein, Robert Bernasconi argues that "subtle strategies to play down the racism of Locke, Kant and Hegel, among others" has "the inevitable consequence that, for example, in the United States philosophers are disproportionately white" (2003, 35; see also Zambrana [2016]). In other words, work to downplay the racism of philosophical texts can be the final straw cementing the exclusion of those who already have to work too hard to locate themselves in the universal human "we." It might seem all very well and good to defend Hegel's or Kant's ideas in the name of their power, for instance, but one is never simply doing that; one is also making an intersubjective gesture, and we should all keep in mind the philosophical community we touch with our words, not simply the issue of the "truth of the matter," as if they could even be separated. This book operates with the sense that it is incumbent upon us to do both, at least in some small way—to engage with powerful traditional ideas and to honor the work of reckoning. This book works to set the stage for a possible future mutuality that has been painfully absent historically, with the hope that it will not rub salt into wounds.

Part of setting this stage is addressing exclusions at the level of language. In mobilizing the history of philosophy for the present and future, I believe it important to approach the issue of gender-related exclusions at the level of pronouns and nouns differently than is typically done. Constantly encountering gender-exclusive language in the texts through which one thinks can really chip away at one's psyche if one is excluded and falsely embolden one if one is included, and I am convinced that these world-historically intelligent people would have used nonexclusive language had they been alive today, just as ordinarily conscientious people mostly now do. Thus, I have chosen to change this language, inserting feminine and nonbinary pronouns and nouns where masculine pronouns and nouns have prevailed. The argument that it is important to note these exclusions and recognize how they are linked to the logic of the philosophy at issue might be sensible, but as I am ultimately of the view that Hegel's philosophy is useful for addressing exclusion and that inclusion needs to be accomplished, I believe it is more than worthwhile to try out this other, largely untrod avenue. In halfhearted acquiescence to scholarly convention, these changes are marked.

The question of why we would go to this source in particular also raises the issue of the supply of sources. Philosophy is difficult, and it is typically learned by reading key sources in the history of philosophy, though the relative inaccessibility of "other people's canons" means that much is yet to be thought. Nonetheless, it is difficult to imagine philosophical powers growing in someone independently of engagement with at least some of the material of one's philosophical tradition, *and* there is not an unlimited supply of profound sources, of which none will be free of the one-sided exclusions associated with their historical moment, free of their communal and cultural ties, their determinate technologies, the religious and economic practices and customs of their time. I believe that, while one could potentially get to this end through other avenues, Hegel has helped me learn how to think and pursue a basic concern for issues of justice, and pairing Hegel with those who treat these political concerns explicitly is my best way forward for mobilizing some of the tradition's powers for the present and future.

Further, one of the genuine virtues of systematic philosophy is that its ambition to be in some sense comprehensive does not permit fragmentary analyses of various pieces of experience and reality, the treatment of specific issues in abstraction from others. Systematic philosophy offers scholars of separate analyses a sense of how they relate to other pieces and how their scope is limited by another dimension of reality. It has the capacity to give pathways to thought, to guide it from one thing to a related other, to see the larger context, the conflicts and tensions, the resonances. It is not that systematic philosophy somehow projects the possibility that all of reality could be analyzed and nothing would be left for freedom and thought. Rather, it insists that, if we undertake practice and theory in abstraction from other relevant and interrelated facets of the situation, then *in theory* we will fail to do justice to the expansiveness of the human condition, and *in practice* we will mobilize forces against us of which we are ignorant, producing what Jean-Paul Sartre calls "counterfinalities" that undermine the possibility of free action (2004, 162). To handle a piece of human experience well, one must have a sense of how it contacts and affects other pieces, and how its character depends on its relations to or tensions with them.

Finally, a note about style. Hegel does not write for casual readers, or communicate very effectively with people who are not already experienced readers of his philosophy. Because he does not, I do (or try to). I want to communicate these ideas in a way that allows their potential to come alive and come across. Just as Hegel uses experiences, particularly in the *Phenomenology*, to express, check, and revise hypotheses, so also this book is filled with examples from everyday human experience, examples designed to help reveal both the rich logic at play in our experience and to make it easier to see what Hegel means, since he (and much of the scholarship on him) otherwise makes it so hard. Further, if the political problems addressed in this book are matters of concern for all of us (since, as Hegel himself would argue, our freedom depends on that of others), then it is incumbent upon us to speak clearly and not only to other scholars of Hegel. Thus this book aims to speak to an audience not already inclined toward him; to give that audience a foothold in his philosophy by elaborating his most fundamental ideas; to enliven these ideas by showing how they resonate in everyday experience; and to address issues of contemporary concern for audiences wrapped up with those concerns. Further, in seeking to cultivate a kind of wisdom and orientation that would develop in readers the capacity for mobilizing Hegel's ideas, it forgoes precise, rigorous moves at the level of scholarly detail. Yet insofar as it offers footholds in relation to scholarly conflicts and quagmires, establishes a stable point of orientation to the bewildering array of complexity in Hegel's texts, and orients attention toward issues of contemporary concern, it nevertheless aims also to be a book for Hegel scholars.

The Ideas and the Interlocutors

There are four basic ideas that operate as the cornerstones of this book: recognition, ethical life, conscience, and objective spirit. Each of them operates as a limit to the modern construal of human beings as fundamentally individual and human existence as fundamentally oriented by the ideal of an abstract rationality that can be located in each individual. Hegel's criticism of this construal is found in his critique of what he calls "culture" in the *Phenomenology of Spirit*—particularly in his analysis of the French Revolution—and in his critique of morality, which is resolved in the idea of conscience. This book begins, in the first chapter, with this context-setting critique of the French Revolution, describing not simply the idiosyncratic features of that event but the ways in which it is emblematic of globally dominant societies that operate in terms of implicit norms that resonate, through their domination, in the societies they dominate. In Hegel's analysis, the French Revolution makes free, rational, and equal individuals its priority. In the name of the individual's power of rational insight, it would overthrow social hierarchies, the rigid authority of existing customs, religious "mystification," and determinate institutions and practices that treat people differently—in short, all of the burdens of the past and of the existing, oppressive world that suppress the operation of rationality on its own clean slate. The Revolution was motivated by a disdain for the determinate, partial, and local in favor of the universal; the interpersonal in favor of the individual; the inherited in favor of what the rational being chooses; the experience of existent value in favor of the idea that values could be invented by that being.

Hegel's philosophy, writ large, could be construed as a systematic account and critique of the abstractions and disavowals associated with the Revolution and with, as I will show, contemporary political life. The Revolution, by advancing a "general human" justified by the general, shared power of rationality and in abstraction from particular human qualities and the particular spheres in which they operate, is in a sense opposed to all actual human beings. We are never universal humanity; we have specific qualities, identities, situations, and circumstances—links with the world's structures—that powerfully shape how we live and what we experience. To abolish determinacy in the name of a rational ideal, as the Revolution does, is to make human life impossible, as our lives are richly specific, implicated in specific others, pasts, worlds, and situations. While any given form of social life may need to answer to the reality of free inwardness, as the French Revolution notices, it also has to make room for and recognize the importance of our specificity, our historical and social situations, the weight of external factors upon who we are, what is local, interpersonal, determinate, unchosen. The question for us is *how to make this dual answerability real politically*.

The four basic ideas that act as limits to the revolutionary abstraction in Hegel's philosophy are *linked dimensions* of a critical response to the world of the Revolution, of modernity. Described in the *Philosophy of Right* and the *Encyclopaedia*'s discussion of "objective spirit" (which I will group together under the label "practical philosophy"), as well as in the *Phenomenology of Spirit*, these four elements are (1) recognition, illuminated negatively by the struggle to the death and the relationship between master and servant; (2) ethical life, as described in the *Phenomenology* and the practical philosophy; (3) conscience, as discussed in the *Phenomenology*, with which I will pair absolute spirit as discussed in the practical philosophy and the lectures on aesthetics; and (4) objective spirit and the significance therewith of materiality, as thematized in the treatment of the body in the *Encyclopaedia*'s "Anthropology," the *Phenomenology*'s discussion of the servant's work, and the practical philosophy's discussion of property, civil society, and the state. Together, these four ideas amount to a well-rounded account of the dimensions by which human beings are extended into the world and which are key to understanding who they are. Human life unfolds inside of concrete, historical, and determinate human relations and on the basis of an external materiality that has always already been organized in a determinate way. Hegel's philosophy, in meditating on the pairing with others and the world that is at the core of human existence, reveals the invisible, immaterial ties that link what otherwise appear as discrete subjects and objects, which do not otherwise admit so easily of perception. His philosophy is not closed to the value of basically liberal commitments, but simply opposed to their tendency to unilaterally set the terms of social and political life, and to their one-sided elaboration without all the supplement, specification, and substantiation that accrues to free individuals in their pairing with determinate, material worlds.

My method in this book is also one of pairing—namely, the pairing of Hegel, a figure who teases out the parameters of thought and existence, with other figures who are particularly apt at revealing the parameters of oppression and exclusion. Each of the following chapters will thus do two things: first, excavate a specific dimension of Hegel's philosophy in which he explores one of the challenges to this modern, revolutionary abstraction; and second, describe the ways in which the vulnerabilities and dependencies operative in these concrete relations have historically been handled poorly, and for which the assertion of free individuality has not been helpful, by pairing his philosophy with powerful contemporary critics of our political present. I will show, that is, how to read Hegel now—how we can use his philosophy to comprehend our own time by pairing it with the best thinkers of certain troubling aspects of our contemporary situation. I believe that this pairing does justice both to the power of Hegel's thought and to the demands of the time, and that the value of this approach should be discerned in the results—the contemporary significance of the four supplements to the revolutionary abstraction—which I will briefly outline here.

First, Hegel discerns that operative in our self-experience is a fundamental dependence upon the perspectives of others upon us, which renders individuality an interpersonal accomplishment. This dependence *bespeaks a condition* and *projects a norm*: the condition and the norm of recognition (*die Anerkennung*). We are dependent upon and hence vulnerable to the perspectives of others. It is vital to our basic functioning that we exist in relations with others and, further, that we own up to this: own up to our own and each other's status as perspectives and to the dependence of our independence upon their independence. Being oneself is a matter of extending beyond oneself into a world, and the world into which we extend is a world of other perspectives. Our assumption of that world depends on the acknowledgment and permission of others. For better or worse, whether we are accommodated by the perspectives of others or not is a matter of great significance to us: our very capacity to exist and act depends on it.

If we recognize that we are shaped by the perspectives of specific others upon us, then it is meaningful to ask: *What happens to us*, personally and socially, when certain perspectives take the reins of human reality and assert that we are unworthy of inclusion in it, and when human reality is built to protect some perspectives and exclude others? When the mutually transformative power of perspectives upon each other is suppressed? If the expectations and attentions others hold out to us are persistently critical, negative, and degrading? If we are repeatedly brought up against the denial of our own sense of centrality? These are failures at the level of recognition, misuse of the power we can have as perspectives upon other perspectives, and suppression of the unknown possibilities of sense circulating in others.

The first part of the discussion of recognition will outline the basic idea as Hegel presents it, and the second will invoke Frantz Fanon's (2008) and Jessica Benjamin's (1995) concrete elaborations of how human encounters are dealt with poorly in actual, historical human circumstances. While Hegel delineates the general outline of flawed encounters, Fanon and Benjamin elucidate concrete personal and social costs of failures of recognition. We will see with Fanon how Hegel's account resonates inside of the entrenched historical problem of racist perception, in which the dishonest suppression of perspective has become systemic. We will see with Benjamin how Hegel's account resonates inside of the historically entrenched problem of sexist oppression, specifically as it affects the practice of caregiving and erotic interaction.

The second fundamental idea that offsets the revolutionary abstraction is *Sittlichkeit*, ethicality or ethical life, an idea that is central to the analysis of this book. Ethical life names the social reality implied by recognition: Formed inside of the perspectives of others, we carry the past into the present, the historical, cultural world around us into our intimate contexts and ourselves. Who I am is not simply a function of a local, interpersonal context but a broader sociocultural reality, a "culture at large," that makes itself real in self-reflection and intimate relationships. With ethical life, the valuing behavior and principled orientations we have as free beings are shown to be articulated always in a determinate, local body of finite conventions, customs, and rituals that have come into being over time. Enactment of ourselves is enactment of this sedimented world, which will always be specific—not culture or humanity as such, but this particular culture and these humans.

Ethical life is as it were the second rebuttal to the revolutionary abstraction. Human powers are always developed and given content by a world that, in its determinacy, channels them along particular avenues. We come into being on the basis of inherited, determinate, historical meanings that shape our relation to the world, ourselves, and others, and we cannot easily bring this reality to the light of our critical scrutiny, since it guided that power into being. Further, we tend to live our determinacy as generality, as the way things should be for everyone, which means that we can fail to see the ways in which other inherited, meaningful worlds open up avenues for the expression of human freedom, perceiving therein only alien determinacy and thus limitation. We can also fail to take the human perception circulating in other worlds as an opportunity for us to see the determinacy of our own. Here again, critical questions emerge: *What happens to us*, personally and socially, if the meaning of those diverse worlds is degraded in the name of the purported superiority of one of them, or if we are asked to live in terms of an alien world? If intercultural interaction is governed by disavowal of ethical life in the name of the revolutionary abstraction of rational individuality? If we bring an ignorance of our own specificity, or an incapacity to see beyond the specificity of another world, to interaction with those from another world?

This section will extend Hegel's conception of ethical life through contemporary thinkers who have articulated these dimensions with regard to the way things operate here and now, historically and spatially, in a global context. It will argue that at the heart of modern colonialism is the wielding of revolutionary abstraction for a destructive end: that a disavowal of ethical life is enacted in intercultural interaction that takes the form of domination. I turn to la paperson (2017) and Glen Sean Coulthard (2014) in particular to set the stage for addressing the problem of settler colonialism, and to Saba Mahmood (2001, 2005) and Lila Abu-Lughod (2002, 2013) so as to better perceive the disavowal of ethical life by the "West." Like Hegel, these figures bring out the significance of our determination as beings of ethical life. With the idea of "grounded normativity" (13), Coulthard captures that we think from concrete, living relations and their institutional history. La paperson illuminates some of the key "technologies" by which historically entrenched and dominant worlds operate (1). Mahmood focuses on how freedom is cultivated in and by relations to which we are essentially subordinated (2001, 203), and Abu-Lughod highlights the violence involved in colonial failures to recognize the significance of attachment to one's mode of life (2002, 788). Like Hegel, they reveal and criticize modern alienation from the determinate, supra-individual contexts that produce human individuals, the modern failure to sustain the experience of belonging, and the relative significance of relations of recognition over self-interested individual life.

The third fundamental idea in Hegel that outstrips and contextualizes the revolutionary abstraction is the idea of conscience (*das Gewissen*). The conscientious self is in fact the "third" and final self of the *Phenomenology* (the first is the alienated self of the Roman world and the second is the self of absolute freedom [*PS* §633/*PG* 341]). Here Hegel presents a vision of selfhood, of the I, that can be said to be poised for right relation with its conditions. That is, while he challenges a simplistic conception of selfhood as self-making and rational by articulating the many modes of externality by which we are made, he also presents a viable conception of selfhood under the rubric of "conscience." "Conscience" is the ultimate form that the I takes, for Hegel, and (as conventional use of the term suggests) it is a uniquely powerful experience of *answerability*. Conscience must discern how to be itself and how to interpret what is to be done inside of this specific situation, relations, and history, on the basis of the experience of being called by standards it takes to be other than itself. How will I be myself and do the right thing *here*, in relation to this person, this situation, and these standards that I experience as "not-me"—standards such as the good, the right, or the just, which I experience as outstripping me?

This section of the book extends Hegel's account of conscience to support the critiques of liberalism operative in Maurice Merleau-Ponty (1969), Fanon (2004), and (more peripherally) Karl Marx (1994), arguing with them that liberal ideals are abstract and that their disavowal of the relation between ideal and its determinate expression allows them to be complicit in practices of exploitation, to impose their own determinate forms of expression of universality under the alibi of pure universality, and to preclude the communicative practices that would reveal the meaning behind determinacy. Here we will center Hegel's notion of forgiving communication (*PS* §671/*PG* 361–62) and Fanon's indictment of Europe as committing "crimes against relations" (2004, 238) to illuminate the import of such communicative practices.

Hegel does not link absolute spirit to conscience in the *Phenomenology*, but there is an implicit link: conscience experiences itself as answerable to absolutes it "discovers" within experience and finds linked to its deepest feeling of self. In the activities of absolute spirit (which Hegel calls art, religion, and philosophy), we similarly investigate *who we are* but in a way that is felt as a matter of *discovery* of truths and principles. Further, these activities of self-*comprehension* are also activities of self-*transformation*: To pursue the question of who we are is a passive matter of self-reflection and discovery as well as an active matter insofar as our answers *change* us, requiring that the question be asked and answered again. Just as answerability to principles we take to be beyond us is always exercised in and translated into the terms of determinate contexts, however, so also are the activities of self-comprehension embedded in and fostered by these determinate contexts, tangled up in its determinate customs, media, and communicative practices. Self-comprehension is also aided by communicative exposure to other forms of life, which Hegel captures by putting world history in the same category as art, religion, and philosophy (*PR/GPR* §341). This brief detour through absolute spirit will portray the dynamic character of inhabitation of ethical life: Our determinate practices of self-comprehension will always be practices of self-transformation, thus revealing the nonabsolute character of the determinate ethical grounds in terms of which we pursue the question of who we are.

The fourth supplement to the revolutionary abstraction is also rooted in the fact that human existence is fundamentally a *doing* and is captured in the very basic idea of objective spirit as such. We do not simply subsist, inertly and in abstraction from our surroundings, but we move and act, which always involves space and stuff. This space and stuff are therefore not incidental to who we are, and we therefore cannot "give or take" our relation to them. It is *necessary* that we have access to space and stuff; they are simply there, included, in the concept of more or less free, existent being. And as though invisibly integrated into this stuff are the perspectives of others: Movement through space is generally smooth because human beings agreed to share it cooperatively; I write because others share their communication; I eat and dress with the implicit support of systems of production, transport, and regulation.

Doing is thus interestingly two-sided. It is at one and the same time ideal (in the sense of involving an immaterial meaning) as well as intensely determinate and material. It is a matter of freedom or free initiative, the influx of the "is not" or the "not yet" into the "is," but this "is not" or freedom is always expressed in materiality, such that two apparently alien systems meet here: freedom and necessity, with necessity as the place for freedom's expression. Navigating a human life is simply a matter of navigating the odd co-happening and coexistence of the ideal and the material, the free and the necessary, the transcendent "anything could happen" and the empirical "fact of the matter." Individuals are material bodies and require interaction with material specificity; their action depends upon organized, predictable environments that organize materiality as well as the relations among perspectives.

One of Hegel's most emphatic points is that we always live in terms of an already organized, historically specific materiality; we always answer to already defined systems. These are systems of human activity—labor, economic and political relations, with all of their exigencies and demands, and all of their projected and historically specific positions and relations—worker, boss, mechanic, civil servant, teacher, bus driver, customer, cashier. What we should ask here, with Hegel, is, *What happens to us*, personally and socially, if the system of necessity and the system of freedom are not well calibrated to each other, such that necessity, instead of being the home of freedom, becomes its prison? If we have to submit to an external, material structure that imposes its machinic priorities upon us, that renders our activity means to *its* ends, rather than itself being for free activity? If free activity depends on the freedom of other perspectives, on the specific worlds of its constitution, and on material externality, then what matters to free activity is whether it can connect with these externalities.

Capitalism and ableism emerge here as the problem to which Hegel's analysis is particularly relevant, since each of them powerfully channels and restricts the coupling between body and world that is the prerequisite of free activity. Free activity is nothing without materiality; it always pairs with things in space, and the history of human societies is the history of making the material world over into the terms of bodies and freedom, building it to the measure of these bodily beings. But the specific ways in which this material world is organized supports specific kinds of pairing and precludes others. With analyses of ableism, we see that the body to whose measure things are built is specific in its size, capacities, and materiality, and so the given world does not accommodate different modes of being human but produces what Rosemarie Garland-Thomson calls "misfits" (2011). The critiques of ableism that we find in the work of Georges Canguilhem and Garland-Thomson oppose the one-sidedness by which the organization of the material world is dictated. To be free, disabled bodies must accommodate themselves to the shape of the world, but the structure of that world works against this accommodation and disavows its character as, as Canguilhem calls it, a "world of qualified objects"—a qualified material world that has been carefully constructed to fit a "qualified living being" and specific material bodies (1991, 198).

Capitalism offers the promise of free enterprise but quickly defaults on that promise, rendering free activity moot for those who do not own and wield the machinery to which such activity must accommodate itself. Under capitalism, free activity or labor power can be bought, and it is channeled to feed these machines, through which their owners consolidate wealth. Free activity lays the bricks of the prison around it. Hegel's conception of freedom, in being alive to its connection with materiality, challenges the basic operation of capitalism; with it we find reason to protect free activity against its own inadvertent consequences. Since we live inside of advanced capitalism, those who are more alive than Hegel to its contemporary form can help in the mobilization of Hegel's thought here. Sartre's (2004) analysis will be particularly helpful—particularly the concepts of counterfinality and the practico-inert—since he too elaborates in rich detail how free activity produces a materiality that turns around and constrains it.

These four phenomena—recognition, ethical life, conscience, and objective spirit—show us the rationality and the vital significance of determinacy. Ethical life, interpersonal relations, and external materiality are always going to be shaped in a particular way, and human beings depend on this, though we can also be conscientiously critical of specific shapes. The fact of determinacy and our entanglement with it cannot be disavowed, because it is simply the character of free activity to require organized, inherited externality and to be developed in and by (and find fulfillment through) determinate interpersonal relations. Nevertheless, as we shall see, there is always a beyond to the determinacy within human experience and a capacity to relate critically to it, even via norms that emerge within it as aspects of its very structure: We come to recognize, within our determinate contexts, that perspectives *as such* are to be recognized; that perspectives do not live simply in terms of the given but relate to what is other than it; that they are always open to becoming their own object; that they cannot perfectly replicate the conventions of their world or perfectly fulfill the expectations of those who experience them.

In the final discussion of objective spirit we will also be doing something beyond qualifying the revolutionary abstraction: that is, answering the question of what kind of social organization, what kind of concrete institutions, would answer adequately to the different dimensions of human experience. In this last section, I will draw out the contemporary significance of Hegel's vision of the state, showing that there is much to be gained politically from trying to think in its terms.

Charles W. Mills observes, with fitting incredulity, that liberal political philosophy does not talk about oppression, operating solely at the level of the ideal (2017, 34–35). Hegel's orientation is to bring a theoretical insight to bear within specific, individual forms of experience and specific cultural worlds so as to witness how these ideals operate in actuality, which is where they always have to be, where they are worked out, and where their full significance can be brought to light.[3] Witnessing the concrete structures that these insights project, and exploring the rifts that open between them and their actualization, Hegel operates in this way in both registers, the ideal and the real. It is proper to retain a place for the ideal so as to be able to criticize deviations therefrom, but this is more a description of who we are than a norm: We are typically "idealizing" beings who are moved by the idea of redressing wrongs and "getting it right," who bring our ideas to bear upon reality. This book will bring principles to bear upon contemporary distortions operating at the level of collective experience, or oppressive relations, with the goal of seeing how these distortions fail to live up to the real structures and forms operative inside of human experience. It will require a reader who is open to attentive phenomenological consideration of specific experiences, for it is our familiarity with such experiences that will offer us the richest possibilities for resonating with what Hegel will ultimately show about them.

We will start, here and now, with a consideration of the experience of thinking, so as to be inducted into both the import and the trouble presented by the abstractions of modern life.

CHAPTER ONE

How "We" Live Now

What is thinking? What could we say about it at first glance, from the perspective we have as ordinary experiencers?

I would say, first, that it seems like something that a person does on their own, that unfolds within them. In thinking, we experience something internal to us, private and inward; we experience ourselves as enacting it, not compelled to think by others or by outside forces, but leading the experience ourselves. We experience ourselves as initiating our thinking, or we experience it as being initiated in us and, even when we do follow the thoughts of others, we ourselves have to engage in the activity of thinking thoughts they (purportedly) think.

Second, thinking seems like a matter of assessing, of standing apart from reality and making judgments about it, whether that reality is inside or outside of us. It is as though in thinking we have the power of withdrawing from "what is," at least momentarily, and having an attitude upon it. We can even have in thinking a relation to what is not—a sense of what something was or should or could be, which no longer or not yet exists—and we can bring this sense to bear on what is. The capacity for thinking implies a kind of separation with regard to the way in which things are, an authority to speak on behalf of a truth that is not yet real, and the possibility of holding reality to a standard different from it.

And yet, third, while we wield it, while we do it, we also experience it as though happening to us, in a way that comes with rules by which we feel more or less compelled. It is as though thinking thinks through us. We can even discern rules in it by which we feel compelled, which is similarly a matter of discovery and not our own invention.

Fourth, and related, in feeling compelled by thought, we experience ourselves as doing what others might also feel compelled to do, and thus we find in thinking the possibility of sharing sense with others. While an inward experience, thinking is also in this way an occasion for being directed toward others who experience these rules as well, who do what we do, and with whom we can thus think together. The experience of compulsion by the demands of thinking, rather than an experience of just our own singularity, is a condition for sharing.[1] Thinking can link us together, allowing for shared understanding of our different experiences.

The point here is not an exhaustive philosophical argument about the character of thinking, but rather to make the modern vision of human subjectivity that Hegel finds expressed particularly clearly in the French Revolution come alive for us in a quick and easy way.[2] While it was not simply absent from other historical eras and places, this vision is taken to have congealed, to have demanded independent consideration, and to have *severed its ties* with other such visions particularly in the modern era. Further, particularly through modern Western colonialism and imperialism, this vision has come to dominate and infiltrate forms of life everywhere, such that each "we" is affected thereby. Projected by recognition of the propensity we have to be and think for ourselves, it has political repercussions: It is a vision (never perfectly enacted) of human dignity, freedom, and equality. The fact that thinking unfolds within us means that the thinking we do cannot be reduced to that of someone else and cannot be controlled by another, no matter what we might want. The fact that in it we register the nature of the world "out there" and evaluate "what is" from a position separate from it means that any worldly determinacies can never solely hem us in as persons, and neither can they be taken as absolutely decisive for the way this world is structured; whether or not I have a particular determinacy should not be decisive with regard to whether I am valued by the world or not, and any given determinacy the world has should not be decisive with regard to the question of what shape the world should take. The fact that we are the kinds of beings who can be compelled by thought conflicts with the idea of being random and arbitrary. And the fact that we can share thinking with others means that we can potentially develop a shared vision of how to live together well. Integrated together, these elements would seem to require opposition to arbitrary hierarchy, to the preferential treatment of people with certain determinate characteristics over others, to a world that would cater to some determinate characteristics over others, and to any condition that would rest on a disavowal of the happening of this independent activity inside of any experiencer.

Beyond thinking their ideas, human beings express and enact them, and so we can witness actual historical events manifesting this recognition of the import of human inwardness. As a result, we do not have to draw up artificial scenarios in order to think this through philosophically, withdrawing into thought and discerning what it would entail; we can just look at history. This inevitable expression of thought is why we see Hegel looking outward and not inward to think: Principles, insights, and ideals never come separately from human social practices.[3] Human beings act on principles and commitments and shape the world to reflect them. What happens when principles and commitments are actualized manifests their real meaning in a way that simple thought, the private exercise of rationality, could never do; we discern what they mean by seeing how the reality they inspire works. How much better will we be at thinking things through if we begin by simply observing what our many-sided actuality—material, historical, and interpersonal—*does* with an idea, or what specific problems that idea produces? In reality, ideas can be "poked and prodded" from many different directions; they redound and resonate in all dimensions of life and in their repercussions for all manner of people. Actuality in its material, historical, and interpersonal aspects "thinks things through" for us as thinkers. As Hegel is reported to have observed in his lectures on the history of philosophy,[4] "spirit" reveals "principle" in "history":

> The stage of self-consciousness [spirit] has reached is the principle which it reveals in history *in the relations of that existence*. This principle it clothes with all the wealth of its existence; the shape in which it exists is a people into whose morality, constitution, domestic, civil, and public life, arts, international relations, etc. this principle is built.... This is the material which the principle of a people has to work through, and this is not the business of one day... it is not a progress in the abstract concepts of pure thinking; on the contrary, this material only advances in pure thinking *pari passu* with its advance in its entire concrete life. (*LHP* 44)

Thus, Hegel turns to history as though with the following question. Something might make sense in thought, but to what kind of world does it give rise? What kind of world is projected by specific ideas or insights—here, in particular, by recognition of the power of thinking and its residence within human beings? What kind of political form is demanded by this free, thinking, autonomous being?

Hegel is a philosopher of the concrete insofar as he sees that insight is never purely intellectual but expressed in material existence, in action that works to make its surroundings fit its ideas so that it can be at home. What we get with Hegel are two recurring questions: First, in thought, or in the case of ahistorical, nonworldly circumstances that are not embedded in actual history but abstract, how *would* this play out? Second, how *did* it play out, if it were an actual commitment or idea playing out in an actual historical situation?[5] How would or does life go if it were or is lived in terms of an idea or insight? Insight moves us to act and to change the stuff of our lives, and so we can track what it really means by looking at what kinds of lives it allows us to lead.

Revolutionary Existence

Hegel analyzes what we have been considering so far—how a world is built, historically, around a conception of the human as a thinking being—by turning to the French Revolution and the world it projects (*PS* §§582–95/*PG* 316–23). Interestingly, we will see here that the failure of the revolutionary vision is precisely a failure to appreciate the concrete: the fact that insight requires expression in action, with all the one-sided limitations that accrue to ideas when they take shape in determinate reality. The Revolution is essentially critical: Rationality critically judges the existing world; actuality is judged by thought and held wanting because it does not suit the rational; the world must be transformed. The existent must be torn down because of its partiality, its arbitrariness, its suppression of the authority of reason in favor of the sedimented conditions of habit and hierarchy. Noble birth and status are inconsistent with the revolutionary vision, and noble land tenure rights are eliminated; the clergy must answer to the nation; social differentiation in the form of guilds must be abolished. The monarchy, nobility, and church are dethroned as enemies of rationality, which does not discriminate on any terms but its own and can find a home in each mind. Forms of social organization that operate on hierarchical, arbitrarily exclusionary grounds are in denial of the universal capacity for thinking.

While a powerful and incisive vision whose elements deserve recognition, there is a problem with the enactment of this new insight in and as a world. As a uniform abstraction, it is unsuited and even opposed to reality in its diverse multiplicity and determinacy and inconsistent with the demand that insight be expressed in action and human reality, which are one-sided and determinate. It disavows the fact that, as Hegel is reported to have observed in his lectures on art, "everything that forces itself out into real objectivity is subject . . . to the principle of particularization."[6] Actuality, because it takes determinate form, is itself cast as problematic in light of the universal, ideal operation of thought. Both decision and action are each in a fundamental way opposed to abstract universality, because they carve up the world: decision by requiring that at some point deliberation end and that someone decide, which may not be when all are ready for it to end and which cannot be everyone's decision, and action by unfolding in one piece of the world and not all, in effects that are for some and not all.

Let us look more closely at the nature of decision. Whenever a decision is made, there are some who are excluded from making it, as a decision is not something in which everyone can take part.[7] Even if it is decided that everything will be decided on the basis of consensus, for instance, this decision is reached in a way that would exclude a different view; someone has to call the question, and someone has to decide by what means it will be decided. In the context of the Revolution, specific people set themselves up as government with the aim of shaping the emerging reality of the nation. But each governmental form is, in the terms of revolutionary logic, a transgression against the freedom of the rest. In this context, government is intrinsically a "faction," a piece of the whole that has set itself up illegitimately over the rest.[8] In a world committed to the equality of every rational being, government is impossible, because to exist this world needs decisions made, but anyone who makes them can be construed as illegitimately putting themselves above others and betraying the universal.

The problem is similar with action. Real, free people require real-life structures: workplaces, courts, shops, trades, professions, schools, cultural institutions, hospitals. But everything that is done for specific people will necessarily exclude others, and so some will be favored and others disfavored.[9] Specific actions channel resources to some over others. The insistence on free, rational, and equal subjects opposes action on behalf of real people—exclusionary, preferential, and determinate acts of care, responsibility, and governance—and so no one can be saved.

Unrecognized in the revolutionary situation is that carrying out the commitment to freedom, autonomy, and equality will always mean risking them. To make the world answer to human freedom is to commit oneself to restriction, inequality, and difference. It is to build a world in which we do not give ourselves the law but are "given it" by the existing structure of the world, by its given forms. The commitment to the equality of human beings cannot be supported abstractly but requires actual support and care for those beings, and this support and care will differentiate, exclude, prefer, and divide. Any actual nation or actual citizen is going to be distinct from the ideal, condemned for being specific, the enemy of the Revolution.

Universal freedom and equality turn out to be opposed to being, and thus we have the Terror, the mass killing of those suspected of counterrevolutionary action, the eradication of single individuals who inevitably produce determinacy whenever they decide and act and thus manifest their deviation from absolute freedom. The result is the "negation of the singular individual as an *existent* within the universal. The sole work and deed of universal freedom is in fact *death*" (PS §590/ PG 320). Absolute freedom cannot be a phenomenon of the actual world, only of pure, abstract consciousness. To make freedom real is to grapple with the constraints of actuality; to make equality real is to transgress and sacrifice it; to honor shared rationality, one must make things that are not perfectly shared. A commitment to the free equality of rational beings cannot be carried out on its own terms.[10]

Hegel's Alternative

The aforementioned should not be taken to constitute a thoroughgoing description of the shortcomings of the French Revolution; here it operates simply as an avenue to description of the elements of Hegel's philosophy that concern me in this book. Human freedom is not in fact opposed by the determinate differences among human beings and their free elaboration. If our lives have content and meaning, it is because we live in a world that is developed by other, different people, because other people have been being themselves and are still doing so, because we inhabit a world that calls on us in particular ways. Who we are cannot simply be articulated in terms of an abstraction from everything that is specific and in terms of an abstraction from the past: As Simone de Beauvoir evocatively writes, "if the world behind us were bare, we would hardly be able to see anything before us but a gloomy desert" (1976, 93). We are specific and emerge out of history, shaped by it. We are beings of the past, not simply of the present, and the determinate character of this past imprints itself upon us in tandem with the development of our sense of ourselves, in such a way that it refuses to allow itself to be made the transparent object of reflection. It is not rational or reasonable to deny the situated specificity in which rationality expresses itself and to deny that the very operation of reason depends upon a sense that cannot itself be dragged into the light of reason. We may in some sense be free, equal, and autonomous; yet our freedom operates in and through what is already here, imposed and unchosen; it operates in and through a world already organized and not at the behest of our will. Our equality as rational beings is expressed in terms of differences; if it comes to exist, autonomy is a result of interdependence. This is not to say that the past and the practices and institutions of the world we inherit cannot be criticized and revised, but that such critical revision has to begin with an appreciation of the inevitable existence of determinate, concrete forms of life and the non-transparency to us of our attachment to and formation by them. Human reality is not simply a matter of universal rationality, but of concrete, non-transparent determinacy. Philosophical reflection has therefore the task of bringing these murky conditions of experience to a kind of relative, limited transparency.

This is where the powers of Hegel and the task of this book come in. My goal is to excavate the specific dimensions of Hegel's philosophy in which he articulates the idea that human life is lived in concrete relations with others and the world—the other side of this modern, revolutionary abstraction—and to show, with the help of more or less contemporary critics of abstract, modern universality, the specific ways in which these concrete relations have historically gone poorly. That which has constituted us and shaped thinking—the past, relations with the human and nonhuman world, the specific cultural and economic differences that are constituted as typical and atypical in these historical, interpersonal worlds, and so on—is Hegel's focus. If specificities such as those of culture, race, gender, economic positioning, bodily capacity, and so on have an impact on the quality and character of the lives we pursue, then abstraction from them in the name of a universal, rational humanity can simply cover over the negative effects of negative cultural valuations thereof and illicitly privilege those determinate forms of humanity that are cast as generic, such that the ideal of universal humanity purportedly invoked for the protection of humanity is in fact mobilized to oppress that humanity. Insofar as Hegel gives voice to the weight of these determinate, historical specificities, then his philosophy should be of interest to critics of racism, sexism, capitalism, coloniality, and ableism, who precisely oppose the way human life is defined by the exclusion of people from consideration on the basis of their determinacies, their belonging to certain kinds of communities, and their being disregarded by those who dominate, and who do not take the idea of universal humanity to be effective as redress thereof. The disavowal of determinacy—the determinacy of relations, of history, of materiality—is powerfully operative in these social problems. What might we be able to say, with Hegel, about these problems, with the historically and interculturally won benefit of access to the articulation of opposition and complaint that is emerging from the depths in which oppression had buried it, making itself heard through new forms of proximity and expanding communities of communication?

Let us turn now to Hegel's multidimensional critique of the abstractions of the French Revolution and with it the modern "revolution." We will begin with the seed or kernel of this criticism, which is found in Hegel's abstract discussion of the structure of the interpersonal encounter.[11] Let us turn now to this moment, leaving analysis of its concreteness to the next section's discussion of ethical life, in which we will see the real, historical, and existential effects of the dependence of perspective upon recognition.

CHAPTER TWO

Recognition

The Struggle to the Death[1]

You are on a stage, perhaps with a microphone in hand; you are going to sing, toast a sibling's marriage, or give the first speech you've ever written to the other members of your grade 6 class. Or you are in a more private space, with someone you really want to kiss, or caught spying on someone else through a keyhole (Sartre 2018, 355).

These scenarios home in on the experience of being perceived by others and experiencing this as charged. Whether or not we allow ourselves to wonder about this in real-life, fundamental questions arise here. How will these people around me interpret me? What will they think of my singing, my toast, my speech? Do they find me interesting and desirable; do they want my attention? Are they displeased or disgusted by my behavior, or indifferent to it? When we encounter other people, we (typically) experience them as perspectives, which means as having their own experience in terms of which we ourselves appear, but this experience is not clearly evident to us. To encounter another is to find something inside of our own experience that, while potentially significant to us, is not accessible.

This feeling of being seen can bring with it a kind of vertigo: I am seen, and this makes a difference to me, but how I am seen and who I am for this perspective is not up to me but up to this other, whose perspective I cannot immediately perceive. If we are alive to its import as a perspective (which we typically are, if we are more or less decent people), then it can have an impact on our sense of self and of the meaning of our actions, which means that *who we are* is not simply a matter of our self-definition. Sartre observes that it is as though the world "has been pierced, in the middle of its being, by a drainage hole and... is constantly flowing out through that hole," and this draining away is a piece of my experience; "it is all there for me, as a partial structure of the world, even though what is at issue here is in fact the universe's total disintegration" (2018, 351). In perceiving this perceiving, or in experiencing this other experiencing us, we do not simply see an object; we see a "drainage hole" through which our experience of ourselves flows away from us, defined by an elsewhere. While we find another person extended in the world as objects are, they are not simply object but experiencer—that is, someone who brings their own interpretive and experiential terms to the encounter with objects and others. We experience them as "in charge of" their interpretation *of us*, and we experience ourselves as open to being impacted by this interpretation. Here, where I experienced the authority of my own perspective, securely established in my inwardness and oriented by it to what is outside of me, I am decentered: my perception gives me another perspective, and how I am perceived affects me in my perception, perspective, and inwardness.

The claim implied in my appearance to myself, in my experience *as* a self, is that I am that to which the world appears, and thus a center of significance; I am not a mere piece of the world within it, but that in terms of which the world has meaning, a source of interpretation of that world, a kind of absolute orientation point around which reality is arranged. To be "I" is inevitably to experience oneself as an aperture through which reality shows itself in particular ways. The fact that another person shows up in my world initially appears as an incompatible counterclaim: "you" emerge within my experience, and thus as a piece of the world that arranges itself around me, but you also appear as an orientation point or aperture. You appear as this immediately, and not as a conclusion of an argument I may make to myself about your personhood (which Sartre shows by noting that shame immediately floods me if I am caught peeping at a keyhole—it is not the conclusion of an argument [2018, 355]).[2] With the appearance of an "I" and a "you," it is as though two counterclaims emerge: I am a structure by which appearance is organized, within which you appear, but you appear within that structure as a structure by which appearance is organized, and in which I appear. In my experience of the world showing its face to me, you appear as that to which the world shows its face. To myself I am that to which the world shows itself, yet a piece of the world that shows itself suggests to me that I am a piece of the world that appears. How does each I grapple with the apparent conflict between them?

As Hegel observes, this experience is doubled:

This doing on the part of one self-consciousness has itself the doubled significance of being *its own* doing *just* as well as it is *the other's* doing, for the other is just as self-sufficient. The other is just as enclosed within [her]self, and there is nothing within [her] which is not there through [her]self.... The movement is thus straightforwardly the doubled movement of both self-consciousnesses. (*PS* §182/*PG* 110)

The other person experiences similarly that the world appears to her perspective and that my perspective upon her is unreachable and ungovernable. What does it mean that this experience is happening for both of us? In this doubling, we gain confirmation of our own self-certainty as a perspective: If another's perspective presents to them my status as perspective, then my perspective is confirmed through their appearance in my perspective, and vice versa. Instead of a threat, then, the other person is the occasion by which my sense of self-certainty can be affirmed as true. In fact, the larger section in which this discussion is nested is called "The Truth of Self-Certainty":[3] through the outside perspective, my own self-certain inwardness can be confirmed as real. While disorienting, this experience is not a threat but supports the possibility of extending into the uncertain world.

NAVIGATING THE CHARGE OF THE ENCOUNTER

I take myself to be explaining Hegel here, though I will explain this more later. For the moment, we should note that Hegel is observing what happens in the experience of myself in relation to another and of another in relation to myself, which could never be revealed in one fell swoop. As Hegel specifies, there are many intertwined meanings and aspects to this experience—"the concept of [self-consciousness's] unity in its doubling... is an intertwining with many sides and meanings" (*PS* §178/*PG* 109). We have already noted the basic picture; what Hegel does next is tease out the strategies we invoke for dealing with the drama of this encounter, and assess whether or not our strategies are adequate to it. We do not prove Hegel wrong, so to speak, if we show that we have never tried to kill anyone, that we are not engaged in our everyday lives with a struggle with the perspectives of others, or that we have already dealt with their counterclaims; the fact is that these counterclaims are there to be resolved; they ongoingly emerge for us in specific interpersonal situations; our lives have taken the shape they do because of the better and worse ways in which we and others have resolved these tensions and lived these complications.

There are several possible responses we can take to this basic incursion of the other into the world, and they can be both literal and figurative struggles to the death. Others can appear in the world refusing to acknowledge the humanity of those they encounter and with the power to actualize this refusal, and the eventual (if not immediate) outcome tends to be resistance. This kind of encounter has been a major piece of human history and has propelled the construction of legal and political agreements, both between and within human groupings such as peoples and nation-states. We live in terms of laws and institutions whose existence is a result of *historical* struggles to the death. Such struggle may be thought of as unusual by people who are protected by their contingent inhabitation of more or less wealthy, postindustrial societies, but history is full of this opposition deemed necessary for liberation, and the security we enjoy is typically due to the legal and political infrastructures built out of that struggle. But we can also try to "kill" someone—kill them figuratively—by denying their character as perspective or downplaying their significance, so as to disable the charge of being seen by another. I can pretend that I do not care about that experience, that it is fundamentally misguided, inferior, valueless. I can insist to myself that I am not concerned with what my date thinks of my wedding toast or what Pooria thinks of my speech. I can insist that the audience is not important, invoking for myself the familiar invitation to imagine that they are naked. Contemplating the possibility of that my desire to kiss someone is not reciprocated, I can construe their desire as undesirable. I can judge the one who catches me peeping as someone who is also shameful and who, familiar with the experience of doing shameful things, is not one to judge. I can quietly assert to myself my own dominance and invulnerability in the experience of being looked at by someone else, degrading the importance of another's perspective so that it does not feel threatening and disabling it of its power.

In these various moves to neutralize the charge of the encounter with another perspective, we should see what Hegel means by the struggle to the death: An encounter with another person can bring with it an intolerable feeling of vulnerability that seems resolvable only by eliminating the threat that they present. To be an "I" and to maintain one's status as "I" is in some sense to be intolerant of a counterclaim—particularly one that threatens one's ability to be a human being—and be moved to kill or "kill" it. To be an I is at the very least to experience the need to negotiate this counterclaim—a need that has partly manifest itself in the elaboration of formal standards of respect.

Another meaning in the many that are implicit in the struggle to the death is the staking of life. In literally staking my life, I announce that

I am not reducible to life but stand for something that is so important that I am ready to stake my life on it; I am not simply one piece of the world among others; I am "fettered to no determinate *existence*..., not shackled to life" (*PS* §187/*PG* 111–12). Rather, I am *perspective*, which means that I "contain" the world insofar as I am that to which it appears; I "hold things dear" or interpret things in a certain way—I do not simply exist alongside them as a chair stands next to a table. To stake my life is to announce that I am not a thing among things, that I extend beyond my status as determinate object, and that "you" should see this. This self-differentiation from life is integral, for human beings, to what it is to be human. I am not simply a part of things but have a view on them.

Neither of these options, however—killing the other perspective or staking one's life and losing it—actually solves this problem of the counterclaim, because what mattered was the other's assertion, if only by virtue of appearing, that she is the one to whom reality appears. One does not eliminate that assertion by killing the person or allowing oneself to be killed. *Assertion outlives life.* Killing somebody, suppressing the significance of their perspective, or asserting one's own significance by sacrificing one's life do not actually result in getting them to agree with our interpretation of the centrality of our own perspective. Death, for instance, "is the *natural* negation of... consciousness, ... which thus endures without the significance of the recognition that was demanded." What is challenging to us is not eradicated by the eradication of our own life or the other's; it does not go away with death. "Life is as essential to [self-consciousness] as is pure self-consciousness" (*PS* §189/*PG* 112). What we actually desire is their affirmation, freely come by, that we are an "I," that we are valued as an "I," that they honor our status as that to which the world also appears, as that which has a view upon things.

Meaningful development of self-consciousness as perspective depends on one's assumption of one's own perspective, on the support of others, and on life, and thus the strategies of killing others, giving up one's own life, or giving up one's own self-centrality all fail. A self-consciousness, as H. S. Harris notes, "can achieve a relationship of respect and trust with the opponent after a fight in which 'honor' is satisfied, but both have survived" (1997a, 355). What becomes evident in our experience of the competing counterclaims is the need for each claim to be affirmed, and the need for the tension to be lived well rather than eradicated. This is in fact the solution that answers to the reality of our shared, doubled situation, as Hegel remarks in the conceptual conclusion to this section. It is in the perspectives of others upon me that my perspective upon myself is fashioned; in and through them I have myself. Through the other, as the "mediating middle," "each mediates itself with itself and integrates itself with itself" (*PS* §184/*PG* 110).

When we encounter another person, we are encountering a source of reality, a person whose perspective inaugurates the world as it appears to them, who brings an orientation with them the authority of which we cannot straightforwardly confirm or deny, and which we cannot simply block from infiltrating our own perspectives. Other people can affect who we are. For a perspective to encounter another is for it to encounter something by which it is outstripped and to which it is in principle porous. To reduce the other to a subjective, isolated view that does not concern me is to disavow this ability to infiltrate my own perspective, an ability they have simply by virtue of being a perspective. We can deny that this is real, but we do not annihilate that reality—and "kill" that other—in denying it.

THE PERVASIVENESS OF THE ENCOUNTER

All of our experience unfolds in a way that is pulled along by other perspectives that we do not inhabit. This reality I cannot plumb, this drainage hole at the center of the world, affects me both consciously and unconsciously in my upbringing: what the other thinks of me, their taking me as a self, has mattered in the sense that I have already become who I am because of them and their perspective. This reality I cannot plumb is the explicit propulsion of my development, in any more or less competent engagement with a world; it opens the world for me in different ways, pulls me along, inspires desires in me, causes me to reflect on myself and the world in ways I did not plan. It presents itself as the ongoing fabric of my life; everywhere I turn, I have to grapple with the perspectives of others in order to pursue my own life: in education, family, job interviews, career, relationships, politics, buying and selling, and so on. It is as though the perspectives of others, which I do not inhabit, inhabit me; my universe is not simply my own, a universe with my meanings, but is peopled by their meanings. Being a child, being curious about or interested in another, desiring another—in these experiences we experience the other's constitution of us most strongly—but it is pervasive in more mundane domains as well. We can never shut out the other as such; we have never shut out the other. Killing and being killed, denying and disavowing perspectives as such, are not real options, as they do not change or address this basic structure. Owning up to this honestly is the norm that emerges here, from within our experience.[4]

Our broader relationship with the world is also being established in and by other perspectives. They may say, "no, you are incorrect; what you are asserting about x is not real or important or you have not captured its meaning correctly"; or "yes, your view on this situation is real and important, and I am impacted by it." In their confirmation or denial, they confirm or deny not simply our sense of ourselves, but our sense of the nature of reality as well, our capacity for sense-making, our sense of the fit between ourselves or our perspectives and the world. In the difference of their experience, they induct us into the world's meanings. Their independent insight into that world, paired with the weight their perspective has for us, opens up a world for us with more angles and receptacles and details than we had previously seen—unless, of course, its orientation is to flatten and depopulate the world of meaning. Ideally our experience will continue in this way: the world becoming richer through our engagement with others, our tools for engagement with it honed through engagement with them. What we witness here is actually a threefold reality: self, other, world.[5]

Before we explore this further, let us look at the next step that Hegel makes here, to reveal another meaningful layer in the encounter with another perspective. One can bring the conflict between perspectives to an apparent close by accepting a situation that is fundamentally defined by one person denying the authority of their own perspective and affirming that of the other, and the other doing the opposite. This Hegel captures by observing in thought the development of a relationship between a master and a servant (*PS* §§189–96/*PG* 112–16). If killing, as we saw above, would not actually accomplish our aim—if we need a live perspective to affirm our claim—we can "resolve" the conflict by giving up or getting the other to give up. The apparent incompatibility of counterclaims is resolved by a relationship in which one dominates and the other acquiesces to domination and serves.

Mastery and Servitude

As we noted previously, Hegel says that there are many meanings and sides to the concept of self-consciousness's "unity in its doubling." In every move and transition, we should see another dimension of this complex reality, a claim about what else is to be seen. We can access the richness of these claims partly by studying the text but also by being intelligently alive to our own experience. Indeed, the development of our capacity for independent thinking is as much needed for as it is propelled by reading the text. Further, however, to see the ultimate meaning of these claims, we have to be able, on the one hand, to separately analyze these moves so as to grasp the specific meanings, and then we have to be able to hold them together, for it is not the case that each piece is the whole story: "on the one hand, the moments within this intertwining must be strictly kept apart, and on the other hand, they must also be taken and cognized at the same time as not distinguished" (*PS* §178/*PG* 109). Later, we will aim to pull the manifold into a coherent account so that we can begin to grasp the whole story.

To the end of resolving the struggle of counterclaims, one might decide to let the dictates of that other perspective shape one's life, living in a way that answers to them. To preserve our lives in the context of violent struggle, we can surrender; or as a way of grappling with the weight of the other's counterclaim, we can adopt a way of life that disavows the claim that our own perspective makes upon us. We may find that we do not have force or confidence enough to get the other's perspective to accept ours, and simply give up, disavowing our independence in response. We can see this in myriad ways beyond the assumption of literal acquiescence in the face of death: when we acquiesce to the terms another sets for us, operating according to their expectations, allowing them to define shared situations in the way that they want, or assuming a stance of cruelty to ourselves, asserting our own stupidity or inferiority. We can see this also with children and parents: children gradually becoming the vessels of a parent's will, such that growing up requires giving up the implicit claims of their own existence and acquiescing to a parent's terms. It is possible that not all such acts are describable in terms of this framework—not all forms of depressive self-contempt, for instance, are necessarily acquiescent responses to the challenge of another perspective—but surely this dynamic is real and meaningful to us. Hegel analyzes this strategy in his discussion of servitude (*PS* §§194–96/ *PG* 114–16).

A second way to answer to the counterclaim is to insist assiduously and effectively on the authority of one's own claim. Literally threatening death and forcing someone to acquiesce is one way of expressing that authority: The fact that consciousness exists only as embodied means that we are vulnerable at the level of the body, and subordination can be forced through body. This person then becomes dominant, having evaded death by being effective in their threat to the other's life, and having evaded the death of the other by offering another option, that of servitude. "I won't kill you if you make my will your own, if you let me use your body to pursue my wishes." This is mastery (discussed in *PS* §§190–93/*PG* 112–14).

Clearly this kind of domination has actually occurred historically and continues to occur. Hegel is illuminating here how the self and its relation to itself, others, and the world contains the conditions for this possibility. But again, there is also a more general and pervasive dynamic to see here, which is the temptation to deal with a counterclaim by trying to suppress or deny the existence of this "drainage hole" and the outstripping power that it has. It is likely that this kind of dynamic characterizes many interpersonal relationships, emerging in minor and significant forms. The otherness of the other perspective is not something we can directly inhabit, and yet its pervasiveness in our experience means that temptations to grapple with it irresponsibly and dishonestly run rampant. The otherness of another person is a central and profound challenge in human life, since living a meaningful life requires living with other people, living with them is a matter of living in support of the world they project, and their sense of self-centrality and the world they project can coexist uncomfortably with one's own sense of self-centrality and one's own world.

Perceiving the other comes with being perceived by the other. I am seeing and I am being seen, perceiving and being perceived, encountering and being encountered. Do I own up to both? Can I inhabit my perceiving even while I am perceived? Do I refrain from acquiescing to the other and allowing their perceiving to dominate? Can I inhabit my being seen and being experienced? Do I refrain from taking the position of mastery? Can I take up the world that the other brings; can I share with them my own? Does the world expand or contract in their presence? Let us now separate out some of these intertwined meanings, beginning by treating mastery on its own.

MASTERY

The master has licensed herself to take herself as central, to be the authority on how the world appears, to define the meaning of things, to outstrip anything else that presents itself as real (and she seems to have eliminated that which would oppose her in doing so). The challenge of the other person seems to have been discharged of its status as challenge (though it has technically done that *itself*, which we will discuss later). The master can now use the body of the servant to reckon with material things and turn them into objects of immediate consumption; the servant's body "is synthesized with independent *being* or thinghood in general" (*PS* §190/*PG* 112–13). Because of this relation to the servant, things can now show up to the master in a way that simply declares: "I am here for you and your defining perspective." The servant deals with the recalcitrance of things, turning "not defined by the master's will" and "not for the master's desire" into "defined by the master's will" and "for the master's desire."

It is not as though the master is freed from things; she still needs stuff, a house, food, clothes, and so on. It is just their independence that she (mostly) does not have to reckon with, since that is the servant's job. The servant "makes the magic happen," discerning the logic of things so as to be able to turn wool into clothing, wood into house, partridge berries into jam. The servant's labor erases the independence of objects for the master: "The master, who has inserted the servant between the thing and [her]self, thereby attaches [her]self only to the non-independence of the thing and purely enjoys it. [S]he leaves the side of its independence to the servant, who works on it" (PS §190/PG 113). The servant is not fulfilling their own will in doing this work, but doing it as a means of survival. Their action confirms the centrality of the master, insofar as it is defined by the master's desire.

There is one object to which the master must still answer, however: the one that has moved the servant to become a servant by imposing the threat on their life. This chain or the threat to their body, which they "could not ignore in the struggle," must continue to be effective. The master has not been liberated completely from the domain of independent objects; her relation to the servant is mediated by that specific independent being (PS §190/PG 112–13).

We can perceive two kinds of relations operative in the master's situation—one with the servant, and another with the world—and each brings with it a problem for the master. Hegel observes that, because "the inessential consciousness is therein for the master the object which constitutes the *truth* of [her] certainty of [her]self," "it is clear that this object does not correspond to its concept" (PS §192/PG 114). The principle being asserted here—the "concept"—is that the master is dominant, the servant recognizes the master as dominant, and events unfold on the basis of this basic logic. But if we look at what would actually happen here in this experience, we would see that the experience contradicts the principle on the basis of which it unfolds. The self-consciousness that has assumed thinghood (§190/112–13) turns out to be essential and powerful, not inessential and disempowered. The master's self-conception is undermined in two ways: She puts herself at the same level as the servant, and she (not the servant) becomes impotent in the face of the world.

The master desires the desire and affirmation of the other, and in so doing affirms the significance of that other. If the other matters to me, then the other holds the key; the other is in charge. In putting herself in this position of dependence upon the recognition of the servant, the master has herself switched the logic, making the servant essential, but she simultaneously declares and depends upon the servant's inessentiality. And what the master really wants, in order for her perspective to be most authentically central, is for the servant to say *on their own* that hers is the perspective that matters: the "object that constitutes the *truth* of [her] certainty of [her]self" (*PS* §192/*PG* 114) has to independently confirm her certainty so as to make it true. In that case, however, the master affirms the servant's freedom to value the master, implying that the servant is not actually under her power. Another way to say this is that the servant must always allow the master to dominate them, such that the servant's free "allowing" cannot be snuffed out; the servant retains within them, even without choosing it, the moment of affirmation or negation of the master, and cannot give it away, even if they want to. The servant gives with one hand and keeps with the other—"I affirm your authority, yet I must always elect to do so." The master takes with one hand and gives with the other as well: "I want you to be free, I want you to be not-free; I want you to be equal, I want you to be non-equal." The master gives authority to the servant, wants the servant's freedom, flags the servant's desire as key—all of which are disavowed in making the servant a servant and in denying their freedom, authority, and desire. And so Hegel writes: "the *truth* of the independent consciousness is thus the *servile consciousness*... mastery showed that its essence is the inversion of what it wants to be" (§193/114).

A similar problem afflicts the master's relation with the world. Her power seems effective: her desires are authoritative and immediately satisfied; they dictate how the world appears: as house, meal, movie, and so on. But the world and its objects are also a massive and opaque mystery to the master, becoming more so over time. The master does not have power in the form of the effective extension of agency in the world; she is more or less impotent in relation to objects, and her "satisfaction is itself only a vanishing" (*PS* §195/*PG* 115). The only thing she can do is command the servant and enjoy. Her stance toward the world commits her to greater and greater powerlessness in relation to the servant, whose power will grow through extended engagement, who "comes to acquire through himself *a mind of his own*, precisely in the work in which there had seemed to be only an *alien mind*" (§196/115).

Here we get fundamental insight into the nature of agency: Independence in the form of authority (reflected in mastery) and dependence in the form of disciplined answerability (reflected in servitude) are interdependent. To be disconnected from reality, from objectivity, from the demands of the world, is to assume a condition that in fact degrades one's power; to be connected to these demands is to have to subordinate oneself to them, answer to them, grapple with the recalcitrance of objects. Power depends on submission, figuring out what the world is and becoming effective in its terms. We will return to this theme—the intrinsic connection between materiality and agency—in chapter 5.

SERVITUDE

Now let us consider these themes as they play out for the servant (see *PS* §§194–96/*PG* 114–16). The servility of the servant also turns out to be less straightforward than it seems. In some sense it is true that, the more the master demands, the more the servant's situation is dominated, but this also entails progressively more competence on the part of the servant, insofar as they are becoming educated into the nature of reality and empowered to grapple with it. The master's authority triggers the master's incapacity; the master's incapacity triggers the servant's capacity, the ongoing development of competencies. In every act of service, the servant learns how to "master."

This process of cultivation began with the servant's assumption of thinghood for itself, being "posited as ... consciousness in the shape of *thinghood*" (*PS* §189/*PG* 112). In taking on thinghood, the servant assumes the same level as things and the capacity to "mingle" with them, opening their body to transformation by things. As the servant answers to things so as to discern how they can be worked on, how they can become different in discerning hands, the servant changes. The way the servant and things meet *as things*—in other words, the very finite embodiment that has made the servant vulnerable to death—is the occasion for the servant's empowerment. By assuming inessentiality, the servant's intelligence and judgment grow, as does their bodily capacity to affect the world and turn it into a home. They can cause the world to change form; their mind develops so as to grasp forms and therefore possibilities beyond actuality.

But there is another aspect to this thinghood that Hegel notices. He says that the servant has "felt the fear of death, the absolute master." The servant has experienced their own thinghood, the absolute dependence of existence on body, on the terms of nature to which they are subservient, and so they cling to thinghood, at the expense of self-assertion as perspective. They drop everything, so to speak, and become thing as tool for master, tool that submits to other tools so as to learn about them. But the opposite—the "essence of self-consciousness"—becomes manifest here behind the back of what seems to be happening. First, in "dropping everything"—in experiencing all "existence becom[ing] absolutely fluid"—the servant essentially manifests themself as self-consciousness and not thing. Things cannot pivot like this, become something different, make something no longer mean what it meant, take a different orientation to the world, decide the meaning of things, make something nothing and nothing something. This is actually, as Hegel says, "the simple essence of self-consciousness, absolute negativity" (*PS* §194/ *PG* 114). Through the very movement of self-negation, the servant implicitly enacts their status as self-consciousness.

With Hegel's discussion of the servant, we see that the "dependence and independence of self-consciousness" is dependence and independence regarding others, but also regarding life, finitude, and "thingliness." The independence of perspective, having a "mind of one's own," depends upon thinghood, embodiment, and the capacity to mingle with the world. "Life is as essential to it as is pure self-consciousness"; we are both "pure self-consciousness" and "consciousness in the shape of thinghood" (*PS* §189/*PG* 112). The mistaken conclusion of the struggle to the death (which shows us something real and important, and thus needs to be portrayed even in its mistakenness) sets these apart. We will return later to the issue of materiality, but for now let us turn again to the encounter with another perspective and the conceptual conclusion of this section, captured in "it is a self-consciousness for a self-consciousness" (§177/108); "self-consciousness is in and for itself insofar as and through the fact that it is in and for itself for another; that is, it is only as recognized" (§178/109); and "they *recognize* each other as *recognizing each other*" (§184/110).[6]

RECOGNITION

We have been accommodated into the human world by other perspectives taking us as perspectives; the ways in which their perspectives have slipped into ours are the ways that we have had of becoming ourselves, and our existence can be deeply enriched by our ongoing openness to being "slipped into." Another person has a fundamental power in relation to us: to shape the way we see ourselves and the way we see the world. The perceiving of others develops into our perceiving; their sense of our value becomes our sense of our value. We can never rid other people of this power; we can never perfectly seal ourselves off from it; we are beings whose perspectives are open to others and whose becoming occurs through this intertwining. The fact that we show up within the perspectives of others, and how that plays out for us, is something that they co-determine with us; they have a say in who we are, what we think of ourselves, and how we take up the world. If they navigate their own independence and dependence well, they interpret us as requiring consideration, formation, and care.

We see this in the most basic way with early caregivers, who induct us into the real through taking us to be perspectives. A child cries, and a parent's arrival announces, "I heard you. You are real. You matter." He sits beside her as she eats and says, "no, peas go in your mouth and not in your eye," redirecting the food to its correct destination. She feels satisfaction as the peas go down her throat and into her belly, and this satisfaction is an outcome of operating in a way that matches up well with things (the peas) but also an outcome of her parent's care. Both are happening, simultaneously. The parent affirms to the child that she is important, she is to be attended to, she is to feel good. He affirms to her that she is a part of reality and shows her how it works. Her development is supported when the thingliness of the world is brought to the measure of her body by her caregivers and her body matches it, growing on the basis of this matching. Development is a choreographed conversation between reality and perspective, in which caregivers offer the cared-for the world that is the other side of her body's development, and affirm, even only by virtue of their presence, that this project is worthwhile because she is. The child's development depends on being affirmed and guided by others in pairing with materiality: the parent says, "this is how to walk, feet on floor, come to me," and to walk the child has to respond to the terms presented by her feet, by the ground, and by the welcoming arms of the parent on the other side of the room. The free being becomes so through guidance, rules, and welcome, material limits and love. The parent slowly gives the child the world and welcomes her in, illuminating the demands of that world gradually and affirming the child's belonginess to it.

We are open to the perspectives of others sliding into our own; in their seeing of us, we develop and learn to see ourselves differently. In their appropriation and perception of the world, we learn to approach and perceive the world; in their witnessing to reality, we learn about further aspects of the world. These are the dynamics that operate and circulate in the interpersonal world, at play in our encounters with others. The richness of my world and my pairing with it is due to its being available to others and due to my intrinsic openness to them.

One of the most fundamental points here is the pivot between others and world: that the careful cultivation of the perspective of others in relations of recognition is key to the development of a rich human world. The domination and crushing of perspective is not the solution to the threat of another, but is the impoverishment of one's own world and one's pairing with it. The existence of other freedoms—including freedoms in other spaces and times—is the proper home for one's full development as a perspective. Perspective is a matter of being dispossessed of itself by the perspectives of others; it is a becoming; it is an interpersonal production. Because of one's capacity to be infiltrated by these beings who can take up the world as themselves and reveal it anew, one's world can expand; one depends in all areas of life upon their independence.

Given this account of the absolutely fundamental character of perspectival interaction, we can ask, what modes of interaction own up to this fundamental character? How do we live our perspectives in ways that own up to our fundamental porosity and the interpersonal history by which we are constituted? Hegel here, as elsewhere, flags the norm implicit in the description, and here the norm that reveals itself is this: The mode of interaction appropriate to our character as perspective is not force but communication, because communication has the capacity to honor the other as a perspective and not just as a thing. The kind of communication that grapples honestly with the character of the other as perspective is one that registers the significance of what is being expressed and is compelled by that significance and not by force.[7] The status of the other as someone who has a world and whose "having" power is a priority is implicitly acknowledged by genuine communication: When I try to convince someone of the significance of a point, or of the significance of my view, for instance, I am trying to stimulate (if I am genuinely engaged with them as a perspective) their free recognition of that point or my view. I want them to come to it themselves, since coming to it themselves allows the significance of the point or of my view to be affirmed for its significance. Any manipulation would cast doubt on the independent significance of the point or my view. Further, conversely, their status as having a world, as being a perspective, means that who they are and how reality appears to them cannot be manifest simply in the terms of objective reality but can only be communicated. If another person is a "take" on reality and not just a "piece" of it, they cannot simply be manifest in the terms that characterize objective pieces of reality.

What is called for here is a recognition of each other as beings who take up the world and each other in ways that we cannot measure or predict, in ways that can powerfully shape our own experience, for better and worse. The I is a defining, world-orienting point, and to recognize that I is to acknowledge that it is a source of meaning that another cannot capture. The other is someone who reveals a measure that I do not and cannot fathom, and who illuminates my capacity to be reoriented. The other is someone who can turn my vulnerability into the condition of my development: I am "for [my]self, and [my] self-externality is *for* [*me*]," and this is happening for both of us (*PS* §184/*PG* 110).

What we also see here, however, will take us to the next sections of this chapter. In being real, these dynamics demand that we own up to them, but they cannot *force* us to do so. Thus, while they are in principle the site of human expansion, in practice they can become the site of human reduction, and in two ways. First, as we will speak of briefly but mostly leave for chapter 3, the fact that we get a world and ourselves through others means that the world and the selves we get are very specific. To make sense, we speak a particular language in a specific way, with particular kinds of affect and consideration for others; we take the world to be this or that kind of place, with opportunities for certain actions; it is these and not other forms of "making and perceiving sense" that we share with others, often not noticing their specificity. We can see this as well in the process of becoming competent at something: we choose to learn something and pursue it—piano, hawking trinkets to tourists, cooking, studying the Torah—but becoming powerful at that specific thing requires the non-pursuit of other possibilities. Becoming competent is paired with becoming determinate. Second, and the theme we will pursue now, exposure and intertwining can be dangerous and destructive for us, since our character as perspective may very well not be acknowledged in our relations, and since the perspectives of others to which we are exposed can project reduced worlds or reductive and defensive modes of pairing with it. Perspectives and our self- and world-relation are vulnerable in their porosity. We cannot ourselves force recognition to be given; the other always retains the power to "turn on the switch of" recognition, no matter how much they seek to evade it. We cannot choose the original others who hold the fate of our development in their hands; the dependence of our paired independence-dependence goes all the way down. We cannot eliminate vulnerability, since our demand to be recognized may not result in its satisfaction, and since we are vulnerable to failures of recognition even before we know we need it. Our sense of self is being forged before we have the means to discern between helpful and hindering relations, between debilitating and constructive forms of porosity to the world and others.

We will see now, in bringing Hegel into dialogue with Frantz Fanon and Jessica Benjamin, some of the real ways in which this vulnerability has been mishandled and abused, and thus aim to bring to life again, through these contexts, Hegel's old idea.

Fanon and Racist Perception

In the portrayal of his trial in the *Apology*, Socrates remarks that the accusations that would result in his condemnation were not the formal ones—impiety and corruption of the youth—but the "first accusations" (Plato 2012, 22): namely, the common views about Socrates that circulate without anyone in particular having invented them or made these claims about Socrates in the first place. These first accusations have shaped the ways that people will approach his current case, and yet no one can be brought to court to account and answer for them, for they are as though beliefs without authors, unattributable to anyone in particular and not consciously chosen, but circulating parts of the world to which they are attached. Recognition operates in this way: Through our dependence upon others, we are inducted into a specific way of inhabiting the world, a specific orientation to reality, and it is always partial, with a varying capacity for generativity or destructiveness. Let us begin here, and then move to Fanon and the discussion of racist perception.

RECOGNITION AS INDUCTION INTO SPECIFICITY

The fact that self-consciousness only exists in being recognized works at the level of the first accusations: When others usher us into the world, they induct us into a determinate way of being human, into one answer to the question of how to be human, not *the* answer. Yet this answer does not present itself as one-sided and cannot easily be held to account for and defend itself, because it is that through which we come to be the kind of beings who can give accounts. This one answer cannot be experienced or presented as one among many, but rather sets the stage on the basis of which other such answers can be evaluated. As the stage, it is not experienced as equivalent to those other answers, but as their very authority and judge. We can say about this stage what Heidegger says about "world": It "is not an object that stands before us and can be seen, but is the ever non-objective to which we are subject" (1993, 170). It is not objective, because it is the stage upon and in terms of which anything "objective" appears as such. It is not subjective because we who are construed as subjects[8] are subject to it. We already perceive and experience the world in a certain way, and these perceptual and experiential habits are difficult to reveal, particularly since our very activity of revealing mobilizes these habits themselves. The powers by which one would study oneself are a piece of the specificity they are mobilized to unearth.

With Socrates and Hegel, we can ask: What is the character of the relations of recognition into which we have already been inducted? How does "having been recognized" operate in our lives? What implicit accounts of the nature of reality and ourselves circulate here, concealed and uncontested, unavailable to be summoned to and questioned in court? What are the worldly "first coordinates" here, that "nonobjective" by which objects are revealed in a certain light? The first challenge of philosophy is to illuminate to ourselves that which withdraws from illumination because it is the stage upon which all the rest of the players are made to appear in a certain way. If philosophical thinking does not attend to the nature of the stage, then it will privilege what asserts itself immediately in our experience as requiring attention, without recognizing that the conditions of the stage dictate how it will appear. As Merleau-Ponty says, we think from the contingent; thinking "moves back and forth between experience and intellectual construction or reconstruction" (1964, 119). Philosophy is an exercise in narcissism if it does not attend to the first accusations that assert, without our noticing, "this is what demands to be thought."

However, while this fundamental porosity to the perspectives of others can debilitate our capacity to think the "general," it is not simply a handicap but its opposite: namely, it supports the possibility of thinking well. If to be self-consciousness is to have one's orientation defined and shaped by others, this means that we are also in principle open to the perspectives of people who do not have the same experiences as us "slipping into" our own, in principle open to reorientation by what lies beyond our experience or off the stage. If, similarly, the practice of philosophy projects the idea of truth, something with a broader scope than just "true for us," and the ideal that to think well is to think on behalf of it, then in principle it compels us toward what lies beyond our experience, to be open to the unfamiliar and willing to be guided by it. The two-sided character of philosophy—its grounding in the determinate and its trajectory toward the general—must be held onto in our discussion. To illuminate what is beyond our experience, it makes sense to engage with those with significant powers of expression who have been moved to articulate that beyond as "what is to be thought" in their experience. It is incumbent upon philosophy to investigate whether our thoughts are actually shareable or whether they attach only to that experience that figures most prominently for us—either our own or that which has assumed prominence, which may not be the same—and to change the scene of philosophy so that peripheral or "disappeared" perspectives can make their way into philosophical inquiry. Our porosity to the perspectives of others sets for us clear and specific philosophical tasks: to recognize our seat in determinacy, to pursue our aspirations to universality, and to build practices of interaction that would support the philosophical potential to be genuinely general, which is a theme that emerges particularly in the discussion of conscience.[9] In fact, these Hegelian criteria can be used to challenge Hegel: While I take his philosophy to articulate these three points, the concrete conditions of his situation did not particularly support the last of these three points, which means that some of the words he is reported to have spoken to his students in lecture courses seem to fall short of truth, would presumably have been different had his communicative context been more expansive, and function to debilitate the possibility of expansion of that context.[10] But we will leave this (and related issues) for the next chapter.

In Fanon's analysis of racist misrecognition, we find a particularly destructive consequence of porosity to the perspectives of others that is situated in particularly destructive "first accusations." The social habits into which we are inducted can be habits of denying recognition to ourselves or others, habits of devaluing certain perspectives, and they operate as the stage, not that which we comprehend from it. When people are their target, these habits of denial and devaluation can negatively affect their self-perception. Human beings are fundamentally vulnerable to this, and Fanon describes a particular type of this vulnerability: being rendered object by being the target of racist perception. Being originally interpersonal also renders us vulnerable to habits of racist perception, whether we are racialized or not, though how we are taken up by others entails the production of different kinds of habits. Like Hegel's, my "stage" and habits will tend to be those associated with whiteness; my perception has inevitably been shaped by the entrenched social habit of racism; I speak out of the space and unthought freedom socially granted to white perceivers, not out of the attunement to racist perception produced in racialized perceivers by the demands of navigating social space and racist perspectives.

In what follows, we are already implicitly invoking ethical life, the theme of the next chapter, which tracks how the perspective of "self-consciousness" is expanded into the way "we" see and thus how perspectives can come to have the weight of a human world behind them. We have to introduce this theme here before we discuss it explicitly, because Fanon invokes the theme of recognition within a concrete, historical situation, but we will clarify the connections later, in the next chapter.

VULNERABILITY TO RACIST MISRECOGNITION

In the most famous chapter of *Black Skin, White Masks,* "The Lived Experience of the Black Man [*du Noir*]," Fanon describes the experience of personal encounter with a nonrecognizing perception, as well as the experience of encounter with the fact that this nonrecognizing perception is a matter not simply of an individual but of a way of life, a "world" or culture. In the experience of distorted relations, he reveals the import of recognition in its absence. In his discussion of the experience of the encounter with a white gaze, Fanon rehearses Hegel's claim about a general structure of experience, that we find ourselves being perceived by others and how that plays out is up to them, such that we discover— sometimes to our dismay—that they can shape our orientation to ourselves and the world and take the world and ourselves away from us in certain ways.

Fanon begins, as Hegel does, with a sense of what the self is as perspective: "I came into this world anxious to uncover the meaning of things, my soul desirous to be at the origin of the world" (2008, 89). Self-consciousness does not say about itself, "I am just a piece of the world"; rather, it experiences itself as absolute, original, a source of reality, not simply taking place in it—a perspective that, in its singularity, remakes the world and is not simply part of an already told story.

In encountering another, Fanon, like Hegel, registers both the possibility of liberation that lies therein and also the dependence upon it: "I appealed to the Other so that his liberating gaze, gliding over my body suddenly smoothed of rough edges, would give me back the lightness of being I thought I had lost, and taking me out of the world put me back in the world" (2008, 89). As Hegel describes it, one self-consciousness finds itself as an other in the other person, who sees it as other and not self, and it requires that the other give it back to itself, through affirmation of it as self: "It gets itself back" through this; "it comes to be in equality with itself again through the sublation of *its* otherness" (*PS* §181/*PG* 109), and this is "*its own* doing *just* as well as it is *the other's* doing" (§182/110). Fanon's words harbor implicit philosophical claims, as his typical of his style; he seems to prioritize bringing rich philosophical insight to expression in descriptions of lived experience over giving a rigorous theoretical account. Here we might imagine that one is originally "light" in relation to being because to be human is to encounter reality and not simply to be a determinate and fixed piece of it. As Hegel states at the outset of the *Philosophy of Right*, the will contains "the element of *pure indeterminacy*..., in which every limitation, every content, whether present immediately through nature, through needs, desires, and drives, or given and determined in some other way, is dissolved" (*PR/GPR* §5).[11] This is a kind of effervescence with regard to being, the capacity to transcend determinacy, even if only by giving it a different meaning. As this lightness, one encounters others who are also "light" in relation to being, and one presumably perceives them as such. In the mode of basic civility, such as one might expect from a stranger on a subway or in an administrative office, we typically implicitly communicate that we respect this "inside" by leaving it alone, and law expresses this respect by protecting basic access to these spaces; in love and friendship, however, this "inside" appears as the occasion of significant mutual enrichment. Unfolding inside the perspectives of the ones who either leave us alone or care for us is implicit or explicit affirmation of our reality as perspectives. Another person can offer us something that we cannot offer ourselves; she can make it exciting and enriching that we are subject to the interpretive overreach of another; we cannot do this for ourselves. They can make it wonderful to be the "not-me" who exists for them, who shows up inside of their perspectives, extending care and recognition that make our lives more meaningful, recognizing and affirming our possibility, the way we outstrip reality, our status as beings who are "at the origin of the world." This is our character as being-with, as beings of encounter, recognition, the intertwining of perceiving and perceived (Merleau-Ponty 1968).

Similar to Hegel, who portrays a scenario in which the demand we project as human is not met, Fanon's target is a situation in which this liberation offered by the other does not occur. Here, it is not abstract but the real, concrete situation of racist misrecognition, which turns the body into "a body without perspective" (Gordon 1995, 102). The universe, as James Baldwin evocatively observes, "which is not merely the stars and the moon and the planets, flowers, grass, and trees, but *other people*, has evolved no terms for your existence, has made no room for you" (1963, 41).

Due to the reality of the other perspective, the experience of racist misrecognition has an effect. About an experience on the train, Fanon writes, "I existed in triple" (2008, 92). I think that Fanon is suggesting here that there are in fact three selves to be discerned in his text: The first, I would argue, is the one "desirous to be at the origin of the world" (89). The second is constituted because of the real vulnerability operative in human experience, what Hegel calls the "dependence of self-consciousness": through the other's look, the self is returned to itself "spread-eagled, disjointed, redone, draped in mourning" (93), "an object among other objects," fixed by the other's "gaze, his gestures and attitude." This is a "suffocating reification" (89) in which the racialized self is turned into an object and his "lived experience" is ignored (90). The third self is the self tasked with recovery.

THE BODY SCHEMA, THE HISTORICAL-RACIAL SCHEMA, THE EPIDERMAL RACIAL SCHEMA

In the scenario Hegel describes, the two aspects of self-consciousness — pure self-consciousness and thinghood — are separated out from each other and attributed to master and servant, respectively. In Fanon's scenario, the "second self," like the servant, is locked in thinghood, and its way of being body, its body schema, is disrupted (2008, 91). In a move interestingly similar to Fanon and other phenomenologists, Hegel analyzes the body here, looking at how the servant so to speak combines their body with the world so as to answer to the master's will. Condemned to thinghood by the master, the servant's dalliance with things reveals something important: Its thingliness is key to its selfhood, and yet it could never simply be thinghood, for this is a thingliness that is the very occasion for its development of "a mind of [its] own" (*PS* §196/ *PG* 116).

Hegel's analysis of the servant's work is not an account of the body schema, of course, but it signals the dependence of human development on interaction with thingliness. The very recalcitrance of things—the necessity they present to it, around which it must maneuver—is the occasion for the development of a "mind of its own." The I is an "I of the world," an "I-world" partnership, or (as Heidegger calls it) "being-in-the-world" (1962, 78). The I becomes itself in answering to the world's structures. As Fanon describes it, the body and the world are engaged in an ongoing pairing that is not conducted by the reflective "I," and this relation gives one oneself. Here we have the body schema as the outcome of a process of intertwining: Body is contact with world; body develops in this pairing; the I is as though an accomplishment on the part of the body/world pair. The body schema is this open availability of the body to the world and its habituated capabilities in and with the world, in which its parts are not separate but unified by its intertwining with the world. It is a lived, bodily intelligence conducted on the basis of this body-world relation, that initiates and sustains the more intermittent activity of cognitive intelligence.

Fanon describes the body schema in the following:

> I know that if I want to smoke, I shall have to stretch out my right arm and grab the pack of cigarettes lying at the other end of the table. As for the matches, they are in the left drawer, and I shall have to move back a little. And I make all these moves, not out of habit, but by implicit knowledge. A slow construction of my self as a body in a spatial and temporal world—such seems to be the schema. It is not imposed on me; it is rather a definitive structuring of my self and the world—definitive because it creates a genuine dialectic between my body and the world. (2008, 90–91)

In invoking the body schema, Fanon is invoking this idea of a lived intelligence that does not generally rise to the level of cognition, but rather "does its thing." Fanon reports on what cognition would make of this implicit knowledge belonging to his body in its "genuine dialectic" with the world: "I know that if I want to smoke..." These moves are typically not mediated by cognition, however, but made on the basis of "implicit knowledge." The world is here and has already been here, projected in a specific way and as a specific kind of availability by my body, because I am a body that has always engaged with it, that converses with the world in a nonreflective manner, that is an orientation to and of that world. The world produces the body schema in being there with and for the body, in implicitly training the body to deal with it, slotting the body as part into its whole, and the body, with the world, makes the world *for* it.

The impact of racist perception is that it interrupts and disrupts the body schema in a way that is similar to reflection. When we spell out our actions cognitively—"I know that if I want to smoke, I shall have to stretch out my right arm" (Fanon 2008, 90)—we do not live through and on the basis of body but make it artificially an object. Racist perception operates similarly. "In the white world, the man of color encounters difficulties in elaborating his body schema. The image of one's body is solely negating. It's an image in the third person. All around the body reigns an atmosphere of certain uncertainty" (90–91). In Fanon's account, racist perception interrupts embodied experience; the racist perceiver assumes the stance of self-consciousness abstract from thinghood, and the racialized body is rendered thinghood abstract from self-consciousness. Racist perception jolts the racialized body out of the body as "first coordinates," thrusting the body onto the stage rather than allowing it to persist as "the darkness of the theatre required for the clarity of the performance" (Merleau-Ponty 2012, 103). Reflection on the body-world coupling is likely to happen only if something interrupts the otherwise smooth coupling of body and world (see Heidegger 1962, 104). Racist perception is one of these interruptions, preventing the world from being ready-to-hand for the racialized body, expelling the body from its "genuine dialectic" with the world (Fanon 2008, 91).

Fanon's insight resonates with Hegel's account: White misrecognition can do this because of our original condition—namely, that we are porous, formed in and by the perspectives of others upon us. A perspective upon us has the power to displace the body schema and change our self-relation, because it is not a thing but a bearer of shareable meaning. White misrecognition disrupts the body schema and replaces it with a "historical-racial schema" and an "epidermal racial schema" (Fanon 2008, 91–92). Let us explore these two schemas in turn: one a narration and the other a flattening of body into thing.

Under the rubric of the historical-racial schema, Fanon argues that the dominant, white "we" has come to attribute developmental narratives to the racialized body; rather than the body as "first coordinates," historical stories developed elsewhere become its basis, inscribing themselves in a gap they insert between self and body. The body schema was not already racialized; racialization is something accomplished by a narrative extending from ignorant perception. The racialized person is reconstructed from outside and, given the porosity of perspective, is vulnerable to taking on this reconstruction herself: as Fanon observes, he himself *"had created"* this schema, on the basis of data provided by the white perspective. "Beneath the body schema I had created a historical-racial schema. The data I used were provided by the other, the white man, who had woven me out of a thousand details, anecdotes, and stories" (Fanon 2008, 91). The other can interfere with one's self-experience, can displace one's own stories about oneself with their own, to the devastating consequence that their stories can become one's own; one can be dragged into complicity. Here we see a tragic effect of the porosity of perspectives: I can lose myself to an external story; a narrative about me can reconstruct me.

Beyond narrative, the second schema Fanon discerns here is a "thingly" one: as he says, the body schema collapses and gives rise "to an epidermal racial schema" (2008, 92). Rather than "a slow construction of my self as a body in a spatial and temporal world" (91), the racialized person is constituted as "black skin." White perception takes the body *to be black* and not specifically body, which is not simply a thing, disabling the body schema through a habituated insistence on the status of the body as epidermis. To be racialized, in Fanon's account, is for body to *become* skin and object, no longer possibility "at the origin of the world."

Others always interfere; we are always a palimpsest of the perspectives of others and our own. We are as though fated to the interference we get, condemned to the work of pulling ourselves out of destructive relations, rehabilitating ourselves and others, reorganizing relations and social structures. Racist perception is thus also deeply unjust in motivating the need for this labor of social and self-transformation, which calls for the third self. The first self was "desirous to be at the origin of the world" (Fanon 2008, 89); the second is "my body... returned to me spread-eagled, disjointed, redone, draped in mourning" (93); and the third is needed to oppose "affective tetanization" (92) and put together the fragments, deal with the fallout of the encounter, and work toward restoration.

But there is more to the labor of this third self than work on herself. Thus far, we have in Fanon and Hegel a shared appreciation of the inevitability of dependence on the other, and with Fanon we have a picture of how that dependence is experienced by the self if it is not accompanied by what Hegel shows is required by the logic of encounter—acknowledgment of perspective. We also have an account of what this experience does to our character as bodies, distorting the mutually transformative relation between (to use Hegel's terms) ourselves as thinghood and ourselves as self-consciousness. Now we come to a further ingredient: that the perspectives of others are empowered to act especially destructively when it becomes a matter of *habitual social practice* to do so. Perspectives are not simply singular and unique but, because of their porosity to each other, tend to become patterned: historical, social, cultural, and entrenched. Once they occupy a position of dominance, they have even more capacity to circulate and perpetuate themselves. Thus the third self is also as if asked to work on behalf of her world and culture. As Fanon reveals, he is suddenly called to oppose a "white world" (2008, 94) and justify the "new species" constituted by that world: "I see in this white gaze that it's the arrival not of a new man, but of a new type of man, a new species. A Negro, in fact!" (95).

"THE EARTH SINGS WHITE": THE WHITE WORLD

Fanon writes that "the white man is all around me; the earth sings white, white" (2008, 94). It is not simply a single being who disavows perspective in a racialized being; rather, this being is ensconced in an entrenched, historically dominant, white world. And so the third self is fated not simply to a reconstruction of self but to reconstruction of the "non-white" world to which she is attached and which is now thematized as the counterpart of the white one. In addition to making body as non-object into object, racialized perception turns nonobjective worlds into objects, such that racialized beings find world, like body, before them as object rather than behind them as the "darkness of the theatre required for the clarity of the performance" (Merleau-Ponty 2012, 113). The work of revaluing one's perspective thus also requires the work of navigating that world that is now in front of oneself rather than behind. This propels Fanon's multiple attempts to answer the question of wherein the worth of his culture lies (2008, 101–19). We will discuss two themes in what follows: the experience of being surrounded by a system of misrecognition, not simply a specific instance, and the experience of being displaced from world as "nonobjective"—having one's world turned into a thing—such that the work of self-reconstruction is also the work of discerning and defending the value of one's world.

Fanon talks about the operation of his body in relation to an interior, domestic space, with drawers, tables, matches, and cigarettes (2008, 90), but we will bring this bodily operation outside to see the systematic character of white perception. Reflected in my embodied interaction with the material world in—let's say—a trip to the store is a human system of interpretation, social reality structured in a particular way, its sedimented agreement about what kind of behavior is appropriate to what kind of space, what kind of action and response I can expect and are expected of me. In navigation of the sidewalks, crosswalks, doors, aisles, counters, wallets, and money, for instance, we see implicit and site-specific norms in operation. Walking down the street reflects significant historical accomplishments; we are welcome here (or not), and we have experiential confirmation of that (or not). I pay the person behind the counter, not the one behind me in line. I don't lie down on the floor. My action reflects my basic understanding of what "we" expect, what "we" define as proper behavior, what "we" understand this kind of space to be, even though these expectations and assumptions tend to recede below the level of self-conscious reflection. The body-world relation is a matter also of a body-other relation, an I-we relation, a historically developed system of human interpretation, and this I-we relation, particularly the character of that "we," is differently experienced by different people. My body can be comfortably at home in the world (or not) because this system welcomes it (or not).

In worlds shaped by racist perception, or "in the white world," as Fanon remarks, the person "of color encounters difficulties in elaborating [their] body schema" (2008, 90). A conflict of interpretations makes itself manifest in the operation of the racialized body. Ordinary human existence is a matter of body-world coupling, but racialized existence is undermined in this, because the "nonobjective" body is turned into an object and the human interpretive system that structures the space of the world designates the presence of that racialized body as troubling. The experience of agency happens below the level of thinking, at the level of inhabiting one's body as a body-world pairing. That pairing is intersubjectively mediated; as we have seen, this is a threefold reality of self, other, and world. It is accomplished by the welcoming of others and thus obstructed by the refusal of welcome. In such worlds, the interpersonal structure is severely dysfunctional. The system of agreement that should render the space of the world a space for one's body has not been established or has broken down.

This problem calls us to think beyond the materiality of space to its immaterial elements. Space is shot through with interpretive, expectant encounter of intelligent bodies, which is materially communicated, and which can turn them into objects even for themselves and against their will. The perspectives of others hang in space, as it were, with the potential to jar some out of nonreflective inhabitation of their bodies. Meanings and materiality intertwine here in ways that cannot be disentangled. Perception of each other does not simply operate as a discrete, single activity, but on the basis of a visual field constructed in a determinate way, a racialized field of perception, where our habits of seeing and what we see are structured by a specific kind of ground. This is what Judith Butler calls "the racial production of the visible, the workings of racial constraints on what it means to 'see'" (1993, 16). Alcoff similarly describes race as "a structure of contemporary perception, ... the field, rather than that which stands out," which "cannot itself be the object of analysis" (2006, 188). This is why, beyond being a simple, single individual, "the white [person] is all around me," as Fanon writes (2008, 94); white perception organizes the perceptual field. Whiteness sustains itself as ground, as Sara Ahmed (2007) notes, in calling for white behavior, in welcoming the comfortable inhabitation of white space by white bodies. Those who "fit" space are enabled to go forth from the world as their ground. White perception and white behavior resonate with the earth that "sings white" (Fanon 2008, 95); they "fit" their ground, whereas the racialized body, as the thematized figure or object visibilized on that ground, does not.

While systematic misrecognition is entrenched in space, in the earth that "sings white" (2008, 94), it is also entrenched in time. Beyond the present encounter with another single perspective, there is the past of such encounters and the way these interpretive structures become sedimented in time. We emerge in interpersonal worlds already constituted in a specific way, and coming to inhabit our perspective is as much accommodating ourselves to that particular world and to the demands of particular others as it is becoming "ourselves"; as we have said, these are three sides of one process. Others communicate to us that to act and interact with them effectively we must do so in "these" inherited ways, handing us thereby the building blocks by which we effectively inhabit both that world and our interaction: language, behavior, customs. Because a "way of life" cultivates in us our powers of perception and understanding, it does not so easily lend itself to being their object.

There is a futural dimension to this temporality as well, which in the logic of racism involves a "white" taking possession of the meaning of history, a "white becoming-ground" in relation to time. History is construed as a trajectory with white Western culture at its apex; as Fanon observes, "destiny... is white" (2008, 12). Other modes of world inhabitation are construed as stages, "phase[s] in the dialectic" that are always "too late" in relation to the white avant-garde of humanity (111); "everything had been predicted, discovered, proved, and exploited" (100).

Alia Al-Saji writes that the "closed" past of "colonized and racialized peoples" is "subordinated to the open time of Eurocentric modernity" (2022, 182). As ground, whiteness brings with it a single temporal arc, a historical trajectory, that becomes the measure of past and future: The past culminates in white culture, which, projected as the only open and becoming culture, is the only one capable of holding the future open.

White perception, white space, and white history entrench one specific projection of the unfamiliar by one specific experience of the familiar. That is, while it is ordinary to be cultivated in particular worlds and find others unfamiliar, the white world is a world that has rendered absolute its distinction between its familiar and its unfamiliar, equating it with the distinction between the true and the false, such that it no longer simply flags who one is and where one lives. While it is easy for the relative status of the distinction between unfamiliar and familiar to become concealed and assert itself in our experience as absolute, the white world precludes everyday challenges to this assertion by establishing itself as the norm in terms of which other worlds will always be deviant or foreign, and thus has powerfully precluded transformation of the familiar and undermined the capacity of those who live in its "unfamiliar" to experience it unreflectively as familiar. Whiteness precludes grappling with the tension that is introduced by the fact that we become habituated to different worlds. It involves the illusory confidence that one has arisen above the shared participation in "depth" (Merleau-Ponty 1968) that renders inhabitation and worlds difficult to perceive. As Sara Ahmed observes, "whiteness might be what is 'here,' ... a point from which the world unfolds" (2007, 154); it is the "here" in the sense of a nonrelative place, an absolute place, by which all others are posited as at a distance.

Let us turn now, more explicitly, to the question of how "non-white" worlds are lived—namely, in the terrain established by systematic misrecognition—and how they are turned, like the racialized body, from ground into figure.

SEVERED BEING-IN-THE-WORLD AND WHITE INTERPRETIVE OVERREACH

One of the significant effects of racist colonization is the suppression of "worldhood." First, that is, world is circumscribed from the outside, perceived as having a determinate character that is fixed and closed. Second, in being marked as such, it is not permitted to be what it is: an indeterminate, open, buzzing potential, the "nonobjective" support of those who belong to it and who are (in fact) always becoming. Like the body, it is jolted out of being the unthought ground upon which perspectives implicitly draw and with which they pair. Become figure rather than ground, world cannot be the smooth support of being-in-the-world. Within white cultural worlds and within worlds projected as unfamiliar by them, racialized being-in-the-world is severed.

As Fanon shows, struggles against racism and racist colonization will thus also have to be struggles to reconnect with world, but that very struggle implies its failure, since one is "too late"; world has already been pulled out of position as ground. The fact that such a struggle is required is part of the problem, insofar as, like bodies, worlds are not typically related to as objects, and are freed to be what they are insofar as they are not thematized. This point is manifest in Fanon's dismay in the face of his attempts to reinvent the meaning of his world in the aftermath of colonialism. He documents his many efforts as a third self to define the world anew, following its white construal as inferior. These are efforts to discern the originality, independence, and contributions of his civilizational "we," all that which makes it capable of supporting original existence. He then shows the interpretive overreach by which white perception casts all of these assertions as derivative of a narrative that contains and transcends the Black perspective.

Fanon spells out these efforts. He equates himself with his ancestors (2008, 92); he asserts himself as a singular Black man (95); he demands explanations based on reason (96–97); he embraces irrationality (102) and the role he plays as emotional, intuitive (106), naive, free, and poetic (108); he excavates Black antiquity to find as yet unperceived value there (109). Besides other theoretical problems with these positions—he cannot simply *be* his ancestors, for instance—the "meaning is already out there, waiting" to be assigned by white perception (113). It is as though white perception projects: "Your people" are an instance of a kind, a type, not original but a piece of the ongoing, underwhelming development of that type (95); we cannot engage you on the level of reason (our hostility is irrational, but we have invested too much in the veneer of rationality to give it up) (111); your immaturity, emotion, intuition, and any greatness you might find in Black antiquity means nothing now, because "we" have already gone further, and now what is left for you is to catch up (108).

According to this analysis, what is needed is for worlds *to be able to recede again*, becoming the background of original beings whose souls are "at its origin" (Fanon 2008, 89). This is world not thematized, not meaningful in a *particular* way, not perceived as that in terms of which the behavior of its members could be predicted—world lived as open, enabling. This would be world free from relations of comparison, world perceived as worlds genuinely are: the determinate grounds we inhabit that offer determinate mechanisms by which we propel ourselves into the pursuit of meaning, worlds as dialogue between determinacy and openness. Here we can see the force behind the notion of "delinking" thematized by decolonial theorists such as Samir Amin (1989) and Walter Mignolo (2007); such delinking may be the condition of world being able to become world again, rather than object perceived and measured by the white world. Indigenous theorists such as Audra Simpson and Taiaiake Alfred also insist on "delinking," "refusal" (Simpson 2014), and the "resurgence of traditions" (Alfred 2005).

We appear to others. This is an occasion for receiving back one's "lightness of being" (Fanon 2008, 89) or for being returned to ourselves "spread-eagled" and "disjointed" (95), or some combination thereof. With Hegel, we see the logical problem of denying to others or oneself this lightness of being; with Fanon, we have seen its actual effects. Misrecognition is a matter of severance from body, severance from world, in which the work of the third self is jeopardized by the fact that its project has become figure and is not left to be ground. To be free, one's soul "at the origin of the world," is to be empowered to live in a way in which one's world and one's body are permitted to be the darkness of the theater required for the clarity of the performance. In their recession into ground, they harbor the open potential that is needed for the being whose being is lightness.

In the next chapter, we will follow Hegel's and Fanon's insights as they resonate inside of the experience of care for dependents and of erotic relations, experiences in which we see clearly the dynamic relation between independence and dependence, the emergence of self-consciousness in relation, and the weight of recognition or its absence.

Benjamin on the Mother-Other

Jessica Benjamin's work in feminist theory and psychoanalysis, where healthy human existence and development are at stake, centers on the idea of recognition. I will focus here in particular on that aspect of her work that addresses both parenting (particularly by women) and erotic interaction, issues that she addresses in many places (1980, 1998, 2017) but particularly powerfully in "Sympathy for the Devil: Notes on Sexuality and Aggression, with Special Reference to Pornography" (Benjamin 1995). We will find in Benjamin's work profound resonance with Hegel's but also independent power as feminist analysis, linking Hegel's philosophy and charged sites of concern for feminists: care for children and erotic relationships.[12]

THE INTERDEPENDENCE OF DEPENDENCE AND INDEPENDENCE: CHILD AND CAREGIVER

In order to exist for the self, one has to exist for the other. This introduces an odd and dramatic tension in our lives, because it means that our existence depends on something that we do not control and cannot ourselves make happen. Existence and health as self-consciousness, our being as independent selves: These depend upon something that we cannot bring about and cannot have brought about, the free recognition coming from another person. We need something we cannot force: the freedom of others. This dependence is inevitable and persistent—it, and thus the other, are the condition of possibility for the development of our independence. In flagging necessary dependence on this relation, Hegel shows that we must attend to the tensions relations introduce, and attend to those aspects of our experience as individuals that deny this relational dynamic. As individuals we must reckon with the freedom of others and with our own dependence upon it, our nonomnipotence (Benjamin 1995, 194). Our power lies in our connection to others in their power, and not simply in ourselves.

This idea is key to every critical perspective with which this book engages. Struggles against sexism, racism, colonialism, ableism, and capitalism all require the reconstructive work of Fanon's third self—dealing with the vulnerability and destruction that can be occasioned by our dependence—and each essentially defends the idea of owning up to our dependence on (hence vulnerability to) the freedom of others and cultivating a social world that would be a home for it.

The relation between dependence and independence makes itself known particularly in the parent-child relation. Benjamin makes the mother the primary focus of her analysis, particularly for feminist reasons, and because people who are typically counted as women are still more likely, across the globe, to be primary caregivers. In the parent-child relation, the parent is relatively independent and the child is relatively dependent, though the parent willingly puts her independence and power into the service of the child, becoming essentially its body and its tool and thereby bringing the child to the possibility of independence. She effectively says, "even though I am other than you, I am present with you; my love traverses the gap between me and you and helps you truck with my otherness and with your troubles. Even though I am independent of you, I care for you, and the meaning of my care is significant insofar as it is something that I give of myself, that comes willingly and lovingly from me. I am not obeying you in expressing my care; my care is real; you are so moving to me that I freely love you. The very independence of my care—the fact that it is not directly the product of your will—makes it valuable to you." The child's development is premised, to put it in Hegelian terms, on the other both affirming the child's perspective as significant and manifesting its own independence, but it can only do each via the other. That is, its being itself and other than the child makes its affirmation of the child mean something, and it honors the child's perspective by choosing to care for the child. This is what the child needs in order to be inducted into reality: a confirmed perspective of its own, a vibrant sense of the non-terrifying otherness of the world, the sense that non-omnipotence is a blessing. It needs the world, in its otherness, to be a place for it.

But let us get into the details here by looking more closely at how care for a baby works, and what the baby is like in its need for care. A baby does not recognize another perspective as such; it is not aware of its existence. A baby does not respectfully grant that the caregiver also has to "do their own thing" in addition to taking care of it. It just says "me," though in a way that is not particularly aware of itself as a "me" differentiated from others and the world. Everything is "me." This non-awareness of the perspective of another is also expressed at the level of the body. The baby needs a functioning body for movement, engagement with the world, and eating, for instance, but it does not yet have a body like that. If the baby does "do" these things, it does them through the body of another. As a caregiver, one is basically the baby's body; physical nearness of the mother-other's body is even helpful in supporting organic processes and development (Simms 2008). One must support its head, move it (every move it makes from one position to another is one made on its behalf), and feed it (every time it eats it is because one provided and served it food). The baby's "doing" requires an extreme level of commitment and availability on the part of the caregiver, particularly because the caregiver also has a body-self with its own demands that bear it toward the world in a certain way and that the baby's needs tend to disrupt. If the parent prioritized itself, the baby would not understand this as the very reasonable thing selves do, but would experience it as its own suffering. To care for a child requires regular suppression of the claims and desires coming from one's own body-self.

Just as an infant does not clearly have its own body, it does not have its own regulation. It cannot answer the questions, "why do I hurt?" or "what does this mean?" It does not have the insight that would allow it to work through challenges from the outside world. It does not have a well-developed sense of the contours of reality that would allow it to understand, for example, that eating a piece of Lego is not in its interest. It does not have a sense of the genuine otherness of other people by which it could tell that scratching a person down their face is not good. Doing so would not in fact be a transgression for the baby, because it is not aware of this otherness.

Even as the child gets older, there are many things it still does not do on its own, and many ways it still does not respect the other's perspective. Those who deal with children are surely familiar with this: the child will hit its caregiver, scream, refuse to get in the car, put on their boots, eat anything but white bread. Every refusal is a kind of assertion, to the independent perspective of the caregiver, that their desire to live out their own lives and even their desire to care for the child have to be reconciled with the child's demand (which it makes without even being aware of it) that it be the perspective to which one answers. Indeed, answering to the child is the very avenue through which the child can become the kind of person who *can* count the perspective of another. If the caregiver insists on the peripheral character of the child's perspective, the child will not learn to acknowledge another.

But of course, a caregiver also has the task of introducing to the child its answerability to the perspectives of others. The child must eventually come to understand that reality has other people in it, and that these people matter on their own terms. Its initial contacts are where this is first learned: It cannot just do whatever it wants to doggy, Daddy, sibling. But this also must be introduced in a way in which it can be appreciated, in a way consistent with the child's capacities, its sense of self, and its desires. The substance and meaningfulness of the child's future life lies in the freedom of others, and thus others must not be introduced to the child solely as a limit, but as recognitive and affirming, engaged in collective making of the world. The child needs affirmation that the coexistence of selves is possible, that otherness is not a threat, that coexistence is wonderful. The otherness the child encounters should be that of a generous being who has basically been present and who is now emerging to the child's consciousness as a self in her own right. She is a source of regulation, answers, and teaching; she will bring the child into meaning, slowly disclose reality to it, emerge in her otherness, and be affirming and receptive in that otherness.

The child cannot satisfy or regulate itself, cannot deal with the tensions of encounter with that world and itself on its own, cannot become a more or less competent self on its own. It requires a relation that can aid it in its satisfaction and its resolution of tension, a relational space in which it can put both its excitement and aggression, where it can become itself. Benjamin writes that the mother-other is "someone felt to exist outside mental omnipotence, someone who can contain the tension that we cannot bear alone, who can receive what is necessary to give" (1995, 194). The mother-other is not simply a tool of an omnipotent child, but her otherness is helpful and not a threat if she helps the child with tensions it cannot resolve on its own. This mother-other is ideally felt, as Benjamin writes, "as both permeable to one's own feelings and unattacking. When we refer to recognition of the mother as independent person, we are including this notion of a mother who is both (partially, imperfectly) knowable and knowing, who can be affected without being annihilated" (195–96). This is a mother who can receive without simply becoming "me," "who can encompass what is inside us without imposing terrifying fantasies from within her. She is neither overwhelmingly weak/needy nor invincible/perfect" (196).

Benjamin links this availability also to communication: The other's availability for the receipt of communication "gives meaning to the expressive act and so transforms the self's inner state" (1995, 197). At a very basic level, expression—whether it be anything from an outburst to a developed thought—is affirmed as meaningful by simply being received; this indicates that the expression is understood to be a communication of meaning and it supports the development of expressive powers, the central medium of relation to others. Further, if the expression does not simply "know" what it is, if it is the inarticulate effect of a felt, vague tension, it depends on the other's reception and articulation to emerge as meaningful. The other's action of receptivity is where the child becomes articulate, and thus what is outside of the child is again experienced as the domain in which it can be itself. The ongoing presence and operation of receptivity teaches the child that the not-I can be a rich source of the articulation of its own experience and of its becoming meaningful. Via receipt of expression, the child is inducted into the rich experience of symbolization and meaning-making. Here also one experiences the emergence of a meaningful distinction between fantasy and reality: What is "in me" can be confirmed in its reality by what is "not-me," and thus confirmed as meaningful as such (not just for me), or it could be corrected. The reliability of this kind of response can encourage the child to note and trust the marking of a difference between fantasy and reality.[13]

It is also significant that the connection facilitated by the caregiver to the symbolic domain and to the child's own symbolic capacities is simultaneously a lived experience of intimacy. The experience of inwardness turned into speech, into impact on another, is associated with a feeling of connection. The fact that enunciation emerges inside of connection and its pleasure is enormously significant in motivating self-articulation and clarity in communication, and thereby in motivating the healthy development of interpersonal relations.

As beings who exist because of recognition, we depend on a world that supports the work of caregiving. Further, given the fact that we inherit a world in which, traditionally, women have done the work of care, largely under conditions of exploitation, this work of supporting relations will inevitably entail some specific attention to women and opposition to their exploitation, even as it envisions the expansion of caregiving beyond women and the expansion of gender beyond binary categories. Before we turn, however, to the question of what kind of world and what kind of feminist labor is required by our interdependent character, let us speak to the phenomenon of adult relations of recognition, particularly of the sexual kind, and the relevance therein of feminist concerns. Encounter with others in adult life relies considerably on whether we are born into relations that are the occasion for enrichment, the pleasure of connection, and shared articulation of personal experience.

THE INTERDEPENDENCE OF DEPENDENCE AND INDEPENDENCE IN EROTIC RELATIONS

In being with our early caregivers, we become habituated to a specific mode of behavior, but we do not typically experience it as one possibility among many, because it is only through that behavior that we develop the capacity for judgment that would allow us later to discern different possibilities, and because the relation sets the terms for our encounter with reality and other others. Thus again we see emphatically that "self-consciousness exists only in being recognized" (*PS* §178/ *PG* 109). If others are those who "bring reality to us," who reveal to us different possibilities for being human but always in their own particular way, then these early caregivers will set the terms of our existence. The habits of interaction we have with those others will significantly impact who we become and how we pursue other later relationships.

But others also take us in new directions. When we encounter someone whom we find compelling, romantically or otherwise, we may experience ourselves transfixed, excited, and moved by precisely their otherness—the ways in which they surprise us and show themselves to be not us, different, enticing. We may find ourselves delighting in their specificity, in how the world reveals itself differently to them and to us in their company. We may find ourselves brought in new directions by their attention, developing different forms of behavior, and coming thereby to have a different world.

Further, it typically matters to us that they, in their otherness, find themselves inwardly compelled by us. We would likely find it problematic if they attended to us because we commanded it, like the master, for then their choice of us would not mean as much. This is the truth implicit in the master's desire—that what she really wants is recognition that is freely given.

In our erotic openness to this other—whether it be romantic or not—we render ourselves transformable by another person. We expose ourselves to their freedom; we make for it a place within ourselves, willingly or not. This is the amazing quality of erotic attention: that through it we become a site for the unfolding of the freedom of another. The capacity the other has to act within us in these relations is a milder version of the extreme version that occurs in childhood, where the freedom of others shapes and forms us. This is the weight and importance of the erotic relation. With this, we expose ourselves to the potentially transformative powers the world has in store; without it, we leave our development solely to the limits of our own imagination.

And yet this otherness is challenging: Through our very desire for their free attention, we make it important to us, but we are not in control of it. If it turns away, we might be disappointed, crushed, our sense of self-worth negatively affected. The other can in this way put themselves at play at the heart of who we are—and again, they can do this willingly or unwillingly, just as we can be willing or unwilling recipients of it. Or we can find it challenging to want both to shape our lives around this other and to live in the way that we define independently, since these two may involve conflicting visions. We may find ourselves passionately invested in some project or piece of the world that leaves them cold, and lose our footing in it as a result; their attention can fit poorly with our historical patterns of worldly engagement. We may find ourselves upon a trajectory with them that has left other trajectories behind, and mourn the unactualized possibilities. Their otherness, in general, renders them separate from us, and separation can stimulate excitement but also alienation—from them, from ourselves, and from the world. Thus their otherness and the freedom it presents is ambivalent in its meaning for us: It can produce problems in how we inhabit reality and take up our own lives.

Like Benjamin's mother-other, however, this other will ideally be someone whose otherness is not generally experienced as a threat, but who is both able to be other and happy to be present *to us* in that otherness. However, if we have become attuned to the meaningfulness of otherness as such, inducted into a more or less friendly world by our early caregivers, and given early models of receptive otherness that we can use to discern whether others are receptive or not, then it is more likely the case that our encounters with other others will work well. To be able to truck with otherness is to be able to make one's life the site of their powers and their vision, so whether or not we can live with the tension that otherness presents is key to whether or not our own lives will become articulate and developed. Much depends on whether we can sustain this openness to being carried along by the possibilities and avenues the freedom of others offers. Much depends, therefore, on things we cannot control or can no longer effect: whether the other, like the mother, is able and willing both to be other and to be present to us in that otherness, and whether we have had early relations that allow us to experience otherness as enticing rather than threatening and that move us to choose friendly others and reject hostile ones.

FEMINIST QUESTIONS

Here we can take the model of receptive otherness presented by Hegel and Benjamin and use it to critique the entrenched sexist and heterosexist orientations that show up in the reproductive and domestic arena as well as in the arena of erotic interaction. There are at least two sets of problems that tend to arise here, interpersonally. The first set is about the source of recognition in caregiving work: namely, it has typically been a matter of "women's work" and done by people usually called "mothers"; it is not typical that these caregivers have been supported in their own otherness and in the work it takes to be present to the child; and it is typically not construed as a matter of "men's" work and done by "fathers." All of this means that human beings may not have as much occasion to experience men as engaged in caring attunement, that men may practice it less than is needed, and that boys may not learn it sufficiently. The second set of problems concerns the adult being who undertakes erotic relations with others: There are historically entrenched, gender-related obstacles to the support of the otherness and flourishing of people in those relations. These problems are related to a basic vulnerability associated with interaction with others: The others with whom we are involved can degrade and even destroy our status as a site of possibility and becoming.

 I want to operate with some degree of generality here, since this experience is relatively widespread, but both caregiving and erotic relations of course take different forms in different societies and contexts and are weighed differently relative to other priorities, so any generalizations would have to be tailored to their appropriate context. My interpretations are shaped by my experience in US and Canadian contexts dominated by white, so-called Western norms.

 In such contexts, the care for children, and for this primary, relational ground in which human beings develop as such, seems insufficiently supported and neglected, particularly if we consider it in relation to its import for human life. Caregivers seem unsupported in two ways, each of which relates to a different aspect of Hegel's and Benjamin's insights: They are unacknowledged and unsupported in their otherness, which is suppressed by cultures that cultivate women to be self-effacing or self-denying, and they are unsupported in the massive effort that seems to be required to be present and receptive to a child in its singularity. Further, given the import of relational coexistence to human life, people are insufficiently supported due to the widespread exclusion of men from this caring work, which has important consequences for everyone. Finally, people are insufficiently supported simply by the whole framework, which is characterized by heterosexist and sexist insistence upon two different binary characters whose traditional roles were and often still are construed as mutually exclusive.

Above we delineated the challenges involved in being present to a child: It does not acknowledge, affirm, or make room for one's own perspective, yet the possibility of its development nevertheless requires that its perspective be affirmed. It is of utmost importance to recognize (which people tend not to do) that to care for a child is essentially to be asked to do something very challenging over and over again, which is to suppress the claims that come from one's own character as a perspective, because it is important that the child learn that it matters, and this valuing is expressed by the outside world's witnessing responsiveness, of which the mother-other is typically the representative. Of course there are people who find their very fulfillment in being consistently responsive and present, but it is deeply unrealistic to imagine that this is characteristic of most people. This work, of course, is often so difficult and demanding that the mother-other is tempted to suppress or sideline the otherness of the child instead. The stakes are high: It is this work that produces human beings. Thus practical support of this labor is significant in the support of childhood development.

Second, the singularity, individuality, and agency of the mother-other has not traditionally been hailed and supported, and so their capacity to be present and receptive *as an other* is also insufficiently supported. In traditionally sexist societies, the lives and activities of people traditionally affiliated with caregiving work tend to be less valued than the lives and activities of those who are not. Mother-others can thus be encouraged to become foils for the selves of their children, rather than selves in their own right. But even beyond its import in its own right, since their singularity operates as an avenue into "reality as otherness" to those for whom they care, it requires support.

When the mother-other withdraws from the relation, Benjamin argues, a sadistic intolerance of outsideness emerges in the child. If what is "not I" is unavailable to the child, the child can experience it as a threat and become aggressive as a means of defense or retaliation. If the mother-other is not present, the child may not have the existence of the not-self gradually emerge as nonthreatening, learn that making sense of the world and others and myself is something accomplished interpersonally, experience pleasure in exposure to the world and in symbolization. It also means that the child is not gently led out of its sense of omnipotence.

Benjamin thus argues that the absence of the mother-other can occasion the development of sadistic erotic fantasies that attract people to pornographic sadism. She argues that this is

> a retaliatory reversal of the omnipotent control suffered at the mother's hands. The impotent rage that the child has split off, unable to express or encompass, reappears in the sexualized fantasy—fueled not by eros but by aggression. (For that matter, women may identify with these fantasies for similar reasons; and men as well as women may play the part of the mother who suffers the child's attack.) The child's wishes for differentiation are transformed but recognizable in the sadistic fantasy: the wish to finally reach the mother as well as to punish her, to separate from her as well as to control her, to be recognized by her as well as to obliterate her. (1995, 188)

Being absent, or being controlling and imposing, are inevitable temptations for the mother-other in the work of care, and supporting caregivers in the face of these temptations is vital. If Benjamin is correct, the patriarchal absence of support for women reproduces patriarchal aggression toward women.

Women's labor continues to be exploited in many contemporary contexts. It is remarkable that we nonetheless have good enough mother-others, people who are affirming and yet other: mother-others who avoid both the Scylla of absolute self-assertion and the Charybdis of self-sacrifice. It is no mean accomplishment to maintain one's otherness and one's status as self while affirming the selfhood of the child who is demanding and imposing, to allow one's perspective to be denied and to introduce it in a responsible, intelligent, and measured way appropriate to the child's development, and to do so in an exploitative and inadequately supportive context.

A similar challenge exists inside of erotic relationships. The I must be I, and must affirm the other I. I must somehow be myself in a way that is responsible and responsive to the other who, as other, is going to bring an orientation and a projected reality that I could not anticipate. How do I maintain my footing? Beyond the mother, gendered codes of participation in erotic relations bear a risk for those gendered feminine or ambiguous because of the failure of their societies to perceive and uphold the singular otherness of all those who have been assigned and/or have assumed feminine or ambiguous characteristics. In worlds that degrade the feminine and the nonbinary, the erotic relation tends to be unsupported in its character as relation and conceived as a kind of masturbation: The erotic encounter is not with an other but with a piece of the world that aids in the satisfaction of the self coded masculine, a satisfaction not directly related to the otherness of the other. The other is conceived as that through whom one satisfies one's existing self, when it should be understood as a site of articulation and development of that self, the site of an experience that gets inside of us, thinking, imagining, and responding in interaction with our own.

Benjamin's focus in the particular essay that I am focusing on here, partly because of its integrated discussion of both caregiving and erotic relations, is sadistic pornography. Her hypothesis is that this type of pornography becomes compelling for people who have not developed a rich, secure sense of the outside other and its capacity to enrich their encounter, who have not developed a complex relationship toward symbolizing on the basis of the availability of the outside world and its lending powers of articulation and pleasure to them. Inside of sadistically oriented pornography, she says, we see figures that are supposed to be selves but are presented as objects, who do not speak from their otherness but only out of their identification of the self's desire, helping the self give expression to its desire while not speaking in their own right. The point is not, Benjamin argues, to get rid of these fantasies, but to work on the conditions of their transformation by supporting symbolization in intersubjective space. The point is not to aim at the elimination of pornography or of sadistic pornography in particular, or condemn those who make and view it, but to understand how particular kinds of relations foster particularly aggressive desires so as to have the capacity to transform those relations, support the development of better ones, and increase the possibility of pleasurable, transformative symbolization in interpersonal space, part of which might involve critiquing pornography.

Benjamin distinguishes the "sexual" from the "erotic" (1995, 198). She uses the term "sexual" to designate interaction or representation that involves "flattening" the otherness that would bring tension, and "erotic" to designate an experience of otherness that brings tension but in a way that is exciting and affirmable (208). The sexual involves a flattening of the otherness that would cause tension because one does not experience otherness as a site of articulation of one's own experience, receptive and affirming—the other as giving "lightness" back to us (Fanon 2008, 89). In the erotic, on the other hand, one would experience this otherness not as threat but as invitation. The challenge of the erotic is, on the one hand, to figure out how to be ourselves in a way that is, on the other hand, responsive to otherness. Who one is as a self is not fixed to a specific version of oneself, but is produced in the erotic encounter and by the otherness of the other. If we have been inducted into a friendly world by our familiar mother-others, we can in turn say, "I am here as me, but as a me that is open, that can answer to you, that may change because of you." As Benjamin writes, eros is aligned with "recognition, life, and reality," whereas the sexual is "aligned with omnipotence, death, and fantasy" (208). The freedom of another can set root in us and carry us along, elsewhere, in unpredictable directions, and whether we can truck with that freedom has significant consequences for how rich the world is for us.

Here I hope to have elucidated Hegel's account of the importance that another person be able to appear in their uniqueness, and yet as present *to us*—or, from the other direction, that we be able to affirm the uniqueness of the other person, because we experience our own individuality as not threatened but sustained, enriched, and affirmed by their otherness. In my view, Hegel's account of the dynamics of human interaction is useful for feminist arguments regarding the work of care and the challenges of erotic interaction. Our encounters with others are largely where our lives unfold, and entrenched sexism and heterosexism undermine that encounter, particularly in early childhood and erotic relations. Reading Hegel's and Benjamin's work together reveals the general framework by which we can hold together the related significance of individuality and interpersonal relations, and on the basis of that framework restructure modes of relating so as to make our vulnerability to each other productive rather than destructive.

Of course, Hegel is not typically used as an ally in thinking through issues of sexism and heterosexism, given the fact that he seems to assign women very restricted social roles that would exacerbate the problems identified here. Let us briefly engage with his words on this topic, so as to directly address the trouble they might cause.

Coda: Hegel on Gender

In the *Phenomenology of Spirit,* Hegel makes comments about women only in the context of a broader discussion of ethical life, and his critique of that form of life is that it attributes to nature or to "reality" as such, not to itself, the "decisions" about how to constitute its form of life. While his analysis here is thus historically specific, let us consider it anyway, since so many feminist readings do:

> While the polity gives itself stable existence only by disrupting familial happiness and by dissolving self-consciousness in the universal, it creates an internal enemy for itself in what it suppresses, which is at the same time essential to it.... By intrigue, the feminine—the polity's eternal irony—changes the government's universal purpose into a private purpose, transforms its universal activity into this determinate individual's work, and it inverts the state's universal property into the family's possession and ornament. In this way, the feminine turns the solemn wisdom of maturity... into an object of ridicule for immature, high-spirited youths and into an object of contempt for those youths' enthusiasm.... However, the polity can only sustain itself by suppressing this spirit of singularity, and... the polity likewise creates it by its repressive stance towards it as a hostile principle. Nevertheless, since this principle, in separating itself from universal purposes, is only evil and is within itself null, it would be incapable of accomplishing anything if the polity itself were not to recognize the force of youth, or the manhood, which... stands within singularity as the *force* of the whole. (*PS* §474/PG 258–59)

To count what Hegel says here as definitive regarding his orientation to women as such is problematic, as many have shown,[14] because he is presenting the character of a specific form of life. Further, his critique is directed at that society's disavowal of its own interpretive agency in the face of the directives it presumes to take from nature. Thus we have here resources by which to criticize rather than bolster the organization of human societies based on what is taken to be a natural difference. Let us note, however, one point the *Phenomenology* makes that remains relevant: There is always the possibility of tension between the state's and the family's orientation to youth. The state may demand an indifference toward the individual that the intimate structure typically called the family could hardly muster, and it may require sacrifice—in war, for instance. This tension is (I believe) real and irreducible, and is one expression of the irrevocable difference between the state and the family and their parallel necessity as institutions of modern ethical life (which we will discuss further in the final chapter).

If we are interested in how Hegel sees the issue of sexual difference in the world contemporary to him and what he takes it to mean, however, there are more words to go on, particularly from the *Philosophy of Right*, where he discusses the institutions required by freedom. Here Hegel seems to be describing what he takes to be the ethical and philosophical relevance of sexual difference. He says that "the *natural* determinacy of the two sexes acquires an *intellectual* and *ethical* significance by virtue of its rationality. This significance is determined by the difference into which the ethical substantiality, as the concept in itself, divides itself in order that its vitality may thereby achieve a concrete unity" (*PR/GPR* §165). In the next section, he goes on:

> The *one* [i.e., man] is therefore spirituality which divides itself up into personal self-sufficiency with being *for itself* and the knowledge and volition of *free universality*, i.e. into the self-consciousness of conceptual thought and the volition of the objective and ultimate end. And the *other* [woman] is spirituality which maintains itself in unity as knowledge and volition of the substantial in the form of concrete *singularity* [*Einzelheit*] and *feeling*. In its external relations, the former is powerful and active, the latter passive and subjective. Man therefore has his actual substantial life in the state, in learning, etc., and otherwise in work and struggle with the external world and with himself.... In the family, he has a peaceful intuition of this unity, and an emotive and subjective ethical life. Woman, however, has her substantial vocation in the family, and her ethical disposition consists in this *piety*. (*PR/GPR* §166)[15]

In the next chapter, I discuss the issue of how to approach words attributed to Hegel that he did not himself publish. In the meantime, the relevant Addition—a dismal portrait of women's capacities—is included in the endnote.[16]

Hegel argues here, unlike in the *Phenomenology*, that this natural determinacy is *rational* and thereby acquires ethical and intellectual significance. He links this significance to the way the different aspects of "ethical substantiality, as the concept in itself" come together in a concrete unity—the aspects presumably belonging to family and society, and that unity presumably being the marriage or relationship as such. Thus, in addition to attributing roles to women and men that "match" their uniqueness, he also attributes a conceptual necessity to the heterosexual relation. These issues force us to ask whether something like sexual difference is integral to Hegel's thought. Is the division of ethical substantiality into two genders needed to give vitality to relationships? Does sexual difference—and thus heterosexual relations and gender rigidity—give the unification its substantiality?

I will not provide here a comprehensive offering in the category of "how we should take up Hegel on the issue of gender." While I will not take the time to argue these points, I take it to be clear that this view is problematic and destructive and we are better off without it, that gender rigidity is bad news for everyone, and that if Hegel were alive today he would no longer hold the same view. I want only to present two ideas here: First, that his philosophy can be mined for feminist insight, particularly by noting what it means that he recognizes family and marriage, the sites in which women historically appear and to which they have historically been limited, as ethical institutions; and second, that his failure to count women as fully free beings is not sufficient to fundamentally contaminate his philosophy.

With regard to the first idea, it is important to note that Hegel designates the family and marriage as ethical institutions on the basis of the argument that, if we are with others at the most fundamental level, in the mode of "the human being *is* a 'being-with,'" then social reality must care for this character that we have and give agency and power to the institutions by which this being-with is actualized: namely, to some kind of familial or intimate "we" (though not one with a fixed form, since that would offend against what freedom has asserted about itself since Hegel's time). There are matters of genuine human import here: namely, we require care in our naturalness, help in rendering nature in the human body a site of specifically human significance; we require care in our singularity, in our irreducibility to other such individuals; we require care in our tendency toward the privileging of specific people in our lives; we require care for the multiple dimensions of our being as universal, singular, thinking, and feeling; and the suppression of these multiple dimensions has typically been destructive for all gendered beings. The larger social structure must recognize this intimate familial body, these interpersonal origins and the various forms of care they provide, even in their insularity, which in the case of the *Antigone* is shown in its capacity to conflict with the larger social structure. That tension must somehow be resolved for us as free beings and supported by our institutions, because we are both familial and public beings, and because the domains of the state and the "familial we" are interdependent. The "familial we" inducts us into the practice of being-with and thereby offers us the world. Grappling well with that original site (which is constituted in its character by the larger social world and thus never purely independent of it) is of utmost political significance. As Mary Rawlinson notes, in an otherwise critical discussion of Hegel's treatment of women: "In spite of himself, Hegel opens up sexual difference and the untilled terrain of women's experience as an essential field of inquiry for metaphysics, epistemology, politics, and ethics. His work calls for a robust phenomenology of women's labor and of maternal love" (2021, 128), and, I would add, of love and the labor of care in general. In Rawlinson's view, Hegel affirms the import of these activities, denying that the "essential and necessary human activities" assigned to women for millennia "contribute nothing to the universal life of spirit," and adamantly rejecting that they could be "already summarized in" what has historically been circumscribed as "man's labor" (129). I take it that we would miss something here if we simply rejected the possibility of taking something from Hegel because he was complicit and not adequately visionary, that he did not help in the emancipation and development of women. We would miss, namely, the politically and conceptually important point that traditionally "women's work" is of ultimate, ethical significance, and that being oneself (that is, being free) is also a matter of being at home in and caring for the interpersonal, familial, natural, and emotional aspects of our being. In any case, again, I do not wish to defend Hegel here—the history of freedom that he so prizes showed that he was wrong about women and marriage and family—but simply give sufficient reason for choosing not to "throw him away." Let us now move on to the second issue, the question of how deep this "gender fault line" goes.

With regard to this question, my cards should by now be on the table, and there are a few. First, the proof is in the pudding; the fault line is too deep if we cannot do important feminist things with his philosophy, and probably not too deep if we can. My thinking has developed through interaction with Hegel's philosophy, and I have been able to use it to think through important aspects of the contemporary situation, including problems related to gender. Second, it would take a vaster perspective than almost all of us have to be justified in deciding whether Hegel's "system as such" were fundamentally undermined or completely contaminated by this problem. As a scholar of Hegel, I would be hesitant to make this kind of vast judgment, and I am skeptical of others who would claim that they can, particularly when they are otherwise not engaged with Hegel. I would be more confident, however, in making the opposite claim, that Hegel's developed insights and principles are inconsistent with what he says about the situation of women in (for example) the *Philosophy of Right*. His construal of the role of women in the family seems criticizable by his own arguments: his affirmation of the centrality of human individual freedom, his description of conscience, and his critique of the way Greek society takes natural difference to be ethically definitive, for instance. We may be able to rethink the distribution of familial activities and describe reproduction in the absence of sexist perception of natural functions, without undermining the actual principles he discerns. It seems here that Hegel's account of the basic principles could be of value, even though some of the determinate ways in which he envisioned their actualization were troubling. Here the very dignity he perceives in the family, relationality, and the domain of feeling is, it seems, that value.

We could bring to bear here the greater clarity that history can lend to perception: There is something fundamentally impoverished about human beings who do not get adequately fed and nourished by affection and emotional interaction in the intimate domain, who do not bring those resources somehow to the public world, who do not develop the skills that intimacy requires. There is something fundamentally impoverished about a social reality that does not give adequate support to the intimate domain and the work done in it, and that privileges aggression, domination, and competition in public domains. I believe that Hegel discerned something correct and important in identifying intimate relations of kinship as an essential ethical structure, even though the actualization of that principle that seemed to be contemporary to him meant impoverished lives for many people. We must ask now, as I believe he would: How do the concrete, historically new forms of actualization of the intimate domain shed light on the principle? How does history, and with it the nonobjective world that affords us our capacities for comprehension, reveal to us what it could not have revealed to Hegel about gender? Like him, we are reliant on the freedom that has struggled over time to reveal this; we do not solely arrive at it in consultation with our own intellect.

Now, fittingly, we turn to discussion of history through consideration of the phenomenon of ethical life—the lived, historical reality of recognition in which we are all immersed. But first, let us briefly summarize the findings of this chapter.

We can try to resolve the tension the existence of another perspective brings to our experience by eliminating that perspective, taking it as meaningless, manipulating it to affirm our own, or suppressing our own. But, in addition to being a dishonest disavowal of what is already ongoing in our experience—the freedom of others operating at the heart of our own freedom—it also severs us from our own possibility, which is found in others and the world. It is our relations that require protection, since individuals are made there. To support relations is to support our very own capacity for becoming, and to oppose those forms of the violent suppression of otherness that are operative in sexism and racist colonialism. These tensions—between the claim of our own selfhood and our desire for otherness, between one self and another—are pervasive in and central to our experience. Learning how to grapple well with these issues, in all of the different contexts in which they emerge, is some of the most weighty and consequential work that human beings do.

In his discussion of the encounter between perspectives and the tensions it brings with it, Hegel remains abstract; "The Independence and Dependence of Self-Consciousness" is a philosophical consideration of the phenomenon as such, without all of the *accoutrements* of actual, historical existence and social reality. In what he calls "ethical life," however, he will consider interpersonal encounters inside of existing social relations, showing what the abstract discussion of recognition means at the level of societies and cultures.[17] He will introduce, to use Sartre's language, the "ternary" relation or "third" that inevitably contextualizes the "binary" relation (2004, 109). Here we enter into the domain of spirit, "the self-supporting, absolute, real essence. All the previous shapes of consciousness are abstractions from it," abstractions in which "that spirit analyses itself, differentiates its moments, and lingers with the singular. Isolating such moments has spirit itself as its presupposition and its stable existence, or the isolating only exists in the spirit which is existence" (*PS* §439/*PG* 239). We always do inhabit an actual, existing world; we think abstractly only as beings who inhabit actually existing, historical worlds—that is, as situated; they are thought and enacted through us; "the living substance is the being that is in truth *subject*" (*PS* §18/*PG* 18). Now we turn, with Hegel, to the developed, material worlds in which these principles are always manifest, actualized, and embodied—or, in other words, to spirit. Here we will see particularly how deeply situatedness affects us, how we should account for that philosophically, and how the operation of racist colonialism has disavowed the philosophical and practical significance of this situatedness.

CHAPTER THREE

Ethical Life

Let us begin this project of understanding what Hegel means by "ethical life" by returning to consideration of the child and its caregivers. Caregivers are always specific and singular, alive to reality in a particular way. Their behavior in a sense takes a stand: "This is what is interesting and valuable; this is what is worthy of attention." They speak a specific language, have specific habits, embody specific values, live inside of specific traditions that they express in their behavior, interact with people in certain ways (humorously, sarcastically, controllingly, anxiously, etc.). But these specificities are rarely announced to the child, and explanations would not make sense to them anyway. These caregivers do not typically flag the option they pursue as one among many, which would be confusing to the child in any case; they do not announce that by pursuing one behavioral possibility and attending to one piece of reality they are precluding others. Their specific orientation is, for the child, reality. The way they behave and the reality they illuminate in so behaving appear as pieces of the world, fixed and necessary: this is how things are and how they must be done. The child fits around their behavior; what they will listen to, accommodate, and accept shapes how the child will communicate, since she wants to be heard. They hold a language out to the child and she speaks it; they manifest an emotional orientation and enact emotional expression that will shape the child's own sense of how emotional life should be lived and what should inspire emotional response; their attention communicates what they will attend to and what is worth attending to. At first, they are the child's only route to reality, her only way to a human life, and thus she has no choice but to grab hold of these mechanisms in some way. And so she grabs hold of them, because *she is the kind of being who must pair with the world in order to exist.*

While these forms of behavior appear as necessary to her, however, they are not absolutely necessary—in the sense that they could have been different and in fact are different in other relational units and in other times and places. But their contingency is not real for the child, and she cannot appreciate it until she has lived through it, at which point it will be difficult for her to perceive it.

Here, the distinction between "is" and "ought," or between "is" and "could be," is effectively elided. When our caregivers announce, through their behavior, that "this is what to do in this situation," "this is how emotion is expressed," "this is how to interact with other people," they are presenting as fact something that is essentially an interpretation, a judgment. In response, we come to approach situations as demanding a certain kind of response, *simpliciter*—"this is simply what one does here." Human development occurs on the basis of the masquerade of interpretation as fact, a concealment of the fact that things could and possibly should be done differently. Or, as Rebecca Comay writes, "ideology arises from the very structure of experience: it expresses the opacity that binds us together as human" (2011, 5).

Further, the very capacity to judge that things could and possibly should be done differently is itself only cultivated by this masquerade, by this condition of concealment. One only develops the capacity for judgment in a context in which the presence of judgment is concealed. That concealment, of course, can be more or less deep, and it is also important—just because it is true—that its existence be at some point revealed, that we see that "fact" is a result of decision. As de Beauvoir says, in the age of adolescence, the child begins to notice contradictions, limitations, and weakness, coming to see that the serious world, called "serious" because it has come to believe that it could not be otherwise, is made by very "uncertain creatures" (1976, 39).

Now, through developing specific forms of behavior in interaction with others, one becomes basically competent: capable of reflection, emotion, speech, thought, and so on. These determinacies of behavior, in other words, allow us to develop the skills by which we can move outward from our determinacy, because these skills are skills of generalization. Through cultivation, we can become the kind of person who reflects on the behavior of our caregivers. Becoming capable of reflection upon the original interpersonal unit is a condition produced through accepting and employing its habits; one only gets to the separability from the original unit through this determinate intimacy with it. Our separated looking at x is a non-separated enactment of x; in this way, we are both inside and outside of this inherited experience. Our capacity for "making transparent" was developed inside of that non-transparent web. The determinacy of this way of life conceals itself by the very fact that *it is lived before it is known.*

There is a broader dimension to be noticed here as well, however: another interpersonal unit that is itself relatively self-enclosed and self-replicating, insofar as it too operates as a kind of determinate channel for the passing down of determinate habits. The behavior one's early caregivers enact is not simply invented inside that interpersonal unit; it is typically a function of a broader social world. The habits of interaction that a parent manifests, for instance, are their individualizing of the possibilities held out as available and as common sense by the outside world that is local in both space and time. For example, in a sexist *society*, the family will likely engage in differential treatment of girl and boy babies, and human adults will likely perform circumscribed roles defined by sexist expectations. Further, social worlds themselves are not typically collections of simply diverse possibilities, but tend to hang together in a relatively coherent way, which coherence is articulated by laws, customs, and institutions to which we accommodate ourselves in living there. And again, we typically accommodate ourselves to them without much difficulty, since they also manifest themselves as inevitable, and since they too have come to inform the behavior of our early caregivers toward us.

Our original interpersonal units (or families) and our social worlds are both domains in which our dependence upon other perspectives is lived out in concrete, historical ways. They are the specific forms of life that we inhabit as beings who are dependent upon recognition, cultivated in and by the perspectives of others upon us. These forms of life are how the dependence and independence of self-consciousness is actually lived, the social reality of recognition.

This is what Hegel means, again, when he says that spirit is the "real essence" and "all the previous shapes of consciousness are abstractions from it" (*PS* §439/*PG* 239). Up to this point in the *Phenomenology of Spirit*, Hegel had investigated the ways of behaving that he calls "consciousness," "self-consciousness," and "reason," each in terms of their own independent function and logic. What he calls "consciousness" is fundamentally a basic receptivity to the world, which operates in different registers: in short, as sensing, perceiving, and understanding. "Self-consciousness" is the self relating to itself in its own right, experiencing itself as different from the stuff of the world, not least because of its capacity to look at itself. And "reason" is that experience of the operation of rationality and its laws in that self, whether that rationality is manifest outwardly (e.g., scientifically) or inwardly (e.g., morally).

With the claim that these shapes of consciousness are abstractions from spirit, Hegel observes that relating to objectivity, relating to ourselves and other selves, and relating to the power of rationality that seems to command thinking and permeate reality all unfold and operate inside of historical forms of interpersonal existence. With the category of "spirit," Hegel makes a philosophically revolutionary point: that we operate in terms of inherited, determinate, historical meanings that dwell in us, and that the "rational selfhood of reason" is embodied in the institutions and relations of material history. Insofar as we are made as thinkers and actors by this concrete reality, we cannot simply shine the light of our reflection upon it, separating it out as perceived object from our perception, since our perception has been fashioned by this perceived object. When we relate to ourselves, we do so in terms of a familial and cultural reality that we cannot easily and absolutely expose to critical reflection. When we are engaged in inquiry, we do so in a way that cannot make its own practice the object of that same understanding. Hegel is effectively saying here, "don't fool yourself; the way your powers operate are due to history, to the specific habits of your social world, which themselves took shape as a response to other forms of life, as a kind of judgement or decision about how to be that was informed by other forms of life and historical developments. This is where judgment comes from—from other people, from other worlds on the basis of which your own world came to be—and none of this can become unproblematically the object of your scrutiny." We cannot get to the bottom of things. History is the absolute, and we are inside it. All of our efforts to render the sense of the world transparent, to discern how we should and do live, to interpret objectivity, rest on a kind of non-sense, a terrain that does not give itself up for interpretation, by which our capacity for illuminating and comprehending is made.

The "absoluteness" of history and the development of the capacity for sense-making on the basis of a ground that does not lend itself to that sense-making means, further, that philosophy must be historical and it must be intercultural. This is one of Hegel's most significant philosophical contributions, a basic point that calls for attention despite critical reaction to the negative comments he is recorded as having made about other cultures, an idea by which these comments can themselves be held accountable. The basic idea of ethical life has tremendous import for the issue of how we approach practices, worlds, and cultures that are unfamiliar to us, and thus Hegel's philosophy has something worthwhile to offer to contemporary discussions of the tensions and challenges involved in doing so.

We become reflective beings, thinking beings, through being cultivated in certain forms of behavior, inside of families, inside of societies that conceal their determinacy from us, inside of intellectual traditions that can even lead us to think that we are disembodied rationality. Thus, studying truth, studying the things that are revealed by thought, requires not just studying its forms but studying the worlds in which those truths are discerned, studying the determinacies in response to which that thinking developed. To understand the nature of that thought, those meanings, we cannot simply observe them as though from above, through abstract thinking, but must go through determinacy, as Hegel does, because human creativity and rationality have their origins in this substantial determinacy.

It is also essential to study this "non-sense," for Hegel, because the true meaning of insight is only seen when it is enacted in materiality, which occurs necessarily in time. We inherit a meaningful world and we make it. We live on the basis of a sense discerned and produced by others, and we mix our own thought and ingenuity with that sense. The ideas we have about it occur on its basis; they are not from nowhere, the products of pure rationality. They have shaped the world, we use them to shape the world, and in that shaping we typically witness both their power and their limits, but shaping and witnessing take time; they are "not the business of one day" (*LHP* 44). When we look back at this history, we can see the material working out of these ideas. As cited previously (from lecture transcripts), Hegel gives voice to the articulation of insight in and by the concrete by observing that spirit is

> a many-sided development of its existence, and the stage of self-consciousness it has reached is the principle which it reveals in history *in the relations of that existence*. This principle it clothes with all the wealth of its existence; the shape in which it exists is a people into whose morality, constitution, domestic, civil, and public life, arts, international relations, etc. this principle is built.... This is the material which the principle of a people has to work through, and this is not the business of one day... it is not a progress in the abstract concepts of pure thinking; on the contrary, this material only advances in pure thinking *pari passu* with its advance in its entire concrete life. (*LHP* 44)

We do not have well-rounded, developed thought in the abstract; in the trajectory of peoples are available the determinate, expressive practices that bring principles to birth, development, and actuality. Determinacy is not an obstacle to the development of principle; it is that through which the meaningfulness, the weight, and the scope of the principle are defined and determined.

But Hegel himself admits of query in this light. If he also is a being of ethical life, then where can he root his evaluation of world history? If history is absolute and we are inside it, what happens to philosophy, to Hegel's philosophy, to philosophical claims to truth? And how should we approach his developmental, apparently progressive interpretation of world history as a movement through four world-historical realms, "the Oriental" ("*das Orientalische*"), "Greek," "Roman," and "Germanic" (*PR/GPR* §354)? Are they to be singled out above others? How, as readers presumably concerned with the violence of colonialism and anything that would seem to justify or defend it, should we interpret the critical things he is reported by students to have said in lectures about other cultures?

In what follows, I will gradually develop some of the considerations that I believe should be brought to bear upon the above questions. Because the terms of ethical life present a genuine challenge to the operation of thought, it is here, in this chapter, that we will wrestle with what we earlier described as the two-sided, "embedded and transcending" character of thought, addressing Hegel's own "transcending" efforts to assess the nature and demands of human existence while embedded within a particular mode of ethical life. Here therefore we will grapple most substantially with some basic questions: whether philosophy can offer transhistorical and transcultural insight, what character it has to have if it is to reliably do so, and whether Hegel's philosophy has that character.

We begin by discussing Hegel's portrayal of Greek ethical life in the *Phenomenology*.[1] Here he portrays a world that seems to operate according to a collective self-consciousness of the centrality of the collective—in other words, a world that lives explicitly in the terms of ethical life. Its emergent self-consciousness of its own one-sidedness will manifest to us the import as well as the one-sidedness of the notion of ethical life, a "we" that embraces its status as such. After Hegel's Greece, we will move to the question of the impact of ethical life upon the practice of philosophy. Then we will turn to what I take to be Hegel's primary contribution to philosophy, which is a systematic study of human freedom made possible by Hegel's own historical situatedness: He lived in a time in which significant light had been shed, by history, upon the dimensions of freedom, and in which he could engage, at least partly, with other historical modes of ethical life that were each in some way grappling with the dimensions and demands of human freedom. We will then engage with the modern view of freedom, freedom as individual, given its contrast with the phenomenon of ethical life. We will approach Hegel's critical orientation to its one-sidedness, looking in particular at how that emerges in his analysis of civil society. Then, finally, we will take advantage of our historical vantage point to discern more about that one-sidedness, engaging particularly with the thought emerging from communities that have experienced its destructive impact: perspectives from North American Indigenous thought and from feminist, decolonial thought mobilized particularly by the tensions between Middle Eastern and US contexts.

Greek Ethical Life

The ancient Greek world produced significant cultural wealth and unprecedented (while limited) practices of democratic self-governance. It seems as though it was a world in which the collective operated as a significant resource for those who were affirmed as free within it, in which significant cultural and political activity was able to unfold because the free "I" was embedded in the "we" and the "we" was affirmed as requiring care and cultivation. And indeed, this is the principle or principled commitment that Hegel attests is operative therein—the idea that human life has the rich possibilities it does because of the world and the collective that is its ground. When he first introduces the idea of ethical life in the *Phenomenology* (which is actually in a digression in the earlier section called "Reason"), Hegel describes those who belong to this world as "conscious of themselves as being these singular self-sufficient beings as a result of their having sacrificed their singularity and as a result of this universal substance being their soul and essence. In the same way this universal is again their doing as singular or it is the work which is brought forth by themselves" (*PS* §350/*PG* 194). The world gives their action content and substance, such that what they do, their "freedom," is empowered by their belonging; free action is enriched by belonging and its meaningfulness is due to the meaningfulness of this social reality. Action's purpose in this world is to perpetuate it, and it is action's honor to be able to do so. The world shows up as charged with value, and action is an affirmation of that value. "The whole becomes, *as the whole*, his own work, for which he sacrifices himself and through which he gets himself back" (*PS* §351/*PG* 195). The call to be oneself is a call to care for its structures, institutions, values, and things, which outstrip anything one could do on one's own.

Hegel takes Sophocles's work of cultural self-interpretation in the *Antigone* as paradigmatic of this way of life and its powers and shortcomings. In the play, Polyneices and Eteocles, brothers of Antigone and sons of Oedipus and (his mother) Jocasta, conflict over who will rule in Thebes after Oedipus's death. Polyneices brings a foreign army against Eteocles, and both die. Creon (Antigone's uncle, Jocasta's brother) takes over the kingship, and rules that Polyneices shall not be buried, upon pain of death. Antigone, also the fiancée of Creon's son Haemon, performs burial rites nonetheless, and Creon imprisons her while deliberating about further action. In the meantime, Antigone kills herself, which triggers Haemon's suicide and thereby his mother's. Creon is left bereft and humbled.

Antigone takes herself to be fulfilling the law of the gods by caring for her brother, and divine law commands burial. In Hegel's reading, she does not stand back and ask whether this is the right thing to do: The meaningfulness of the domain in which she participates is to be honored. She experiences her action as an enactment of divine law; it compels her to action. She does not take herself to be in charge of the making of the meaningful world, and if she were her life would be significantly impoverished. We should also notice, however, that she brings significant stubbornness to her action (as does Creon), which is revealed in contrast to her sister Ismene's attempt to cajole her into calmer and humbler consideration (and Creon's action is similarly revealed in its difference from his condition at the end of the play).[2]

There are two important considerations here that illuminate the broader context of Antigone's action. First, the interdependent "we" or social reality is differentiated into different forces and fields: the gods and the family, which appear as though given, and human self-governance and creative inquiry, which is collective, scientific, self-directed, and open-ended. These two dimensions—let us call them family and society—each offer something that human beings require. Second, while the powers to which we respond in our action may be substantial, our action itself is always specific, and can only be specific. Action demands *just one thing*, and it demands it when not all relevant knowledge is available. In acting in one way and in one context, we can inadvertently disable ourselves from acting in another way or in another domain. These two considerations will each, it turns out, be of great significance.

Family and society, as Hegel will discuss in detail in his dedicated political texts, are each "absolute" in more or less developed human reality, by which I mean that both are necessary to it. Human life is both received (in response to which human beings have construed themselves as indebted to nature and to God or the gods) and made (something for which human beings themselves take and have had to take responsibility). Further, there are two basic forms of interpersonal context in which reception and making are lived out, and which are required for basically meaningful and organized existence. We must be able to inhabit immediate contexts of care in which we receive attention directed to us as persons, with our needs and desires, and we must be able to inhabit relatively organized societies, because the richness of experience depends on the existence of and our access to others beyond our immediate contexts of care, as well as on systems: of transportation, sewage, the exchange of goods, the transmission of knowledge and culture. Think of all of the systematic dependencies implicit, for instance, in the "simple" act of making a cup of coffee: water, electricity, trade agreements, money. Human life is lived in the embrace of these two structures and as a matter of navigating self-receipt and self-making.

Yet while these two basic forms, family and society, are deeply connected, they are also significantly different. The one tends to be more articulated than the other, and to be oriented toward a broader generality. Societies, that is, must accommodate, and thus more or less answer to, different kinds of people; their ongoing functionality depends on whether they can broadly satisfy those who inhabit them. Their members' freedom to depart from or transform the existing state of affairs can surge up here more than in the family because the link to social reality is felt to be more flexible, because social interaction more than familial interaction tends to bring with it a broader array of possibilities and opportunities. Societies are led then to greater self-articulation; they are implicitly challenged to make sense to their inhabitants, and to communicate that sense in understandable ways, whereas families tend to be asked less to justify themselves. Because of a family's intimacy with the identity of its members, and its ties to their past as children, it can be difficult to even realize that the question "why *this* way of being a family?" could be asked.

As Antigone shows, the difference between family and society can also become opposition. Even though each is a necessary aspect of a more or less functional human existence, they will not always operate in lockstep with each other. This is due to the different ways in which each responds to a different kind of need that we have and a different aspect of the reality that we are. The family operates in terms of a kind of favoritism, a privileging of its members, and it must to a certain extent do so; Jamar will probably not have a very nice life if his parent takes all children to have a claim equal to Jamar's on their time, attention, and resources. The general functioning of our sociopolitical structures, on the other hand, depends on a kind of opposed availability to all members. The family's favoritism can oppose society's (typically highly imperfect) tendency toward nonfavoritism; the dynamics of the family can assert their authority outside its borders; the dynamics of the social world can fail to honor and support the real need we have for care. This conflict plays out in the *Antigone*, in which the weight of these irreducible yet conflicting pieces of social reality is on display particularly in the Second and Third Choruses.

The Second Chorus celebrates the wonder of humanity and the capacity for self-making it manifests by harnessing the powerful world around it. Here are some portions:

> Many are the wonders, none
> is more wonderful than what is man.
> This it is that crosses the sea
> with the south winds storming and the waves swelling…
> He it is again who wears away
> the Earth, oldest of gods, immortal, unwearied,
> as the ploughs wind across her from year to year
> when he works her with the breed that comes from horses…
> A cunning fellow is man. His contrivances
> make him master of beasts of the field
> and those that move in the mountains…
> and speech and windswift thought
> and the tempers that go with city living
> he has taught himself…
> He has a way against everything
> and he faces nothing that is to come
> without contrivance.
> Only against death
> can he call on no means of escape;
> but escape from hopeless diseases
> he has found in the depths of his mind (Sophocles 1991, lines 368–411)

The choral ode is a catalog of the powers with which we deal with externality and limitation, and it declares that the human being "can always help himself," though this ingenuity and self-transcendence is always a collective accomplishment. The tools and "contrivances" it identifies are many: nets, boats, plows, bait, yoke, language, thought, feelings, shelter, foresight, medicine, law. The "city living" flagged by the ode is imperative to this wondrousness and must be protected. This is essentially Creon's job: to protect city living against those who would destroy it.

The Third Chorus, however, illuminates something that looks much different from what was celebrated in the Second, though it is intimated therein ("Only against death / can he call on no means of escape"): namely, the powerlessness of human beings, their receipt of themselves, their incapacity to "help themselves" when it comes to their own finitude and death. Its topic is those aspects of existence in relation to which we are powerless and passive: for one, the fact that we "receive" ourselves from our ancestors, and that our lives will have already been shaped by their lives. The human being cannot overcome finitude manifest as family, as the cycle of life from generation to generation, as the inheritance, we might say, of behavior. Here is the first part of the Third Chorus, which bemoans the negative aspects of vulnerability to this lineage:

> Lucky are those whose lives
> know no taste of sorrow.
> But for those whose house has been shaken by God
> there is never cessation of ruin;
> it steals on generation after generation
> within a breed...
> No generation frees another, some god
> strikes them down; there is no deliverance.
> Here was the light of hope stretched
> over the last roots of Oedipus' house,
> and the bloody dust due to the gods below
> has mowed it down—that and the folly of speech
> and ruin's enchantment of the mind. (Sophocles 1991, lines 640–56)

We do not make our own bodies, the situations of our own lives, our psychology, and to live is not simply to make oneself and one's community and make the world into one's home, but to find out who one is, by what forces one's life is moved. City life and its accomplishments are shrouded by this less transparent domain, which turns speech—the very means by which collective living is enacted—into folly.

Like Hegel's analysis, these two choral odes flag elements and priorities operative in human life that are potentially in tension with each other. Are we made or making, passive or powerful? Does our interpersonal nature condemn or uphold us? In the Chorus's remarks that "wisdom is far the chief element in happiness / and, secondly, no irreverence towards the gods" (1991, 1420–21), the play seems to conclude that each is true. Wisdom would allow human beings to discern how to deal with their conflict, but it must be accompanied by reverence toward the fact that we receive the meanings and ingredients out of which our lives are built. The city must be a home for the collective accomplishments of humanity, and so it cannot tolerate internal threats like those represented by Polyneices, and yet the debt of that city and that self-conscious human making to all it cannot comprehend or fathom must also be recognized, and so the family's and religion's gestures of respect toward the dead, toward ceremony, and toward their own passivity should be respected.

However, it is only reverent wisdom that would be capable of answering to this challenge, not the rules or priorities of the domains of family or state, since, as the play shows, they can infringe upon each other. The human being is thus herself presented as someone who, with wisdom and discernment, has to think through the tensions in her world. She does not simply live inside that world, but can also reflect on it. It is not simply the case that the I is a we; the we is also an I. But Greek ethical life exists on the basis of a denial of the power of the I to subject its world to its reflection. In fact, the very power of the "we" here—the very immensity of the resources it has—creates for it this problem of the disavowed I. Of course this "beautiful" world—to use Hegel's term (PS §440/PG 240)—will produce powerful and insightful individuals!

As mentioned above, there is a second issue here—that human action is only ever simple and specific, and it is unrealistic and unjust to expect of ethically charged action that it can honor all of the powers to which it owes its existence. In obeying the gods, Antigone cannot easily also acknowledge the authority of the city. It is possible that she could have found an action more reflective of the domains that bolster her existence, a more capacious action, especially if she had encountered greater receptivity in Creon, but there are limits on the capaciousness of action. Here communication would help, as we will see in our discussion of conscience in the next chapter: I can act and confess my action's one-sidedness, such that the "more capacious" action can be or be found in communication.

But this world does not particularly support or affirm the development of a discerning wisdom on the part of individuals, nor does it really tolerate action that does not live up to its substantial powers—that is, action that is "just mine," single, human, and finite. In not doing so, it fails to own up to the fact that flawed, finite beings must do the work of interpretation and discernment. Greek ethical life, that is, allows interpretation to masquerade as fact. It even posits nature as authoritative, taking its structure to be based on what it takes to be "natural" differences—for example, sexual difference ("ethical consciousness is *immediately* directed toward the law, and this determination of immediacy means that nature itself enters into ethical life's action" [PS §475/ PG 260]). It cannot truck with nature's inability to be decisive, which is manifest, as Hegel notices, when nature offers *two* sons as potential kings. There is no immediate fact of the matter: Human discernment needs to assume responsibility. New things are happening all the time; traditions are not being fulfilled or perpetuated perfectly; "*immediate unity with its substance*" (*PS* §472/*PG* 257) is not possible; individuals are interpreting and deciding. They have to interpret and decide, in fact, because sometimes the duties demanded of them in this ethical world conflict with each other. Each may turn to their existent system for answers as to how to deal with the problems that arise, but it cannot give a sufficient answer, because it has produced the problem. The fact is that Antigone and Creon are both guilty, insofar as they acted against a law upon which they depend, but their guilt is rooted in the system producing the problem: What it demands that they do in order to fulfill the ethical command is, it turns out, a transgression of a different command. And so they are thrown back onto the demand to be thinking, to be judging.

We are actively knowing, discerning, creative, and (in some way) rational; nonetheless, we owe our lives to things that cannot be made the transparent object of critical reflection. That is the two-sidedness of human life captured by both Creon's and Antigone's commitments. As two of the absolutes in terms of which we live, each side commands affirmation and acknowledgment. Greek ethical life is one-sided in denying the need for individualized agency and critical reflection. The modern world will err in the other direction, disavowing the idea that our lives are made full and meaningful by the rich substantiality in which we as individuals are rooted.

The analysis of ethical life shows our intrinsic porosity to each other, a porosity that channels us into specific forms of life and bespeaks significant vulnerability. It reflects as well the human need to inhabit and be attached to a determinate world. Finally, it curtails and limits an opposed principle that has been mulled over in its distinct and complex character often but not solely by cultures associated with the West: that of freedom not as membership but as individual subjectivity. In all of these ways, it is of profound significance to the issue of colonialism, which reflects our interpersonal and intercultural vulnerability, is a suppression of specific forms of life and attachment thereto, and tends to seek legitimation from the priority of individual freedom. But Hegel also presents the one-sidedness of ethical life, and with it the inevitable demand for individual discernment and political protection thereof. Let us bring these considerations to bear, now, upon three related questions: First, how do the priorities of individual subjectivity and ethical life contribute to reflection on societies that seem to privilege them unequally? Second, how do colonized societies grapple with the West's history of self-positioning as an evangelist of modern subjectivity? Third, how does the factor of ethical life impact the practice of philosophy, or how do we take up the demand to think as beings of ethical life, non-transparently inside of non-transparent interpretive webs? And specifically, how does the phenomenon of ethical life impact Hegel's claim to interpret world history and make general claims about the nature of freedom? Let us begin with the final question, the relation between ethical life and philosophy, turning thereafter to the problem of colonialism.

Ethical Life and Philosophy

We should observe in ethical life both a challenge to philosophy as well as its condition. It is a condition insofar as this non-sense is the very avenue through which our capacity to appreciate sense develops. We are not simply locked in non-sense, not condemned to non-knowing; rather, the knowing that we do is mobilized and made possible by these non-transparent grounds. Our embeddedness in specific relations closes us off from other different others, but also reflects an intrinsic porosity and receptivity, which in turn keeps the possibility of openness to them open. This is the human situation: Inherence in local relations and attachment to their goods produces provinciality, partiality, and the failure to perceive others adequately, but this inheritance and attachment is the very soil in which a more expansive moral orientation can develop. Being embedded in a way of life makes what it presents obvious and what it does not present difficult to discern, but we gain our tools for grasping the difficult from being in the obvious, and if we simply had to think all of our thoughts on our own, they would be unimaginably impoverished. Philosophy must go through embeddedness in ways of life whose ground is not related to intellectually but lived from. Let us explore now the philosophical tasks opened for us due to this challenge: most basically, that the *ethos* of philosophy is a willingness to thematize the familiar and encounter the transformative powers of the unfamiliar.

One challenge to philosophy presented by ethical life is that it is easy to confuse the familiar with the true. The familiar conceals itself as such and presents itself simply as the parameters by which other things are judged, as the perceptual ground rather than the perceptual figure: It is the basis that recedes from perception, upon which the figure perceived comes to a certain clarity. We confuse the familiar with the true also because of the temptation to feel experienced, authoritative, and knowledgeable, comfortable on our own terrain. We theorize as we have always done, in that comfort, inside of our traditions—in my world, for instance, in interaction with Locke, Plato, or Hegel. To an extent, this kind of culturally insular self-exploration is necessary for self-knowledge (what are the building blocks of this world I inhabit and by which I have been made?), though these sources can also help conceal the "whys" of this way of life.

The first task that follows from the magnetic force the familiar has when we are engaged in the pursuit of truth is this: to ask what we are enacting as beings of ethical life. The task is to do an inventory, in Gramsci's sense:

> The starting-point of critical elaboration is the consciousness of what one really is, and it is "knowing thyself" as a product of the historical process to date, which has deposited in you an infinity of traces, without leaving an inventory.... Philosophy cannot be separated from the history of philosophy, nor can culture from the history of culture. In the most immediate and relevant sense, one cannot be a philosopher, by which I mean have a critical and coherent conception of the world, without having a consciousness of its historicity, of the phase of development which it represents and of the fact that it contradicts other conceptions or elements of other conceptions. (2005, 324)

What is the historical moment—the "non-sense"—that projects the dimensions of sense for us; what does it conceal from us; how does it develop? How is our thinking, our engagement in philosophy, affected by our character as beings of ethical life? What contingent situations move us to think and of what do they move us to think? From where and what and whom does our thinking unfold? What shadows are produced by our spotlights? The worlds we inherit, themselves shaped by intellectual insight, become stable, with the insights that shaped them hardening—no longer live answers to a living problem but an assumed way of life and a fund from which we draw (as Book VIII of the *Republic* so powerfully shows with its discussion of regime change in terms of the metaphor of passage from fathers to sons [Plato 1968]). As beings who have grown through the perspectives of others upon us, our thinking enacts our world's priorities and accepted truths rather than operating in terms of our own "pure autonomy" and "pure reason." The "what" that leads us to thought is our relations, our social institutions, the expectations projected around us and at us regarding what it is to be a citizen, sibling, child, parent, student, friend, lover. The "what" is prevailing cultural expectations regarding the characteristics of a meaningful, worthwhile life and of reasonable, respectful interaction. What are the world's preoccupations, the principles by which it takes itself to be defined: God or the gods? Individual rights and free enterprise? Traditional customs and rites around nature? Consumption? The technological production of self-image? If the roots of agency are non-transparent and even our tools of scrutiny have been made in the murky waters we seek to investigate, then how do we find out what we are doing?

A second task emerges from the fact that inventory is aided by interaction with the unfamiliar. Here the task would be to engage with the texts, artifacts, and cultural products of others, and oppose the domination that might interfere with their cultural practices, particularly when the worlds we inherit have been actively engaged in their suppression. Insofar as determinacy potentially shows up for outsiders *as one-sided determinacy*, as idiosyncratic difference magnified and depth or meaning minimized, and insofar as our determinacy has become virtually imperceptible as such for its bearers, interaction with outsiders may allow us to better perceive our own peculiarities as beings who live in terms of an inherited orientation, for instance, of coloniality—an orientation in terms of which "West" is implicitly a developmental apex. If philosophy is always enacted by beings of ethical life, then it requires engagement with "other minds" who make a different division between the familiar and the unfamiliar. If philosophy is always a thinking *from* (a concrete world organized in terms of certain priorities), then its aspiration toward generality demands that it be a matter of thinking *with*; and this thinking with requires *practical* support when the very existence of other worlds is under practical threat by our own.

A particular kind of *affect* seems quintessentially philosophical here—one not of confident expertise and authority but of humility. Cultivation of this affect would be a third task, resisting the temptation to stay within the familiar, exposing ourselves to that about which we are not authoritative, trucking with the uncertainty of being on unfamiliar terrain. In doing so, philosophy could be rendered more open to the range of insight available in human thinking.

A fourth task stems from the fact that the weight of familiarity manifests itself as the failure to recognize the meaningful in what is unfamiliar. The task here would be to refrain from taking alien determinacy as simply mystifying, without sense, and presume instead that there is meaning lying behind it. Ethical life makes it challenging for us to discern the genuine meaningfulness concealed in the determinate practices of other forms of ethical life—or indeed, as Saidiya Hartman (1997) has powerfully described, in the determinate, creative practices of those in tightly constrained circumstances. Determinate practices do not necessarily announce the meanings they reflect; and when these meanings are expressed, even their communication takes a determinate form: one's own language and the gestures that mean something in one's culture. Thus even modes of communication are determinacy concealing meaning and should be understood as such.

Fifth, philosophy must *go through* human history—ways of life whose ground is not related to intellectually, as an object of reflection, but lived *from*. Discerning the meaning of principles and insights requires studying the worlds in which they are played out, studying the historical determinacies in interaction with which thinking developed, looking at specific intertwinings of ideality and materiality, meaning and matter. To understand the nature of that thought, the nature of those meanings, we cannot simply observe them as though from above, through abstract thinking, but, as Hegel does, through determinacy. Because philosophy is the domain of principle, and because principle is submerged in determinate actuality, philosophy must become intercultural and historical. Hegel gives significant attention to the aesthetic, religious, and philosophical insights of other cultural worlds, demonstrating the insight that lies behind unfamiliar aesthetic, religious, and philosophical practices. In its form, this is a model of philosophical pursuit, even if the insight available in our own historical moment—and indeed, in Hegel's own arguments—would lead us to criticize some of his observations of these other worlds.

There is a final task that accrues to us by virtue of the historical *effect* of non-perception of one's own determinacy and non-perception of the meaningfulness of the determinacy of others, which has been the imposition of relations of domination and subordination between worlds. This effect does not tend to foster openness to discerning the reality that each brings to light. The task associated with this effect is to work against domination and oppression, and to counter the narrative of the West as the great leader, to expose the destructive consequences of its sway, to expose the way this orientation has become a mode of ethical life, such that even its internal critics are complicit.

Now we turn to Hegel. How does Hegel himself reflect an openness to ethical life when he seems to think, as he is reported to have said in his lectures on world history, in terms of a history of cultural development in which the sun rises in the East and sets in the West, in which "Europe is the absolute end of history, just as Asia is the beginning," since "it is in the west that the inner sun of self-consciousness, which emits a higher radiance [than universality in itself], makes its further ascent" (*LPWH* 196–97/*VPW* 242)? Is not the very effort to draw a comprehensive picture of the nature of reality at odds with the value he puts on world history and the reality of cultural multiplicity? How can he or one arrive at generalities from the point of view of embeddedness in one space and time in history? Is he doing philosophy in the mode of a false expertise with regard to the rest of social reality, illegitimately producing an authoritative, comprehensive, and systematic framework, interpreting the rest of reality in the terms of its local logic, which masquerades as universal? It might seem that Hegel falsely privileges his own reality as the apex, construing the rest of human history as a development toward it—that for him, as Fanon would put it, "destiny is white" (2008, 12). Hegel identifies development as a key reality, and interprets history as developmental, highlighting the "Germanic" realm as the most appropriate home for freedom as the freedom of all, other societies and cultures only discerning part of the story (*PR/GPR* §§358–60). Even the Greek and Roman worlds that Hegel purports to have discerned significant aspects of the truth of freedom are worlds that have been appropriated by Europe as *its* history; it is only what he calls the "Oriental realm" (*PR/GPR* §355) that is significantly "other" to the West. This construal of both the "important" developmental points and the "apex" might lead one to interpret other periods in terms of that trajectory and its ultimate aim, disregarding their determinate singularity—their logic, their past and future. The particular comments he is reported to have made in the lectures on world history portray many non-Western cultures as inferior, lacking development, and even, as in the case of Africa, not "consonant with humanity."[3]

We could look at Claude Lévi-Strauss for a different yet resonant demonstration of what the category of ethical life could offer in the form of a limit on one's own powers of observation and therefore also as an invitation to wonder at another form of life (here again we have a "Western" source engaging in some kind of critical self-reflection). He argues that the human being "grows to [its] estate surrounded, not by humanity in the abstract, but by a traditional culture" and challenges thereby the modern desire to interpret the history of world civilizations in terms of a "false evolutionism," which, he says, purports to value the diversity of civilizations but immediately undermines that value by construing cultures as "stages in a single line of development" (1952, 13). He criticizes this idea on the basis of the paucity of evidence—"we can know only certain aspects of a vanished civilization; and the older the civilization, the fewer are those aspects since we can only have knowledge of things which have survived the assaults of time" (16)—but also the limiting nature of our perspectives; the quality of a culture for observers tends to depend "not on its intrinsic qualities but on our situation with regard to it and on the number and variety of our interests involved" (25). Similarly, a culture may seem to us to be "stationary" because "the line of their development has no meaning for us, and cannot be measured in terms of the criteria we employ" (24)—"a complex system of criteria" instilled in us by "a thousand conscious and unconscious influences in our environment" and "consisting in value judgements, motivations and centres of interest, and including the conscious reflexion upon the historical development of our civilization which our education imposes" (25). Lévi-Strauss illuminates multiple threads of meaning that we can miss if our culture's priorities send it on a different trajectory:

> If the criterion chosen had been the degree of ability to overcome even the most inhospitable geographical conditions, there can be scarcely any doubt that [the Inuit], on the one hand, and the Bedouins, on the other, would carry off the palm. India has been more successful than any other civilization in elaborating a philosophical and religious system, and China, a way of life capable of minimizing the psychological consequences of over-population. As long as 13 centuries ago, Islam formulated a theory that all aspects of human life—technological, economic, social and spiritual—are closely interrelated—a theory that has only recently been rediscovered in the West in certain aspects of Marxist thought and in the development of modern ethnology.... The West, for all its mastery of machines, exhibits evidence of only the most elementary understanding of the use and potential resources of that super-machine, the human body... on the related question of the connexion between the physical and the mental, the East and the far East are several thousand years ahead. (27–28)

Lévi-Strauss importantly qualifies these observations as well, arguing that

> these things in themselves are less important than the way in which each culture puts them together, adopts them, or rejects them. And the originality of each culture consists rather in its individual way of solving problems, and in the perspective in which it views the general values which must be approximately the same for all [hu]mankind. (29)

Hegel does not manifest this kind of receptive sensibility, though he does note the philosophical significance of the phenomenon of cultural differentiation in, for instance, his lectures on aesthetics, which include rigorous study of the art, religion, and philosophy of many ancient and modern cultures. What he offers, however, is a systematic study of freedom as it is revealed by human beings over time, in which context freedom itself is shown to be a product of exposure to otherness.

Close scrutiny of the details of this historical study of freedom is worthwhile, I believe, for there are matters of great general interest to see here if we bring careful consideration to them, as well as a content that is significant for our own time. History has happened to free beings who can look at and understand themselves, and so they respond to what happens to them, change their conditions due to the limitations they encounter, learn who they are in so doing, and give evidence to later people, like Hegel, who will look at them and learn something: Philosophical world history "has universal concepts about history that extend across the whole" (*WH* 142).

Before we launch this discussion, however, now may be an opportune time to raise the question of sources, since so far we have made some reference to lecture notes and have not explicitly considered the status of these words that are not claimed by Hegel but attributed to him by others. Many of the words that are invoked in discussions of Hegel's orientation to other cultures were recorded by students and published after Hegel's lifetime, both in the lectures and the notes (called *Zusätze* or "Additions") to published texts, and thus we encounter genuine scholarly limits if we want to avail ourselves of these words, even though we know something of the conditions of their development. The difference between texts that Hegel did and did not publish lies particularly in the significant piece of information we get from the action of publication: namely, it declares that "this is what I (Hegel) think"; "I am showing you here how I want to be understood." For better or worse, we do not have that same information with regard to the texts he did not publish; we do not know the conditions of enunciation of the lectures; we do not know to what local issues, concerns, and conditions he might be speaking, whom he was trying to reach and why; and we cannot know whether he would have chosen to publish those words for unforeseeable readers to read. Thus we do not have the kind of information we need in order to know how Hegel "held" these words. We might think, of course, that the fact that he at least had these thoughts personally disqualifies his philosophy, but I believe that this is to deny the weight of ethical life as it operated in him and his speaking with local others and to unwisely empower a nonintegrated piece of his philosophy to disable us from using the integrated pieces that I believe speak powerfully against an oppressive and derogatory orientation to human beings. The standard identified by Ludwig Siep (2021, 370) is helpful here: We can turn to the notes if they are more or less consistent with the published work and help us understand it (which they often do since, directed as they were to students, they can be clearer than the scholarly texts), but if there is a disparity between the published work and the notes we should privilege the published work. In any case, this book is written out of the conviction that Hegel's philosophy opposes oppression, which means that I am interested neither in concealing the derogatory words nor in taking them as a reason to stop reading him. Let us now move on to Hegel's systematic study of freedom, for I believe it is of interest to all human beings, not just those in the room with Hegel in the early 1800s.

FREEDOM

The reason we are speaking of freedom in the context of a discussion of ethical life is because the nature and demands of freedom are not revealed all at once, but are discerned by human beings over time, inside and because of specific forms of ethical life. Human beings find that they both do and do *not* find themselves reflected in the specific structures of social life, and in the tension with these structures they discern what they need, which in turn could always produce another form of restriction that would require further social, material transformation. Freedom is central to Hegel because it *asserts itself* as central: It is the engine of transformation; it reveals limitations in the way things are by experiencing them; it will not be reined in by the way things are. Insight into the character of freedom, however, unfolds only historically and materially; it is a product of a clash between "who we are" and specific, traditionally and temporally established forms of materiality that themselves were shaped by freedom, a clash that produces new material forms. Freedom is discerned historically—in historical conversation with itself, so to speak—and inside of specific cultural worlds.

This discussion of freedom is aimed toward discerning a framework that could handle a variety of factors that are in tension with each other but whose tension may be navigable if recognized. If freedom is a matter of historical human discernment empowered by interaction with specific material constraints and enablements, then it will be discerned within ways of life, and wherever it appears it will typically not be present in full form. This means that, looking for freedom in history, one sees one-sided enactments thereof: social forms that, without being exhaustive, are revelatory of the character of freedom. This means that the perspective that is studying and learning from them is two-sided, a "critical witness": witnessing how their specific form reveals the nature and import of an aspect of freedom, and revealing the aspects that are wanting by observing the freedom that contests them from within and by setting them beside free others who do or have done things differently. Worlds produce insight into the character of freedom and can be critically challenged by reference to these insights taken as a set. However, critical witnesses themselves are formed inside of ways of life, which means they tend to evaluate others in a way informed by the aspect or aspects of freedom that occupy pride of place in their own, such that their evaluation of others can itself be one-sided. Many readers of this text and of Hegel will be those who inhabit worlds that prioritize individuality, and so the idea of freedom as a phenomenon of ethical worlds and as much more than merely subjective will be most relevant as a critical rejoinder to them. However, if we can *grasp* both of these phenomena—the one-sidedness of what we see and of our own seeing—then in principle we can also approach, on the basis of the work that others have done, the idea of a more or less "full-sided" freedom beyond the one-sided vision enacted by any particular world, and the idea of a more or less "full-sided" capacity to register this full-sided freedom that could critically engage with the question of its own perspectival character and thus in some limited sense transcend it. Further, because full-sided freedom and a full-sided capacity to evaluate it are brought about by the work of others and aided by meaningful interaction with their insights, they do not reflect any given self's superiority but are a matter of profoundly intercultural and historical indebtedness to historical, interpersonal labor and collaboration. Taking them up is a matter of doing justice to others.

We will see that there are many factors to hold together here. First, we have respect for societies as the places in which freedom emerges in its clarity but also as a principle that an appreciation for freedom would demand of us. This principle of intercultural respect exists in tension with, second, a critical orientation to the one-sided actualization of freedom and an expansive appreciation of the affordances of history (itself a matter of intercultural respect), such that we are challenged to hold intercultural respect together with a critical orientation. These two principles exist also in tension with another specific principle about the character of freedom revealed historically by the free praxis and thought of human beings: that it is also individual. Further, we do not approach these principles in the abstract, but from the specific circumstances and practices of oppression circulating our own context, which give the conceptual issues a particular kind of historical and political "charge" and should shape how we navigate them. Here in particular the problems presented by colonial imperialism, white supremacy, sexism, and capitalism seem central, and the historically motivated privileging of individual subjectivity seems particularly complicit, even as it is a piece of the character of freedom, in Hegel's construal. Thus we are heading here; or, our aim will be to focus in particular on these problems and on the "subjectivity" piece of the freedom puzzle.

Hegel's philosophy is akin to a lattice, built through consideration of the non-optional aspects of human existence, what structures they require, and how they can be held together, materially and practically, even in their tensions. In this lattice work, he has resources for navigating this complexity and for holding together the fact that freedom is revealed over time with the principles that this revelation reveals: respect for individuals, human societies, history, materiality, and thinking. In any case, let me describe now Hegel's basic framing of the nature of freedom, after which we will discuss its relation to history.

Who are we? We are beings-in-the-world, material bodies, intertwining with material resources, existing in a particular space and time and engaging with the material bodies of that space and time. We are beings who depend on our own initiative in order to act. We are beings who are loved and who love, who are taught and who teach, who are surrounded by others and who seek others out; we are cared for and caring, guided and guiding, and these activities move between us through touch and through language, in proximity and at a distance. We are beings who pursue meaning and the goal of self-understanding, mobilizing the available media that are effectively communicative in the time that is contemporary to us.[4]

We are free, according to Hegel, when we are allowed to be who we are, when we are supported in being what we are. Freedom in Hegel requires recognizing these various irreducible pieces of our existence and developing and sustaining the material and social infrastructure required for their enactment.

Hegel's philosophy systematically unveils, disentangles, and works through the essential characteristics of human existence, demonstrates what they require in order to be preserved, and addresses the various tensions that arise among them, typically through consideration of the observations made by a (limited) selection of other societies and manifested most clearly in the traces of their art, religion, and philosophy. These structures include, for instance, material support of finite, material bodies; a local domain of care; a developed social world with a political infrastructure; education; and open-ended, exploratory, and self-reflective activities such as religion, art, and philosophy. When human beings build these structures as home for their essential aspects, they are supported in *being themselves* in both their actuality and their possibility, which means in *being free*. Let us briefly consider the pieces of that lattice and their intertwining to discern something of what we would get if we looked closely.

One aspect of free activity is that it takes the form of different activities of engagement in the question of who we are, which Hegel calls "absolute spirit" and which he takes to be happening in art, religion, and philosophy. This engagement is pursued through imaginative and intellectual reflection, description, and creation around questions concerning what we take to give our lives meaning and purpose and the things we take to be most true and fundamental, by which we are oriented. This is the terrain of our character not simply as finite, material beings with determinate needs, but as beings whose meanings are not immediately apparent but invented and discovered. As such, it is the richest form of freedom, because it is the mode of free activity by which, as individuals, we travel in the unlimited dimension of meaning, open to a reality beyond ordinary limits, pairing with it through our capacities for creativity and thought, which we experience as our own but also as compelling us to something like universality and truth as such. This dimension is not indifferent to but also not simply occupied with the finite concerns attached to our neediness, and in it we arrive at insights that shape the other subjective, objective, material, cultural, and individual dimensions of life. That is, the activities of absolute spirit are not simply independent of what Hegel calls "objective spirit." First, insight in these domains is typically relevant for the question of how to build the objective worlds we inhabit, the material and determinate interpersonal structures upon which freedom relies; and second, we bring the power and freedom of the "we" we inhabit to these activities of self-understanding, because these activities mobilize resources that are expressive in our space and time, and thus we operate here on the basis of the capacities of specific historical others. In his various lectures on aesthetics and religion and philosophy, Hegel discerns how freedom has been manifested historically, finding in the initially alien cultural, religious, and philosophical activities and products of historical peoples—the fire of the Zoroastrians, the Pyramids of Egypt, the statues of the Greeks—sustained reflection on the meanings by which their lives were oriented and the expression of who they ultimately took themselves to be.

But freedom, beyond being defined by the activities of absolute spirit (and as they in fact discern), is also a matter of what Hegel calls "objective spirit," a matter of pairing between a determinate, single, bodily being and the world around it. For this being *to be itself*, it must be able simply to access this world, its space, and its things—the space in which it meets its most immediate needs and in which it engages with others and the world, the things that are always on the other end of free action, things that, while necessary, take more or less contingent forms such as chairs, books, trains, and so on. Thus, as we discerned in discussion of *Antigone*, the human being requires both a protected domestic domain—some kind of familial environment—and an organized and regulated public domain for pursuit of its own activities and its encounters with others, each of which organizes materiality for engagement and use. This means that free beings effectively demand particular, organized societies that will sustain and protect the spaces and material that free, mobile bodies need. Access to these spaces and material is itself dependent, further, on an acknowledgment and welcoming from others. Different spaces come with different kinds of acknowledgment—in the everyday public world, this is general acknowledgment as one among many and treatment that is predictably more or less civil; in the familial world, this needs to be caring acknowledgment that affirms and cares for singularity. This acknowledgment is expressed also in materiality, in our affirmation of the way the human being extends into things, into respect for those things. This "objective spirit" is the objective, material, organized, and regulated domain projected by the human being as material, needy, and free, with the accompanying suitable attitudes on the part of the others who inhabit it.[5] Further, this domain always preexists us and (if it has taken shape for free beings) is already structured to be accessible to us prior to our emergence, and so it does not and cannot simply answer to our free, individual will but is a kind of imposition coming as it were from the past, at the same time as its very existence is the expression of respect for freedom. Multiple environments with all kinds of degrees of intimacy and publicity operate to support this being in its pursuit of meaning and life in and beyond the circumscribed environment of familial life.

These structures of shared activity, which Hegel calls objective and absolute, reflect his persistent observations, as we have already explored at length, that the content of our actions and our pursuit of meaning is always deeply indebted to specific others; we develop and navigate our perspectives on ourselves by grappling with the perspectives of others; our individual activity is buoyed by the material expressions of the freedom of others around us. Experience is always a matter of being inducted into particular ways of being human, and thus always a matter not simply of individual singularity but of more or less coherent cultural wholes, and of more or less culturally coherent yet also open-ended philosophical, religious, and aesthetic inquiry. These wholes are somewhat narcissistic, metaphorically speaking, though their "self-circling" is how they support the pursuit of absolutes beyond specificity, since we require shared practices and their structures for extension beyond the "we."

Yet, in interaction with these others and this history, there is also the single being (which Hegel typically calls *der Einzelne*, the single being or the singleton)[6] at the simple core of this developed world and all of its activities. To be able to be ourselves is also to be able to be this simple being, which means that this is also an aspect of human freedom. The wealth of human cultural activity is a collective accomplishment, but single individuals are needed to engage it. The organized world is organized for these single beings, who cannot but act on their own initiative and more or less think for themselves even in seeking to follow the views of others. Thus freedom is a matter of selfhood, singularity, or what we tend to call "subjectivity": the "we" is always also an "I." Meanings, values, practices, and institutions will always depend on individuals for their expression and elaboration, and thus those meanings, and so on, require the affirmation and protection of those who would elaborate them. When worlds are constructed of meanings, values, practices, and institutions that subjugate these individuals, they make themselves vulnerable to individual action, which cannot be permanently suppressed. Thus worlds, as many of their members tend to argue, need to come to terms with the centrality of individual selfhood, simply as a matter of avowing the fact that the organization of the "we" is dependent upon the capacity of the I to recognize and sustain it.[7]

But these elements must be integrated with each other; we are challenged by their very existence to hold each of them true in a way that is consistent with respect for the others. There is the connection between singleness, on the one hand, and particularity and objectivity, on the other: One can only affirm and support single selves by affirming the existence of a specific, historical, objective "world" or determinate "home," since it, in its developed history, holds and supports subjective pursuits; hence the ultimately problematic character of the concepts of subjectivity and objectivity, intertwined and co-constituting as they are. To care for those selves and their agency is to care for their capacity to extend into and couple with a determinate context, to make of that world an extension of themselves and vice versa. We can also see here the importance of connection between subjective, objective, and absolute, or similarly between singularity, particularity, and universality:[8] A single self that *can* enact itself in a particular world will be a self with *intelligence*, a self that *understands* how to act effectively; it mobilizes insight in regard to the determinate, particular site of its action so as to be able to collaborate with it. This means that individual subjectivity does not demand to be upheld simply in its arbitrariness but in its educability, in its capacity to develop from arbitrariness to *insight*, and it demands to be supported in its capacity to actualize that insight with regard to objectivity, which includes things, contexts, and other beings. Human beings cannot be themselves simply on their own, but only in *collaboration* with what is not them, and thus their action requires "fit" that in turn requires learned engagement. Thus effective action requires basic rationality in understanding and basic goodness and justice in acting, because freedom depends on free beings being able to coexist with the real. This means that the being who acts is one who learns and develops, such that to care for it is to care for its transformability—not simply to answer to how it happens to be but to preserve its opportunities for growth, exposure, contact, and transformation. The centrality of learning and educability means that freedom is a matter also of universality: that involved in understanding the world (being rational), respecting those aspects of the world that are the home of free action or that allow us to be ourselves (being good and rational), treating other beings in a way that is consistent with *their* character as free and needy beings and as the condition of our freedom (being good and just and rational), and being open to transformation (which we could call the aesthetic moment). Finally, however, because freedom is freedom, one cannot exactly force it, but *can* work to construct the institutions it requires, as well as criticize their absence, which the history of freedom effectively does in noticing what was absent and needed and producing it.

In his consideration of the intertwinedly material and conceptual history of freedom, Hegel concludes that something has been accomplished: that because of the work of freedom in history we have seen its many-sided insights and projected institutions demonstrated. In an observation that likely sounds imperialistic to many contemporary ears, Hegel takes "the Nordic principle of the *Germanic peoples*" to have taken on "the task of accomplishing this reconciliation" among the various aspects of freedom (*PR/GPR* §358). What Hegel means by "the Germanic realm" seems to be the world that developed as the Roman Empire fell, out of the westward migrations of the Germanic people. Terry Pinkard draws a picture of Hegel's possible referent, describing what he (Pinkard) takes to be the concrete, historical conditions of preparation for the arrival of a commitment to the freedom of all, "the rule of law and the bureaucratic apparatus necessary for a free" and satisfying life: namely, long experience of the harshness of feudal rule, everyday horizontal interactions governed by the virtues of loyalty and camaraderie, and aesthetic exploration of the mundanity of everyday life (2017, 122; see particularly Hegel's analysis of Dutch art in the lectures on aesthetics). In his editorial notes, Allen Wood notes that the Germanic realm refers to

> "Germany proper" (*das eigentliche Deutschland*)—which Hegel understands to include the Franks, the Normans, and the peoples of England and Scandinavia (*VPG* 421/[*PH*] 349). But it also encompasses the "Romanic" peoples of France, Italy, Spain, and Portugal (in

which he includes not only the Lombards and Burgundians, but also the Visigoths and Ostrogoths) (*VPG* 420/[*PH*] 348). The Germanic world even includes the Magyars and the Slavs of Eastern Europe (*VPG* 422/[*PH*] 350). (*PR* 479–80)

As Eric von der Luft argues, however, Hegel should and need not have associated this task with a people; rather, it is more importantly a philosophical idea best understood theologically (1984, 341) or, we could say, a historically emergent, important thesis regarding what is to be taken as ultimately orienting that has come to animate a way of life, even while many practical dimensions of that way of life will continue to threaten it.

Before we investigate this further, however, we should look closely at what Hegel thinks it is the task of this "Germanic" spirit to accomplish. His argument here is that it has grasped "the principle of the unity of divine and human nature and the reconciliation of the objective truth and freedom which have appeared within self-consciousness and subjectivity" (*PR/GPR* §358). It is the dignification of human finitude in the unity of divine and human, the sense that this finite, material, self-conscious being, that *this* objective world, and not the far-off kingdom of God, is the domain of its freedom. It is the reconciliation of struggle between, on the one hand, the "otherworldly and *intellectual* realm whose content ... has not yet been *thought*," and, on the other, the "realm of ethical barbarism and of crude arbitrariness which has being for itself" (*PR/GPR* §359). This reconciliation, in other words, means that human beings and communities in their *finitude*, and not the kingdom and ultimate authority of God, have been found to have dignity, though not in its arbitrariness or its crude pursuit of self-interest, but rather *in concrete institutions in which our connection to each other as free beings in the pursuit of meaning and self-comprehension is nourished and fed*. This vision developed over time, due to the work of many cultures, many human seekers of freedom, and the transformation of the material world.

Reflected in this vision seem to be many of the historical efforts on the part of historical peoples—religious, philosophical, and aesthetic efforts—to grasp who they/we are, as well as the aims inspiring contemporary critics of oppression. That is, I think that Hegel goes a long way toward grasping the real conditions of freedom, conditions that are consistent with contemporary emancipatory visions, and that are importantly at odds with the state of the world as it is, a state of the world for which actual so-called Germanic peoples are heavily responsible. Also, we should not take Hegel to be arguing that this vision has been accomplished by any specific, historical "Germanic" society, and history since then has also shown how destructive "Germanic" failures to actualize it have been, particularly since many destructive and exploitative techniques have only increased in effectiveness. We may have at our fingertips, because of the historical efforts of peoples working out the character of freedom in their own determinate contexts, the conceptual and determinate, material resources with which to conceptualize the basic threads of this vision, as Hegel might, but this does not mean it has been actualized as such. But we have historical accomplishments here that give us resources by which to challenge determinate, real circumstances in real human societies. In some sense we do see this freedom actualized: We can see built up all around us the "ordinary secularity of actuality" and "rationality of right and law" that offer the self a substantial home and connections with others, without which its independence is empty; we have domains of the pursuit of meaning, historically constructed over time, that allow selves to be active participants in the articulation of truths to which they experience themselves as receptive, in practices of "religion" and "science" (*PR/GPR* §360). It is important to see these real things, even as we use their principles to challenge their shortcomings.

We can witness clear failures to bring "heaven down to earth in this world" (*PR/GPR* §360). They can be tied to problems that Hegel highlights: including the fact that the "ethical barbarism and crude arbitrariness of being for itself" frequently asserts itself (*PR/GPR* §359; see also Moland [2011]). In other words, modern forms of social life easily come to support barbarism and arbitrariness, turning the state into the tool of this barbarism and degrading the dignity of finite bodies, nature, locale, and environment, and the power and reach of that barbarism and arbitrariness have only increased. In this world, we have the poor (and rich) "rabbles" that Hegel observes (*PR/GPR* §§244–45).[9] The cause of the rabble, for Hegel, is the absence of interpersonal dynamics needed to support the possibility of effective and meaningful life. Engagement with each other at the level of the finite (through institutions such as Hegel's corporations or estates, for instance, which we will discuss later) opposes the temptation to trample on each other; engaging in efforts at self-understanding opposes the temptation to stifle what in us is moved by meaning, what inspires us to assume our status as the site for the appearance of meaning, and not solely for the satisfaction of immediate desires. Human individuals and human societies need the freedom to be engaged in this way, and failures to support this kind of engagement with meaning and with each other in turn risk the more determinate and finite bolsters of freedom.

Hegel's insights about objective and absolute spirit are partly the result of watching the one-sided privileging of individual subjectivity play out in the so-called West, with all of the destructive consequences of its one-sided sway over its contexts. We, more than Hegel, have had the opportunity to watch this privileged insight play out, and so, after we have considered one of his central treatments of that one-sidedness, we will move on to consider contemporary observations thereof. The obstinate assertion of this one-sidedness as absolute has supported the assertion of superiority on the part of the West that has prevented the value and significance of other meanings from being reliably perceived, and it has suppressed and distorted humanity in its capacity to be the site for the appearance of meanings, whether absolute, objective, or subjective.

The important thing, again, is that these elements—absolute, objective, and subjective—must be held together as aspects of one whole, in relation with each other (just as the similarly resonant moments of universality, particularity, and singularity should be). The single self is not overpowered but empowered and fulfilled by the grand aesthetic, philosophical, religious, and political reality facing it; in fact, in one of those grand religious narratives, that of Christianity (which, akin to other religious forms, Hegel takes to have discerned something ultimately true), we see that the ultimate religious insight is that God is finite, human, and mortal. Hegel believes that Christianity ultimately opens itself to secularity in its affirmation of the sacred character of finitude and its attribution of dignity to actuality. This world is no longer thought to be outstripped by a world beyond and, as such, is no longer simply the meaning-void terrain of a mundane being pursuing arbitrary, self-interested freedom (*PR/GPR* §359). And these human beings are no longer subject to a remote, divine, and absolute authority but fundamentally valuable in their own flawed right. This is a present that "has cast off its barbarism and unjust arbitrariness" and a truth that "has cast off its otherworldliness and contingent force" (*PR/GPR* §360). The singular being, through its worldly, objective, and particular reality, is the home of the universal, but only in this richly mediated way—a being of this world, these practices and customs, the specificity of which is not simply specific but bears universal meanings and is thus so to speak "sanctified."

Earlier we considered the Chorus's observation about wisdom and reverence in *Antigone*, observing that they are demanded by the human condition. That is, while we find that the demand for wisdom may ultimately fall upon us as singular beings, we have been cultivated in our powers by the efforts of historical humanity, the existing cultural world and the meanings that impinge upon us, in relation to which our own efforts and meanings are wildly inferior, such that here we see the suitability also of some degree of reverence toward these efforts and meanings that fill out our lives.

We have now a better sense of Hegel's construal of the elements of freedom. But what does it mean, particularly for decolonial and antiracist commitments, that Hegel takes these elements to have been revealed over time, inside of specific societies, through the historical labor of free beings? Let us now move, at least more explicitly than we have already done, to what Hegel construes as the condition of freedom's appearance—namely, to history.[10]

FREEDOM AND HISTORY

Traditions of engagement in absolute spirit, the construction of organized social environments, and ethical commitments and the mechanisms for upholding them do not occur in nature; they do not unfold naturally. They must be *discerned* and they must be *produced*, which means that they require freedom and power for both discernment and production, neither of which is immediately present either but must be developed. Further, the need for discernment and for production most fundamentally means that *they take time*: time for discernment and time for building what discernment requires.

Human societies have not discovered all of these mechanisms all at once—although, as Hegel observes, their history is a history of the discernment of specific *aspects* of these mechanisms. Hegel portrays a handful of societies (because discernment is always a collective endeavor), showing that, while they "work on" an aspect of freedom, it typically generates problems in which they (and we who later reflect on this) can discern what piece of the multilayered reality of freedom is missing. Here is the generative power of failure that we see Hegel tracking throughout his philosophy, or the one-sidedness of our ideas when we try to make them real in the world: that failure or that manifest one-sidedness shows us what we missed in our elaboration of something true; it helps us see better what we might have meant. It belongs to other generations, peoples, and cultures to set to work on other sides. We can ask, for instance, as Hegel does in his lectures on aesthetics: What is the import of the Egyptian pyramids or Greek sculpture, as far as the question of who human beings are is concerned, and what is the tension or flaw of the vision of freedom manifested there? How do practices change, and what does this change reflect? What can we learn from these changes and experiences of others?

Human societies *enact* their visions of who they are; they shape the world around them to reflect their insight into their own nature, which means that they leave a record of human self-understanding in materiality and in the technology used to shape it. Hegel writes, "spirit is only what it does, and its deed is to make itself... the object of its own consciousness, and to comprehend itself in its interpretation of itself to itself" (PR/GPR §343). Being in that world, intertwined with it, they can also reflect on it, and so the materialization of thought is paired with further reflection on it. Such reflection is, of course, transformative, and so it contributes to the further elaboration of self-understanding, or to further insights, which again entail materialization and transformation.

Further, because human cultures share the material world *physically*, and because through thinking and communication they share *meanings*, insight, and self-understanding, they can "get inside of" each other, whether consciously or not. Any development or progress that we witness, or any increase in the capacities and techniques of destruction, is not a specific culture manifesting its superiority or inferiority; rather, it is cultures building on each other by virtue of their shared materiality and their more or less shareable rationality, a building that becomes more shared as these cultures come into greater proximity.[11] The invention of writing and the domestication of sheep, or the suspension bridge, the cannon, eyeglasses: Each of these changes the world we occupy; shared materiality and ideality allow us to appropriate and build on each other's discoveries. Similarly, when another person shares a compelling idea with us, we can go on to think in its terms. While internalized and experienced as our own thought, it is also the thought of the other, the way the other insinuates herself into us. When the historically revealed aspects of freedom shape materiality, they are in principle taken up and extended, though not necessarily reflectively: one generation's insight can become another's nonconscious ground; the (partially) reflective praxis of others often becomes one's own "unthought given." Rather than a privileging of what is later, this could be construed as a surreptitious takeover of what is later by what is earlier. What we see here is the status of cultures as palimpsests (Russon 2017, 73), texts written on other texts, indebtedness to other historical forms, how those other forms assume inhabitation in them. Hegel says that "spirit is... what it does"; that in doing "itself" it makes itself the object of its own consciousness; and that in comprehending itself in this form it changes: "The completion of an act of comprehension is at the same time its alienation and transformation" (PR/GPR §343). There is no "standing still," as we will explore further in the next chapter's discussion of absolute spirit.

Hegel does not simply consult his own mind to develop his view of freedom; rather, he goes *to* the worlds in which its aspects are manifested and developed. For demonstration of the phenomenon of the "we" and its limits, for instance, he goes to Greece, and for excellent reasons. It is possible he could have gone elsewhere, as contemporary scholars would likely do, but he does not, which I imagine is due partly to the genuine power and appeal of Greece, but also partly to his belonging to a way of life that is culturally homogenous and that construes Greece as its heritage, to his culture's undervaluation of many other cultures, and to the fact that the tradition of scholarship in his culture on other cultures and the global circulation of scholarship were not yet richly developed. (And we should not claim that they are developed now, given the ongoing heritage of colonialism and imperialism and the silos created by linguistic difference and the domination of English.) We need not retain the Eurocentric focus of Hegel's reading; we can discern insight in other worlds, following Andrew Buchwalter, who claims that the "concepts of mutuality, social membership, and communal virtue" in Hegel are much more developed in "Asian and African accounts" of freedom (2009, 94). Or we could look (with Lévi-Strauss 1952) to the Inuit or Bedouin to find out what kind of experience is supported by integration with one's environment, or to the "East and the Far East" for what happens to experience when the connection between the physical and the mental is a central cultural theme.[12] We could pursue literary engagement with other worlds; for instance, Erdrich's (2016) and Simpson's (2020) portrayals of specific forms of Indigenous experience can offer a glimpse of a way of being-in-the-world that is typically inaccessible to settlers and that one's own can shut out. Another powerful example is Chinua Achebe's *Things Fall Apart*, which allows the reader, insofar as they come to inhabit the world of the story, to experience the brutal disruption of Igbo society by the British as though it were happening to themselves and their own world. Propelled by the embedded and historical nature of thought, to think with Hegel is to pursue this open consultation with meaning, judgment, and reason in history, this expectation that there is something to learn from the freedom of others, some generative power in both its discoveries and its failures, some efficacy in its transformation of materiality. The effort to study the insights of other worlds, to perceive their revelation of something our own does not reveal, and to see how our vision might be transformed thereby— these efforts are consonant with Hegel's conception of how thought works. As Timothy Brennan notes, "it is Hegel, for example, rather than, say, Edmund Husserl or Friedrich Nietzsche, who gives an explicit theoretical space to non-Western thought and provides an opening for scholars to explore such sources seriously" (2014, 89). Critique of Hegel's own expression of one-sided, underinformed views of some other cultures is consonant with this Hegelian spirit: One must learn from others what characterizes their freedom and what their vision reveals about one's own one-sidedness. While, as Brennan observes, "structures of colonial influence" continue to dictate the centrality of Western thought (86), implicit in Hegel's philosophy is a self-critique thereof and a vision of freedom filled out by non-Western cultures, which could recenter thought once deemed peripheral and redirect the so-called West from its collision course with the effects of its one-sided principles.

I take it that these are some of the reasons behind Buchwalter's argument that we should distinguish between, on the one hand, Hegel's Eurochauvinism and his Western and even Eurocentric conception of world history, and, on the other, his *idea or logic of world history*, which Buchwalter believes is not itself Eurocentric (2009, 87).[13] Hegel, says Buchwalter, enacts a "normative reconstruction of history" (88), which implies that we should pay attention to what peoples have discerned, respect the "mulling over" that their existence over time represents, and perceive how their insights have been integrated into our understanding (without assuming that everything that happened in history is sensible and just). The themes we see being "mulled over and tried out" are largely consonant with Hegel's own sense of the benchmarks of freedom: objective, subjective, and absolute. But this is a normative reconstruction in the sense that it discerns in history what is essential for freedom, which is not simply everything that has happened. Also, the ability to normatively reconstruct history should not entail an assertion of superiority on the part of those who do it but of the import of the existence and insight of others, who have empowered us to perceive freedom and construct reality in terms of that actuality or normative view (which is an unending task).

Further, just as Hegel has done, we could "consult Hegel's world" to discern the reasons particular phenomena seemed meaningful to him, and to discern what differences there are between him and ourselves that inspired him to pursue tasks that we would not and that leave us with tasks appropriate to our historical juncture. Hegel lived in Prussia, his adulthood spent largely in the early nineteenth century. The storming of the Bastille occurred when he was about nineteen years old, and for about a decade of Hegel's adult life, Napoleon was working on the project of expanding revolutionary France into what we now call Europe. Hegel lived with the more or less recent heritage of modern European philosophical thought, which had begun to plumb the depths of subjectivity, but this was a political context that was in upheaval, only in the middle of practically recognizing the priority of subjectivity. Prussia, for instance, had no constitution (which, as discussed in the final chapter, is central to Hegel's political thought) and was ruled by King Frederick William III. Because of his meaningful engagement with the cultural and philosophical efforts of other societies and times (including that of the ancient Greeks), and because of the simultaneously embedded yet transcending character of thought, Hegel could take a philosophical distance on this modern heritage and discern the outside of subjectivity, the elements and conditions of its existence, and the limits of its availability to itself. But while conventions, institutions, and laws were in the middle of massive shifts, they had not yet settled around the priority of subjectivity. Discernment of its nature and demands happens materially and temporally, in its institutional and political actualization, which was only in the process of developing, and so the various intricate problems with it and its mechanisms of protection had themselves not become manifest.

Given our historical situation and in Hegelian spirit, therefore, there are three things that we can offer to further historical discernment and actualization of the diverse aspects of freedom and the limits thereof. They are slightly different from Hegel's insights, yet I would claim that they follow his lead.

First, given the terms of our shared world, the accomplishments of our ethical life, we might have more resources with which to study the insights and offerings of other cultures than Hegel does (even if our ingenuity and ability are admittedly lesser than his), discerning more about the basic principles he links to the "Greek, Roman, Oriental, and Germanic" realms by looking at different cultural actualizations of principles and the revelation thereby of their scope and meaning.

Second, we have more concrete, historical resources by which to elaborate the one-sidedness of the "modern" vision of freedom as individual subjectivity, and so we can add to Hegel's description of that one-sidedness, for a decisively Hegelian reason—this one-sidedness, and the power this vision has to endanger freedom rather than protect it, manifests itself *in time*. Relatedly, the most nuanced reflection on the damage associated with that value is likely to come from those who have experienced that damage most directly, and so there is further historical reason to engage with the practical insights and scholarship of historically nondominant cultures. But the "freedom as subjectivity" aspect of freedom can be an ingredient of struggles against oppression if it is grasped as one-sided and if its necessary, extraindividual conditions are elaborated. Hegel shows that the values that move us are multiple, none the whole story, and that diverse truths can be held in their relations and tensions with each other.

Third, given widespread informal and formal education, in this era, into the phenomenon of intercultural interaction, and given how the value of individual subjectivity has played out destructively in that interaction, we can also find in the Hegelian critique of this value's one-sidedness, in his supplementary category of ethical life, and in his focus on the "absolute" practices of other cultures, a vision of intercultural communication that would support a more comprehensive freedom that may be our historical task to enunciate (see Hoff [2018a]). Hegel's notion of ethical life manifests a norm for intercultural interaction insofar as it asserts that cultures are the sites of revelation of absolutes—those absolutes that their very existence has revealed, in terms of which they live, and the significance of which develops and unfolds in finite, determinate practices, rituals, and customs.

Thus, in the next section I begin by discussing Hegel's own revelation of the one-sidedness of the West's characterization of freedom as subjective, after which I engage with the contemporary scholarship that diagnoses the problems with this characterization and with how it has played out. Each of these projects—Hegel's and the contemporary decolonial and Indigenous thought that we will foreground—invokes the phenomenon described by Hegel as ethical life, with contemporary scholars offering a vision of ethical life more or less appropriate to our contemporary situation. Again, learning about the limits of oneself and one's culture, about what more comprehensive freedom requires, through encounters with other forms of life, such that one becomes more oneself and more at home through being displaced and possessed by the other: This trajectory is, I believe, supported by Hegel's philosophy.

Finally, we will also see that to thematize the idea of learning through encounter is to commit oneself to affirming in principle the ideal of a more comprehensive freedom. The one does not exist without the other. We are capable of recognizing the significance of the ideas of others; we are fundamentally receptive to their capacity to reshape how we think. If we look at history and other peoples, we find human beings making the world over to reflect their insights into their nature and needs—what is demanded of them by their freedom—and we can make some headway in discerning these insights and registering how they contribute to the fullness of freedom. Indeed, we find these insights imprinted in the very material form the world has taken. The idea of history as revelatory does not mean contemporary humanity should congratulate themselves on their superiority over earlier peoples, but rather that they are indebted to the humanity of the past and have the opportunity to work to "comprehend the principle of this self-organization" (de Boer 2009). We do injustice to people if we do not acknowledge that they were discerning how their concrete situations needed to be fashioned and to change in order to be a home for them as free beings, and if we do not respond to their discernment and shape the world differently on its basis. The shape that specific forms of life take is due to the sense they make of specific historical situations, which are products of an extensive history and the massive material changes human beings have made to their worlds. The distant people of the past have helped usher our specificity into being by shaping the world into which we appeared. We live on the basis of others, supported by what they have materially and theoretically accomplished, in the context of a humanity that exceeds us in every direction, and in making our own lives we draw on them and that material history.[14] This is reason in history, concrete and material, expressed by human beings in action inside of meaningful, conflicted, problematic, and changing material worlds of which they are aiming to make sense. With history behind us, we can look back and, as Hegel does and as Pinkard notes, comprehend historical and "collective self-comprehension and different ways of being a human subject," or

> self-comprehension of what it is to be a temporal, self-conscious being and a struggle over the right terms of our lives with each other.... As the people living through these developments and unfoldings try to make sense of this, they give shape to an "Idea" that itself ultimately has come to take the shape of justice as based on the principle that "all are free." This is a freedom in which a modern form of independence has taken root within a modern web of dependencies which is the very condition for that kind of independence and which is only real, effective—"actual," as Hegel would say—within those webs of dependencies.... Even though justice and freedom have very rarely been front and center in the "restless succession" of human history, nonetheless, as components of a conflicted striving for collective self-comprehension and thus for recognition, they have emerged as what the struggles have been all about. (Pinkard 2017, 168)

The historical study of freedom's manifestation over time shows its mettle in our attempts to critique contemporary political problems (or so this book is arguing). Hegel opens philosophy to world history, and we can continue this effort, in communication with contemporary sources attuned to the suppression of freedom.

We can also do so with the confidence that the fullness of freedom in Hegel's sense, while expressed in "all are free," has not been actualized by the modern focus on individual subjectivity. Hegel's critique thereof should aid in contemporary efforts to track the damage associated with it. As Buchwalter argues, Hegel challenged the prejudices of his age—egoist and apolitical notions of individual freedom, bureaucratic and institutionalist conceptions of law, traditionalist and exclusionary conceptions of community—and emphasized the importance of education for practical engagement (2009, 100): We require an *education by history* and its revelation of the one-sidedness of different kinds of social forms. The vision of a (not-yet-realized) integration of the different, historically discerned dimensions of freedom is, I believe, convincing. It is even convincing to think that we have the principles by which to envision and articulate it, given what experience has revealed, even though we will always have to figure out the technological and material means for actualizing them, even though these specific forms of actualization are infinite, and even though time will ongoingly challenge our efforts: As Comay observes, "anachronism" is the "signature" of consciousness, as "experience is continually outbidding itself, perpetually making demands that it (i.e., the world) is unequipped to realize and unprepared to recognize, and comprehension inevitably comes too late to make a difference, if only because the stakes have already changed" (2011, 6). The vision of this integration, however, does justice to the various demands voiced in this book regarding how to support human existence in its various dimensions. Ultimately, however, the proof will be in the pudding: in the ways in which this vision reveals and answers to the political demands of the present.

In his philosophy, Hegel illuminates the conditions that individual subjectivity itself projects as its own, conditions troublingly absent from many actual Western cultures, to the extent that we can see how they have concretely failed to actualize the very ideal teased out so thoroughly in their philosophical, religious, and aesthetic traditions. Hegel, in recognizing these conditions, provides mechanisms for how to actually support individual subjectivity, and how to oppose its own capacity to destroy the world and itself when asserted in abstraction from its conditions. For an example of this we shall turn to his discussion of civil society, in which we conveniently also find a discussion of colonialism Hegel actually published, which notably links colonialism to the ills, risks, and dangers of civil society when it is left to its own devices.

HEGEL ON CIVIL SOCIETY

While we cannot dive into the details of Hegel's practical philosophy, we can portray its basic project. Briefly, it is Hegel's reckoning with the fact that freedom, the "essence, purpose, and object" of each person, is "not an Idea that [we] *have* about it [freedom], but an Idea that [we] *are*" (*PM/E* §482). Freedom is free *activity*; it is worldly and thingly. The freedom of the free being extends beyond its own borders and requires that extension, since it exists only in its link to the world, being itself only in it, with things and others. The dimensions of this worldly, existent freedom are many and must all be held together, and thus the text is something like a catalog. Most basically, freedom is of three different kinds: It is individual activity that essentially pairs with things and perspectives in the outside world (abstract right); it is the activity of following one's insight and being oriented by the values one discovers there, independently of external circumstances (morality); and it is participation in a world built by historical beings who recognize both the externality of activity and the inwardness of insight, and who support activities of creative exploration in relation to truth that even propel members beyond its borders, figuratively speaking (ethical life).

"Ethical life" is the part of Hegel's practical philosophy in which he, simply put, becomes concrete: What kind of worldly forms of living together are projected by this being whose freedom is both a material *doing* and a *subjectivity, perspective*, discerning, assessing, "holding" of the world? In ethical life, we see that different dimensions have developed in the real that answer to our different orientations to the world around us or to the different ways in which our freedom attaches to the world: namely, family, civil society, the state, and international relations and world history, by which we see these worlds contextualized by space and time. It is a world of intimate familiars; of free individuals engaging in self-directed activity and existing side by side; and of an organized, sociocultural reality that has developed a dignified life of its own, through which we share in what we have produced and which is maintained by a collective that together cultivates a perspective on the whole as such and fosters its membership's awareness and care for that whole. With ethical life Hegel asserts, against the moral stance, that we know all of this not through our own insight but because of our character as historical beings—because this is what free beings have demonstrated about themselves through their historical struggles and their self-reflective grappling with their circumstances. As beings who are within time and space, yet whose time and space is defined by its past and distant others, we are both within and outside of it, and *can* take lessons from history.

Civil society enters here as the worldly, material consequence of historical recognition of the general and important impulse to self-defined activity on the part of free individuals. Civil society is the form that recognition of individuality takes within a socioeconomic system. It is the concrete *social reality* of that recognition, because there are never simply individuals. Recognition cannot be abstract: Free activity is *of* and *in* the world, within a context in which we are circumscribed on all sides by material and interpersonal facticity of all kinds: by supply and demand, the division of labor, the current state of technology, the activities of others. The idea that there could be abstract, individual action that is not implicated in this broader context, any part of which could at any time contingently wreck any given individual's capacity for free activity, would be hopelessly naive.

This means, however, that we pursue self-defined activity in a world that outstrips us and whose contingencies could at any time crush our capacity for free activity. This part of Hegel's philosophy, like the rest, shows how the generative power of failure is harnessed in thought and in life: Free subjectivities in civil society themselves project different needs, on the basis of the wreckage that would ensue if they were not to notice the destructive possibilities borne by centering self-focused individual pursuits. The promise of free activity would mean nothing without some way of protecting us against contingency and, importantly, means of doing so emerge at the level of civil society itself, not simply at the level of the state. The most powerful and interesting of these is the "corporation," an institution by which individuals organize their pursuit of self-defined activity in relation to the similar pursuits of others and by which they pool their resources, experience, knowledge, and agency (discussed in *PR/GPR* §§250–56).

To put it briefly, corporations are communities whose membership is defined by expertise. Corporations give people a sense of membership and belonging and protect them from the effects of unpredictable economic life and its contingencies, by regulating the domains of their livelihood and supporting their members both materially and psychologically when they meet with trouble generally or, specifically, with poverty. Resources and capability are

> recognized, so that the member of a corporation has no need to demonstrate h[er] competence and h[er] regular income and means of support—i.e., the fact that [s]he is somebody—by any further external evidence... it is also recognized that [s]he belongs to a whole which is itself a member of society in general, and that [s]he has an interest in, and endeavours to promote, the less selfish end of this whole. Thus, [s]he has honour in h[er] estate. (*PR/GPR* §253)

We associate in corporations, Hegel argues, in the awareness that self-defined activity is protected by collaboration with those similarly engaged, and we gain dignity thereby that protects against the degrading effects of humiliation associated with poverty. The corporation also protects against the tendency toward excess accumulation, which Hegel argues is motivated by a distorted desire for recognition. Isolation (as opposed to corporate membership) would reduce a person

> to the selfish aspect of his trade, and his livelihood and satisfaction [would] lack stability. He will accordingly try to gain recognition through the external manifestations of success in his trade, and these are without limit.... Within the corporation, the help which poverty receives loses its contingent and unjustly humiliating character, and wealth, in fulfilling the duty it owes to its association, loses the ability to provoke arrogance in its possessor and envy in others; rectitude also receives the true recognition and honour which are due to it. (*PR/GPR* §253)

Loss of dignity through poverty and contingency's negative effects, on the one hand, and excess accumulation, on the other, are central risks of the activity proper to civil society. The corporation is meant to restrain the tendency toward "an indeterminate multiplication and specification of needs, means, and pleasures — i.e., luxury, a tendency which... has no limits, involves an equally infinite increase in dependence and want" (§195); this "luxury and love of extravagance of the professional classes... is associated with the creation of a rabble" (§253). "Despite an *excess of wealth*, civil society is *not wealthy enough*... to prevent an excess of poverty and the formation of a rabble" (§245). As Lydia Moland writes, it is Hegel's sense that the "*theoretical* commitment to the value and dignity of all humans" could only be realized if people "could be kept from collapsing into a single-minded pursuit of desires in civil society.... But Hegel seems to have thought that this was a big if: on his account, the most dangerous obstacle to European states' achievement of this goal was the temptation of unfettered self-interest" (2011, 152).

Hegel observes also that, in disrupting the family, civil society earns further obligations thereby. It

> tears the individual away from family ties, alienates the members of the family from one another, and recognizes them as self-sufficient persons. Furthermore, it substitutes its own soil for the external inorganic nature and paternal soil from which the singleton [*der Einzelne*] gained his livelihood, and subjects the existence of the whole family itself to dependence on civil society and to contingency. Thus, the individual [*Individuum*] becomes a *son of civil society*, which

has as many claims upon him as he has rights in relation to it. (*PR/GPR* §238)

Civil society has the character of a "universal family" (§239), and the corporation "has the right to assume the role of a *second* family for its members" (§252). Civil society has these obligations because (1) it has transformed natural, immediate life by removing the "immediate mode" (§217) or "natural means of acquisition"; (2) it "dissolves the bond of the family in its wider sense as a kinship group" (§241); and (3) through it, "specialization and limitation of particular work" increase, as do "the *dependence* and *want* of the class which is tied to such work," which undermines the capacity of this class "to feel and enjoy the wider freedoms, and particularly the spiritual advantages, of civil society" (§243). Civil society must protect individuals against the vulnerabilities they have within and because of it. This is not a task government per se assumes, but the self-organization of free activity by free beings in the name of their own freedom.

"In civil society, the *aim* is the satisfaction of need," as Hegel writes,

> but the mechanism of the necessity of society involves... the contingency of this satisfaction. This is due to the variability of the needs themselves, in which opinion and subjective preference play a great part. It also results from localities, the connections of a people with other peoples, from errors and deceptions which can be introduced into individual parts of the whole clockwork and are capable of throwing it into disorder—as also and in particular from the limited capacity of the single individual to acquire for h[er]self a share of those general resources. (*PM/E* §533)

The "police" can step in, pursuing on behalf of individuals the aim of civil society, the satisfaction of needs. But the corporation is another mode of redress internal to civil society that treats the cause rather than the symptom, through which free individuals cultivate social connections that prevent the reduction of the human to the contingencies of materiality.

Now, it should be noted that Hegel introduces colonialism at precisely the point at which he observes that, "despite an *excess of wealth*, civil society is *not wealthy enough*—i.e. its own distinct resources are not sufficient—to prevent an excess of poverty and the formation of a rabble" (*PR/GPR* §245). That is, it is the "inner dialectic" of civil society that drives it "to go beyond its own confines and look for consumers, and hence the means it requires for subsistence, in other nations" (§246). It is important to note that Hegel links colonization to what he has just construed as *problematic* tendencies of civil society: a contradiction between excessive and inadequate wealth; the production of luxury, dependence, and want; the creation of rich and poor rabbles, and so on;[15] it is not advocacy of colonization.

Civil society is not the last word, and so it is not the case that this inner dialectic is authoritative. Civil society itself projects the need for the many bodies that mitigate its effects: the police, corporations, and the state. In fact, the corporation is supposed to rein in the imbalanced, disproportionate reeling between luxury and indigence, the motive propelling colonization, and to cultivate an ethic that would preclude capitalist expansion. Further, Hegel embeds insight regarding specific forms of production and labor into government: Of the members of the legislature, some are representatives of the *estates*, which are groupings of human beings constituted by different areas of labor. Thus Hegel connects "the *sense* and *disposition* of the *state* and *government*" with "the *interests* of *particular* circles and *single individuals*" (PR/GPR §302).

We broached the topic of civil society and the project of the practical philosophy as such in order to show the rich contexts that are projected by the priority of free individual subjectivity. Emphasized here is meaningful work, recognition, and belonging, the prevention of runaway economic inequality, and freedom's responsibility (a responsibility projected by its very nature) to cultivate contexts for meaningful, productive labor and concrete relations of answerability that would limit self-interest and give life meaning. (This material will be relevant again in the chapter on objective spirit.) With his discussion of civil society, Hegel illuminates the capacity for subjectivity to undermine and destroy itself, but finds in its interpersonal nature the practices and institutions it requires for its flourishing. We would have to say much more in order to give a full and convincing account of civil society, of course—such as a more detailed description of the state by which civil society is further contextualized and its proper activity circumscribed—but we will leave this for the final chapter. Let us return again to the notion of ethical life as such, and with it to the notion of history, before turning to contemporary scholarship.

Hegel's concrete presentation of the different institutions of ethical life—whether family, civil society, or state; whether police, corporations, estates, and so on—is due to his recognition of the impotence of individual moral subjectivity and the moral stance, which leads him philosophically to the category of ethical life that recognizes, in opposition to moral self-consciousness' self-congratulatory stance, that human beings inherit their insight from each other and the historically developed world around them. Subjectivity is relatively impotent against the way the world is, not least because it is itself fostered by what is, and recognition of its dignity requires the cultivation by many over time of a substantial, concrete world. Subjectivity is no match for a world without institutions. Due to the weakness and vulnerability of subjectivity, the world *must already be built* in a way that stems from its needs and character in order for it to be allowed to develop its native powers, while at the same time it *is built* in this way thanks to subjective initiative mobilized over time. Hegel writes that "the good lack[s] subjectivity and determination, and the determinant, i.e. subjectivity, lack[s] what has being in itself—they cancel themselves out and are thereby reduced to moments" (*PR/GPR* §141). What is needed and good must be determined, which means it requires determinate action, and so subjectivity must be acknowledged as the route the good must take to "get into" the world. But moral subjectivity should *will actuality, not the ongoing need for its own action*. If we assume the moral stance, we reflect a profound lack of awareness of how ineffective it really is: first, because its capacities are inevitably constructed by the world it inhabits such that moral independence is an illusion; and second, because its own vision of the way things should be pales in comparison to the vision enacted over time by historical human beings and sustained by the very recalcitrance of materiality as the aid and repository of thought. "The objective ethical (*das objective Sittliche*) is the concrete substance *through* subjectivity as infinite form" (§144, my italics), which means that subjectivity *requires* objective institutions and forms of practical life (the real, interpersonal, material world), because *it lives there, outside itself, in the world with others*. This subjectivity can be itself only through material, interpersonal, and worldly mediation. If the human being is in fact a "co-self," one who lives with others and in a world and whose "living with" gives its life meaning, then the world will be a world of interpersonal institutions that affirms both our character as individual subjectivity and our character as co-selves and cares for the tensions that emerge between them. Individual freedom depends on the intimate and anonymous relations between subjectivity, institutions, and others, and the world to which we belong should lay out possibilities and obligations for us that we would in freedom choose, because we will typically answer to its dictates in any case. The vision of how the world should be so as to answer to this demand is, again, not simply produced by any individual human intellect, but the outcome of the shared efforts of free historical beings to discern how their flourishing could best be supported, such that it is not an imposition but could be a more or less democratically developed conclusion.

We should see in Hegel's philosophy his own refusal to allow himself the moral stance: His thoughts are empowered not by his sense of his own moral genius but by his consultation with the freedom of others and what it has accomplished in the world. But he too is both "inside" and "outside," such that when he is "looking at 'x' in his world 'w,'" he is "enacting 'w,'" or his observation of the phenomenon of ethical life and the principles its existence projects could be his way of life enacting itself through him, such that everything that we have said here could be used to hold Hegel to account, in Hegelian spirit. We and he are not impervious to the shortcomings we diagnose, and we can legitimately ask how he might fail the demands of philosophy. We might think, for instance, that Hegel's investigations were more informed when their object was what he took to be "his culture's" history, that he did not and was not particularly well-equipped to look very closely or informedly at cultures other than his own or cultures outside of those that had been appropriated by his culture as its history (particularly Greece and Rome), and that he assumed, without investigation, that there was nothing much to be noticed or attended to behind unfamiliar practices.[16] We might think that he got things wrong, and that he should have known better (though I am sufficiently in awe of the power of ethical life and the power of other perspectives upon our own to not claim this, since they tend to rigidly preclude the appearance of the unfamiliar as well as powerful possibilities of transformation that would be generated through inclusion), but we can be deeply opposed to the exclusion of large swaths of humanity without rejecting the philosophical thought of those for whom multiculturalism was not quite a living reality, particularly if their articulation of the dimensions of freedom effectively opposes the oppressive consequences of such exclusions. Further, I believe that Hegel discerns the standards by which we could most effectively subject him and others to judgment; in discerning them he has done some effective navigating of the inevitable tension for ethical beings of being simultaneously inside and outside of a way of life.

In what follows, we will turn to comparable contemporary analysis of the social breakdowns occasioned by emphasis on individual subjectivity and on the assumption of relative superiority by societies that have preached this emphasis. I will invoke two specific contexts and types of analysis here: North American accounts of the excesses of settler colonialism and feminist accounts of the colonial tendencies of transnational feminism. We will see that the basic phenomenon of ethical life is effectively central in these analyses. Each offers insight into the shortcomings and one-sidedness of the priority of subjectivity, and insight into the values, practices, and institutions that can protect it from its excesses, that could help derail the West and those it has subordinated from its collision course with the effects of its own principles. Let us begin with the issue of settler colonialism, in dialogue with Coulthard, la paperson, and other critical decolonial thinkers.

Coulthard, la paperson, and Settler Colonialism

Ethical life names that into which we are inducted as determinate, historical beings. This touching that has always been happening between our bodies and the material world, that perceiving that has always been occurring between us and other perceivers: These preexist and produce our powers of reflection, and our behavior emerges from and floats upon that unfathomable sea, as it were. The aspects of this "sea" count for us in a way comparable to how the "*unwritten* and *unerring* law of the gods" counts for Antigone: "They *are* and nothing more than that" (*PS* §436/ *PG* 236).

Coulthard's notion of grounded normativity (2014, 13) and la paperson's notion of scyborg (2017, xiii) are deeply consonant with the idea of "the *I* that is *we* and the *we* that is *I*" (*PS* §177/*PG* 108), though each of course introduces nonhuman elements into the unit (as Hegel does too, but elsewhere and in a different and lesser way). Coulthard writes, "I call this place-based foundation of Indigenous decolonial thought and practice *grounded normativity*, by which I mean the modalities of Indigenous land-connected practices and longstanding experiential knowledge that inform and structure our ethical engagements with the world and our relationships with human and nonhuman others over time" (13). The notion of grounded normativity captures the fact that we are a sedimented orientation to the world, empowered by this world, with our sense of answerability and of ourselves already established, our meaning intertwined with materiality. It reflects the sense that we have already come from somewhere, that we are implicated already in relations and obligations that we, with the support of this ground, can come to discern, and that these relations afford us a rich sense both of reality and of our obligations thereto. Coulthard's "ethical life" is characterized by connection to place, experiential knowledge, and an emphasis on relations, which means that it explicitly affirms the "I-we" interdependency. Colonial dispossession, in this context, is alienation from and disavowal of the historical, experiential ground of interpersonal and material intertwining, or ethical life.

La paperson[17] captures something similar to what Hegel would construe as the relation between the I and we in ethical life by adapting Donna Haraway's (1991) notion of "cyborg," an organism that comes into its own by virtue of integration with technology, though he adds to it an "s," which stands for "system" or "structure." The "I," for la paperson, enacts a world, an orientation to reality shaped by a "we" and manifest in its practices and the materiality of its body-world integration. "I" is a scyborg, in fundamental collaboration with its material, interpersonal reality, an oft-unwitting agent of a structure or system, though any given individual can go some way toward mobilizing a different system or refusing the one that is ready-to-hand for it. The scyborg does not and cannot simply replicate that system, as the "we" does not perfectly express and reiterate itself in the "I," as the "I" never perfectly enacts the "we." The system's elements circulate as they are, but also as open to being refused or wielded otherwise. Scyborg agency is the agency *of* that structure, but structural agency admits of permutations and combinations unrestrainable by structure.

I am a settler, neither a member of an Indigenous community nor a scholar of issues facing Indigenous communities. What I take to be my responsibility here is to frame the insight of others regarding ethical life, grounded normativity, and the scyborg and thereby to discern three lessons and ensuing tasks regarding settler colonialism. First, and most basically, we can illuminate how intrinsic to settler colonialism seems to be a fundamental *disavowal* of the ground of normativity, of the existence of a "they are" (*PS* §436/*PG* 236), of its own ethical life and that of others—due to an unnuanced, reductive, and self-destructive emphasis on the principle of subjectivity. Second, we can discern the *technologies* behind the operation of settler colonialism as a grounded normativity or an "ethical life" and thus become clearer about what it is, what categories and technologies it offers to unwitting settlers and others, and what technologies we would have to wield and oppose in order to oppose it. Third, we can investigate the *challenges* faced by societies that find themselves needing to coexist with each other in the same space and time but whose different visions of reality entail different forms of organization of space and time; this would require confronting the challenges to coexistence and discerning what would be needed to support it. Let us move through these three points in turn, beginning with disavowal.

At the root of human individuality lies a kind of subordination, a lack of consent, to something that already is; agency and choice are built over time on the basis of a prior subordination to an interpersonal, intermaterial reality. Initially the body itself is "disciplined" so as to wield the elements that allow it self-expression and activity. Independence is not there at the start, because accommodation to a richly developed interpersonal reality is its necessary ground. We have analyzed this phenomenon in this chapter and the chapter on recognition.

But the principles of the modern, colonial mode of ethical life lend themselves particularly well to concealment of grounded normativity and ethical life. When what counts as ultimate to people in a way that recedes from attention—their "they are"—is freedom as individual, as critical orientation to existing ways of life, as separation from sedimented determinacy, then this "they are," this ground, conceals *itself* as such. When the "they are" comprises commitments to individuality, free agency, and rationality, then its status as a "they are" is disavowed. Oriented toward individuals, modern colonial ethical life does not attend adequately to the interpersonal and intermaterial structures in and by which individuals are made. It does not prioritize the dynamics of care, concern, and cultivation that it takes to produce individuals. It does not permit the circulation at play in systems of relations that would challenge the carving up of the world into measurable units for discrete individuals.[18]

Interestingly, according to la paperson's analysis, to some extent the "settler, native, slave triad" that is the "analytic mainstay of settler colonial analysis" contributes to this disavowal by focusing on "racial identities: settlers, Indigenous peoples, and Black people" (2017, 5). La paperson argues, in ways resonant with Hegel, that while the technologies of settler colonialism operate through individuals they are not simply attached to individuals by virtue of their identity. According to the triad, "settler" is opposed to Indigenous peoples in a different way than it is opposed to Black people; Indigenous peoples and Black people are not oppressed in the same way. It cannot be straightforwardly said, particularly in North America, that Black people are settlers; their ancestors were typically not complicit in the appropriation of Indigenous land and, due to the structures of racism, they have not inherited much of its productivity and wealth. While for la paperson the triad has its uses, it can also be anthropocentric and individualizing, requiring that we identify people in fixed ways when "settler-native-slave technologies operate everywhere on everybody in intersecting, sometimes contradictory ways, and always with a dynamic specificity that radically changes with context" (9). The prejudice toward modern individualism conceals the fact that these technologies circulate inside of systems and institutions and can operate even in the absence of any settler, Black, or Indigenous person (2017, 13). As scyborgs, we make a home for such technologies in our action or not—though of course, as la paperson emphasizes, "individual settlers tend to uphold settler supremacy" (10n12). These technologies are the "they are" of worlds—modes of ethical life—that produce individuals with agential tendencies, and they travel, circulate, and mutate above, beyond, and through our action. To some extent we can, la paperson notes, come to occupy systems differently and avail ourselves of different technologies than the ones with which we are affiliated upon entering the world, though our mobility will be limited, of course, due to the fact that ethical life operates non-transparently.

What is settler, if not simply an identity, per se? With regard to its form, it is a "they are": a certain conception of the world, things, and people, by which settlers and others unreflectively live, and by which access, belonging, power, and non-power are decided, a conception that moves and cultivates us as the individuals we are and curtails what seems possible and permitted for us. La paperson's view seems to reiterate Hegel's logic in thinking of agency not in terms of individuals but in terms of the broader sedimented norms, values, and customs that perpetuate themselves *through* us, the "first accusations," in Socrates's sense (Plato 2012). And settler colonialism's first move is to disavow these first accusations, particularly because they are premised on individualism.

Let us turn now to the technologies of settler colonialism, which focus on space (2017, 12), and to the "technologies of Indigenous erasure," which focus on land (2017, 11). La paperson gives many examples of these technologies: property law and "the weapons that enforce it, the knowledge institutions that legitimize it, the financial institutions that operationalize it" (2017, 4); the "partitioning of earth into 'natural resources' that can be separated, owned, sold, and developed"; externalization of the cost of accumulation through contaminated water, disease, and other traumas to the "natural" world; "boarding schools and other institutions of cultural assimilation"; the racial science of disappearance in, for instance, blood quantum (2017, 11). They are all rooted in a particular vision of space, a vision that makes settler "settler," the particular "they are" of settler colonialism. "Settler," according to la paperson, is

> the idealized juridical space of exceptional rights granted to normative settler citizens and the idealized exceptionalism by which the setter state exerts its sovereignty. The "settler" is a site of exception from which whiteness emerges.... Not all settlers at all times enjoy the full privileges available to the "settler"; rather, settler supremacy is sustained and maintained by a number of technologies: citizenship, private property, civil and criminal innocence, normative settler sexuality, and so on. (2017, 10)

"Settler" names what space is, for whom it exists, how it is organized, and by what power it is operated. "Settler" is idealized juridical space that solicits action appropriate to that space, action that will sustain that space in the way that it is "supposed to be." This space construes certain people and action as belonging to and welcomed by it, and their belonging is protected by its systems of governance and policing: Different forms of action are criminal and innocent in it. Space is accessible, shareable, and *ownable* by those who are recognized by the authority that governs that space and taken to be its beneficiaries: white settlers, not Indigenous people or people of color. It is separated into parts, with public parts policed to protect settler interests and non-public parts construed as requiring ownership and development: Those who will make these parts produce capital have privileged access. Tuck and Yang (a.k.a. "la paperson") observe that "the settler is making a new 'home' and that home is rooted in a homesteading worldview where the wild land and wild people were made for his benefit. He can only make his identity as a settler by making the land produce, and produce excessively, because 'civilization' is defined as production in excess of the 'natural' world" (2012, 6).

Again, the disavowal of ethical life and insistence on the focal point of the "legal human" individual (la paperson 2017, 10) helps conceal this interpretive vision of space, support its operation, and mobilize technologies of Indigenous erasure. The organization of space necessary for this focal point recedes from attention; quietly concealed settler norms regarding space prop up the obliteration of Indigenous "worlds" and forbid emphasis on the construction—both interpersonal (our fates are tied up with each other) and "intermaterial" (we are material bodies joined in and with an ecosystem)—of a livable future.

A central piece of this technology, this interpretive vision of space, is its insistence on the mutual indifference or alienation of individual and space, and between the individual and other bodies in that space. As la paperson proposes, this is a world in terms of which "land and nonhumans become alienable properties," a world that creates and maintains "these separations, these alienations: Black from Indigenous, human from non-human, land from life" (2017, 4). It is a vision of severance, a rejection of membership, belonging, intertwining, mutuality. Settler "common sense" recasts "land as property" (2017, 4), asserting the priority of the human in the human-land relation, rather than recognizing the thoroughgoing character of human dependence on and integration with land. Even though traditional agrarian values may have shaped North American settlement, settler worlds now operate in terms of the norm of human/nonhuman separability. The techniques of settler colonialism are incompatible with modes of ethical life that reverse the priority and recognize interdependence (and incompatible with its own existence, as we see in climate change and runaway economic inequality).

The "they are" of settler colonialism implies an orientation to "land" or "Land" that is wildly inconsistent with that of Indigenous worlds. Indeed, it is as though the focus on "space" by settler technologies is aided by disavowing that space is in fact "land"—not abstract, indifferent, and quantitatively uniform and measurable, but material, natural, affectable, and determinate. While Indigenous beliefs, practices, and values are inevitably diverse, Julian Brave NoiseCat argues that "they find common roots in a relationship to land and water radically different from the notion of property... land and water are regarded as sacred, living relatives and ancestors whose well-being humanity depends upon for our continued health and existence upon this earth" (2017). Clifford Atleo and Jonathan Boron describe the orientation to land management and protection of different communities in "Canada." They cite Jeannette Armstrong (2018) who gives voice to the Syilx concept of tmix^w, an understanding of land as a life force: "Each life form is a single strand of the life force of that place and requires others of that place to have existed and to continue to exist. In that way tmix^w captures the dynamics of the myriad relationships that make that place what it is" (2022, 2). They refer to S. Denise Allen (2005), who says about the Wet'suwet'en traditional territory of the Yinta that "Wet'suwet'en land tenure is more than simply a form of joint property vested in descent groups. It is a social frame of reference that includes the lands, the waters and the other non-human entities that live on them" (2022, 7). Coulthard calls land a "system of reciprocal relations and obligations" (2014, 13); it is the context in which meanings and relations circulate, from which we cannot carve ourselves out as independent units. Sandra Styres and Dawn Zinga distinguish land in the "geographical and material" sense from "Land" "as a spiritual and relational place" (2013, 295) "grounded in interconnected and interdependent relationships" (300–301, cited in Liboiron 2021). Following their lead, Liboiron uses "Land" to refer to the "unique entity that is the combined living spirit of plants, animals, air, water, humans, histories, and events recognized by many Indigenous communities" (2021, 7n19). In his discussion of the movement to protect the Missouri River from the Dakota Access Pipeline, Nick Estes cites Ruth Wilson Gilmore's (2017) claim that "freedom is a place" (2019, 252): It is as though "Land" names the fact that free activity and substantiality are nothing without space, things, and others. The commonality between these accounts and

Hegel's notion of ethical life allows us to notice where cultural worlds might separately arrive at what is to be noticed, which could support worlds becoming more familiar to each other, not with the goal of eradicating singularity or affirming the oneness of a developmental narrative but of propagating possibilities for future solidarity and action against the disavowal that threatens all of us.

Jack Forbes captures the non-alienability of land from life and non-human from human (and thus the destructive character of settler technologies and technologies of Indigenous erasure that assert its alienability):

> I can lose my hands, and still live. I can lose my legs and still live. I can lose my eyes and still live. I can lose my hair, eyebrows, nose, arms, and many other things and still live. But if I lose the air I die. If I lose the sun I die. If I lose the earth I die. If I lose the water I die. If I lose the plants and animals I die. All of these things are more a part of me, more essential to my every breath, than is my so-called body. What is my real body? We are not autonomous, self-sufficient as European mythology teaches.... We are rooted just like the trees. But our roots come out of our nose and mouth, like an umbilical cord, forever connected to the rest of the world.... Nothing that we do, do we do by ourselves. We do not see by ourselves. We do not hear by ourselves. That which the tree exhales, I inhale. That which I exhale, the trees inhale. Together we form a circle. (2008, 145–46; cited in la paperson 2017, 17)

The technologies of settler colonialism and Indigenous erasure put at risk all that is essential to the body—air, sun, earth, water, plants, and animals. They disavow co-belonging, demanding that everything be subject to one-way human appropriation. Prioritizing the human will in its arbitrariness, they support the exploitation and destruction of animal and plant life. The "they are" that belongs to settler colonialism, which relies on the alienation or separation of what can only become genuinely indifferent to this alienation in death, is not capable of supporting life. The rationality celebrated by the French Revolution, by which we experience our separability from the world and even from our bodies, can be an immensely destructive suicidal power, insofar as it severs itself from its own conditions. As Hegel concludes in the struggle to the death, self-consciousness needs life (*PS* §§188–89; *PG* 112).

The terms and technologies of modernity, of self-concealing settler ethical life, construe humanity as the capacity to "write the world," to make history upon and over the natural world, mobilizing nature as the tool of will. Humanity is construed as creative, active, differentiating itself from nature, remaking the world, and this construal is protected and upheld by traditions, institutions, laws, and government. The unlivable "they are" of settler ethical life is given legal solidity and protection in the form of rights and the state, which defend these alienations (and as such are fundamentally inconsistent with Hegel's conception of the state and its mechanisms, which we will see in the final chapter). As la paperson writes, "alienable rights are produced: the right to own (property), the right to law (protection through legitimated violence), the right to govern (supremacist sovereignty), the right to have rights (humanity). In a word, what is produced is whiteness" (2017, 4).

It is not the case that the notion of property is simply problematic, that the human capacity to write the world is simply unreal, that human initiative is not significant in its own right. As Hegel shows in his discussion of abstract right in the practical philosophy, a certain kind of property is simply necessitated by the bodily, embedded character of selves, whose freedom is a matter of bodily pairing with things in space. But this active bodily pairing immediately opens us to a much larger picture involving the limits to property required for action, limits generated by a revelation, by action, of what property itself depends upon. The idea of property is meaningful precisely because the will is extended into the world and made there, but it is also *contextualized* by what it meets there—materiality and the freedom of others—which we will discuss in the final chapter.

Another technology of settler colonialism and Indigenous erasure that resonates again with the idea of ethical life relates to the figure "native" in the "settler, native, slave" triad. "Native," again, should not be construed as an identity, according to la paperson; it is rather a world that, according to settler colonialism, is "to be obliterated, exceptionalized as the necropolitical target, and also to be splintered into pieces that are constructed as 'naturally' eligible for 'primitive accumulation'" (2017, 10), or, as Tuck and Yang argue, made into a ghost (2012, 6). The technology operative here is explicit destruction of ethical life: What is threatened is the way in which meanings hang together for different peoples, the modes of implicit and explicit self-understanding of any given "we," their "they are." One sees this obliterative technology operative in the residential schools to which many Indigenous children were taken and in which they were put at risk of abuse and death[19]—this is interruption and endangerment of the processes by which meanings are handed down, of the cultural, religious, aesthetic, political, economic, and developmental articulation of a people.

Denial of ethical life operates here: Settler technologies constituting juridical space are modes of Indigenous world obliteration. The non-alienation of human and nonhuman and the idea of materiality beyond property are aspects of Indigenous "worlds" under erasure. Disdain for the very idea of ethical life turns those who live an ethical life that projects human affiliation with worlds, nature, and other beings (and that in its difference from settler ethical life becomes apparent as such to settler perception) into targets to be revised, disappeared, erased. La paperson argues that settler reality offers two options: "becoming killable or becoming a killer" (2017, 7). To live in the terms of possessive individualism is to undermine the conditions of life and to be a killer. To oppose living in this way is to be at risk of state-sanctioned violence. If one insists on non-alienation, one becomes threatened, tracked down, disposed of, and so on. Non-alienation from land, relations, and accountability is rendered illegal.

While la paperson construes the figures of "settler" as space and of "native" as world, he argues that anti-Black racism construes "slave... as an ontology of total fungibility and unending property constitutive of the very world order of settler colonialism" (2017, 11), or, as he and Tuck observe, labor without personhood (2012, 6). While "settler" centers around space and "native" around world, the core meaning of Blackness in worlds organized by settler colonial and racist logic is *body*; "technologies of antiblackness have a corporeal priority" (2017, 12). The Black body is construed by the logic of racial capital as object, instrumentalizable, capable of being bought, used, imprisoned, and inserted into economic interactions. The Black body is destined to be exploited for its brute utility, and if it will not make itself useful it is targeted for suppression.

Technologies, la paperson argues, are made to fit their target. In targeting world, settler technologies include unsafe water, residential schools, the killing of the buffalo, the incontestable sovereignty of countries like Canada and the US. Anti-Black technologies target bodies: They are technologies of illegality and criminality, industrialized prisons, trafficking (2017, 12).

We have said generally about ethical life that it and its technologies are difficult to perceive if one emerges as belonging to them. Settler colonialism, la paperson argues, happens *for* a person as a settler (2017, 4); it is not simply something that "happened" *to* Indigenous peoples. If who one is is such that this world is made for "one's kind," if space is organized around "one's kind," if one does not confront limit but only assistance in that world, one may not notice how the world "fits," how it works as a kind of assistive technology. If the world matches us, it recedes from our attention. Much easier is it to perceive something when it gets in one's way, threatens one's existence, refuses to be ignored; then one cannot easily live without confronting it. The fact that its ethical life has shaped settler action means it suits typical settler action and moves settlers to perpetuate settler technologies.

La paperson calls attention to the coexistence of conflicting models: "Occupying the same space and time are the colonizer's territories and institutions and colonized time, but also Indigenous land and life before and beyond occupation" (2017, xiii). Inhabiting "the 'selfsame land' are spatialized white immunity and racialized violation, non-Native desires for freedom, Black life, and Indigenous relations" (3),[20] "desires for a colonizer's future" and "desires for Indigenous futures" (xiii). The ease with which the possibility of coexistence is projected in the name of reconciliation often bespeaks the colonizer's interpretation of space: Namely, interpersonal existence is a matter of individuals living side by side in space, each in terms of their individual characteristics and projects. When self and action are understood to be ways of inhabiting, projecting, and coupling with a world, or matters of ethical life, it is easier to see the challenge of coexistence and the fact that denying this challenge operates in the interest of the settler. Indigenous sovereignty has already been sacrificed if we are allotted authority only over private domains, since this already bespeaks a settler mode of projecting a specific carving up of public and private space. Different forms of ethical life conflict at the level of what space is and means.

We have spoken of disavowal and settler technologies; let us now move to the topic of the challenges to coexistence. Taking seriously the notion of ethical life requires acknowledging the complications of conflicting claims to sovereignty in contexts of shared space, as in settler colonialism. The solution cannot simply be a matter of giving each other room to exist alongside each other, because this already privileges settler logic. The idea that we can exist alongside each other, each partitioned off in our own space as property, is already a settler conception of space and thus opposes the sharing of space. If we are being-in-the-world, then space — the way it is lived, construed, and inhabited — is a matter of who we are.

Hegel's discussions of ethical life and recognition should illuminate the genuine challenges of coexistence. The I is rooted in and dependent upon a "we." This "we" exists and expresses itself in and through its practices, institutions, and habits, with all of their materiality, their organization and articulation of space, their specific character as historically determined. This is the practical reality of recognition, and it describes the essential dignity of forms of life as places of recognition, as where we grapple with the "absolute." That is, pursuit of self-understanding and consideration of what we are oriented by is expressed in the terms *of* these forms of life and could never be reduced to the small, private domains of individuals.

If any intercultural contact is to be made, however, it can only happen through these forms of ethical life. We cannot leave our worlds behind, so to speak, because we could not even identify that from which we would need to sever ourselves. We must move through dimensions of familiarity, as Uday Singh Mehta argues, in order to transform them; any commonality we establish will rest not on shared abstractions of principle but on our shared "parochialism" (1999, 26–27). While I do not have any specific proposals at the moment regarding what this would look like on a broad sociopolitical level, the experiential basis of such broader political work could be described in this way: I operate with a vague feeling of how things hang together in a meaningful way, and so do you; this "hanging together" is different in each of us, but it exists for both of us and we can identify with each other in this. I can become alive to the weight of my own and to the weight of yours for you, and I can try to discern what it would be like to operate in terms of a different sense, of "your" feeling of how things hang together meaningfully. And a vague sense of what is operative in your world, such as can be inspired by the experience of literary engagement described above, can even trigger a sense of alienation from or lack within my own.

Theory tends toward abstraction, and philosophy especially toward first principles, or the conceptual kernels of the situations that it considers. As such, philosophy can fail to notice the concrete situations that launch it toward this search. Given that we are beings of ethical life, we are implicitly committed to and mobilized by a specific "concreteness" that refuses illumination. The abstraction of philosophy is built on a concealed concreteness, but the effectiveness of philosophy depends on its openness to being educated by different forms of the concrete. Philosophy must go through ethical life, through the concrete: both to see what it has propelled in us as far as thinking is concerned, and to see what other meanings or expansions to already familiar meanings are suspended in different modes of the concrete.

We will discuss in more detail the worldly, spatial character of human existence in the final chapter. For now, let us move to some prominent critics of Western feminism to see a different kind of colonialism and, with it, another mode of suppression of ethical life.

Mahmood, Abu-Lughod, and Colonial Feminism

With the idea of ethical life, Hegel illuminates how we belong to determinate social worlds, with that belonging itself envisioned in a singular and characteristic way. Who we are is not simply ourselves as individuals but ourselves as members, as participants, whose action and judgment reflect as much the character of this world as our own singularity. To try to understand ourselves is to own up to the reality of membership and try to understand it. What world are we already inside of? What are the ideals this world projects as its founding commitments and aims? And, particularly with regard to the questions we are grappling with here, what are the shortcomings that characterize cultures complicit in modern European colonialism? Let us reiterate now, in the context of transnational feminism and its critics, what principles are operative in the "common sense" of the worlds from which modern colonialism has issued, and second, what they lack with regard to what human beings need and desire. Here again I will argue that the categories of recognition and ethical life can reveal and help explain these shortcomings. My analysis, it should be noted, will be a matter of me trying to shed light on the world I basically inhabit, and will presumably bear the markings of that belonging in ways that I do not notice. The world I project and from which my thinking emerges is one that has been afforded to me as a white, university-educated, nondisabled, cis woman, a settler of Dutch and Protestant heritage living in what I took to be Canada.

The values that operate as the "common sense" and in the "imaginary" of colonial forms of ethical life and that have been used to justify colonial supremacy and the structures of social and political life are those that focus on the individual, individual rights, self-determination, autonomy, and democracy. These principles assert the status of the human being as a separable, self-defining agent, undetermined by what is not it, doing what it wants, and protected from the incursion of others, with the ability to call on the state for protection against transgression of its boundaries; state power, that is, is mobilized for the protection of private, individual interests.

This is simply a gloss of the matter, of course, meant as a description of the character of this ethical life, not a theoretical analysis of what is at play in such principles. The point is to reflect on the idea that principles like these circulate in the mode of an assumed common sense, that they have "gotten into the walls" and "made a home inside of" broadly Western structures, institutions, laws, and habits, so as to become "the way in which that 'we' lives."

As a matter of contrast, we can also look at what they lack, which the discussions of recognition and ethical life show insofar as they are effectively concealed by these principles. These principles, that is, do not emphasize the importance of relations, of mutual care and cultivation, of shared and cooperative access to the goods in the world that others help cultivate and the wealth that others bring to our lives—their intelligence, support, creativity, and productivity. In fact, focus on, for instance, individual property rights conceals from us how much we depend upon the goods that come from others and discourages us from developing a sense of the pervasiveness of public goods and the goods that overflow as it were from private stock. As Hegel argues,

> the more we reinforce freedom, as security of property, as the possibility of developing and exercising, etc., one's talents and good qualities, the more it appears *to become a matter of course*; then the consciousness and estimation of freedom especially turns towards the *subjective* sense of freedom... But... this very freedom... only arises under conditions of objective freedom. (*PM*/E §539)

And so we can ask, do we desire connection? Relating and relationships? Access to the shareable goods produced by others? Do we value belonging, participation in a world that extends beyond ourselves? If such things are important, then they too require protection, respect, and support. Do the political principles operative in the colonial world protect and support the goods of the world and participation in them and it? Do they help us perceive and share the "wealth" we produce together? Do they cultivate recognition? Do they make possibilities for participation in the things that we collectively do? And finally, do they illuminate the significance of ethical life, allowing world to be valued as world and thus to *be* world? Belonging gives content and significance to our capacity for free agency, such that freedom is not a matter of doing what one wants in an isolated way but of being in a world that offers rich possibilities for action and finding meaning in that "being in." If agency is enriched, supported, and made meaningful by the dimensions of the world around us, then such worlds and our access and belonging to them must be nourished and sustained (see Hoff [2014b]).

In resonance with the idea of ethical life, Saba Mahmood argues that what has come to be called "the West" operates in terms of an impoverished, unidimensional, and parochial conception of freedom (see also Hoff [2023c]). The construal of freedom as individual bears the implicit meaning, she argues, that "real" freedom is resistance, critique, opposition to the way of the world, subversion of existing norms—that freedom is taking a stand *against* the way things are. Agency "is understood as the capacity to realize one's own interests against the weight of custom, tradition, transcendental will, or other obstacles (whether individual or collective)" (2001, 206). Her critique is aimed ultimately at "the normative subject of liberal feminist theory" (2005, 33), which fails to apprehend that its construal of freedom as opposition to the weight of the world is itself expressive of a tradition, an unrecognized commitment to a specific mode of life. In other words, this is how insiders to this form of life *express* their belonging, their way of life: "We" conceive of freedom as opposition and in doing so we express our faithful enactment of a way of life. Resistance is thus implicitly obedience, involving the pleasure of being at home in the world, inspiring affirmation from that world. Mahmood's goal is to expose the fact that this is a parochial vision in ways it does not acknowledge. If it is a *norm* to construe agency as the subversion of a norm, then subversion is at its core compliance. Opposition to x is accommodation to y, the larger context one inhabits.

Mahmood adds that we should notice the operation of power in this compliance concealed as opposition. Rather than resisting the dominant, this model of freedom implicates us in domination. Here she uses an example from Abu-Lughod of Bedouin women wearing lingerie to defy their own social norms. This is not simply opposition to dominant relations of power, but imposition of "alternative forms of power rooted in capitalist consumerism and urban bourgeois values and aesthetics" (2005, 9). It becomes acquiescence to the more powerful, to the way a dominant mode of ethical life has of construing freedom. There may be meaningful resistance to power here, but it is not simply that, because it is also subordination to the norms of a way of life that serves capitalism and urban, bourgeois values.

Beyond the logical point that subversion can be at its core adaptation, and that what appears as opposition to dominant values can be acquiescence to even more dominant values, something of vital importance is lacking in the model of freedom as opposition, which undermines the exercise of freedom in worlds that organize themselves around that model. If our actions as free beings are filled out by the world around us, then to fail to thematize and support continuity with and participation in worlds is to undermine freedom and reduce its content. Indeed, freedom would be empty if it were simply a matter of our own self-definition: the content of our agency depends on the resources the environing world offers to us, such that to exercise freedom is precisely to be able to mobilize those resources. The "normative subject of liberal feminist theory" (Mahmood 2005, 33) is not what would naturally grow in human societies if it were perfectly unobstructed, because it is through specific forms of determination, ambivalently obstructive and productive, that anything grows.

Hegel's argument is that agency develops through the determinate avenues, mechanisms, and others that summon it into existence. Mahmood's argument, similarly, is that we should "think of agency not as a synonym for resistance to relations of domination but as a capacity for action that historically specific relations of subordination enable and create" (2001, 203). This essential subordination at the heart of agency brings us into being as free beings, which means determinacy is powerful and important to us. Wherever we get human beings, we get one-sided, determinate modes of being human. Adaptation is inevitably the way we become free, even as there are other elements at play here that limit this one (some of which we will explore in the chapter on conscience). Subordination and agency are pairs—co-essential, coupled sides of the same process. The abilities by which agency is articulated are not the natural capacities of an undominated self that existed prior to the meanings and forms of organization of this world, but are themselves their products. As I grow through, in, and around the meanings that structure and organize my world, they become my meanings, and my grappling with and articulation of them is an expression and development of my agency. To be cut off from the rich nutrients of ethical soil, so to speak, is one of the most significant obstructions we could experience. Any attempts to distinguish good from bad subordination need to begin by acknowledging the necessity of this subordination.

Mahmood's focus is Muslim women in Egypt engaged in shared study and discussion of Islamic scriptures, social practices, and forms of bodily comportment. She observes these women to be engaged in a practice of freedom—namely, feeling out their sense of the value of being inside of a particular world that makes sense to them, querying its mysterious corners, exploring its dimensions and depths, mixing with it their own capacity for sense-making so as to render it more satisfying to their impulse that it make sense, that it hang together more or less coherently. They are supplementing the meaning and articulation it gives to their lives with their own activity of engagement with it, meeting it with their interpretation. They are pursuing the avenues it projects, avenues that have come to shape their sense of what it is to live a meaningful life. As Mahmood writes, the "agency I am exploring here does not belong to the women themselves, but is a product of the historically contingent diverse traditions in which they are located" (2005, 32). While Hegel does not speak concernfully of the situation of women, these could otherwise be words he would say. Individual agency is a matter of being in a world and rising up to meet it—grappling with the meanings that it has already planted in one's experience and by which it has given that experience its feel and shape.

We cannot even begin to engage with the question of "other people's freedom" if we do not recognize that it is a matter of ethical life; this is thus the order required by responsible attempts at intercultural understanding. To make one's way in the world is to do it in a rich and intricate world that hangs together in a certain way, to which one is habitually attached, by which one is always already motivated, and which operates in terms of domination and subordination. Agency will always be a matter of coupling with the world, finding and mobilizing the possibilities it offers (Morris 2006); it is as if the world stood behind one's action, lending that action its weight. Freedom is not a matter of simply resisting that world as an individual; the resources one has as an individual are microscopical and meager in comparison with those of the shared world.

The material determinacy we have at hand is going to be different from that of others; the determinate worlds we inhabit will cultivate different orientations and desires within us. Yet freedom is a matter of mobilizing the determinate conditions at hand. The Egyptian women of Mahmood's study may desire the cultivation of a kind of bodily comportment for the sake of a virtuous life; doing so would then be an expression of freedom within and with a world that has already inspired them to perceive certain things as meaningful and not to register other things. We cowardly disavow the complexity of the relation between individual and world when we take one version of such relation to threaten our (parochial) sense of the independence of norms. We can never judge that someone is free by looking to see if the determinacies of their practices of freedom are the same as our own; because freedom itself always has a determinate content and materiality, there is no one way to be free. If we are interested in the question, then we must find out what it means for people to engage in their action, and how they navigate their existing world and find self-satisfaction—the meeting of self and world—in that world.

Both Hegel and Mahmood bring us back from abstraction to the concrete: Principles, values, and ideals are expressed through actions, materiality, and the determinacy of worlds. That "stuff" is going to differ from place to place. Yet this does not preclude development of a shared understanding with others, and it does not entail a simple relativism, because worlds are one-sidedly working on matters of general human significance and because we often mobilize this "stuff" for the sake of similar aims, the sense of which can be shared, and the sharedness of which is often just concealed by differences at the level of determinacy. A person may dress the way they do, for instance, to look respectful, rebellious, or proper, to engage in a scholarly, worshipful, or casual practice, but the specific means by which the shareable meanings are expressed, the pieces of clothing and traditions of dress, will always be culturally and historically specific. What we have in specific acts is the expression of ideational content, of "spiritual" content: people expressing their affiliation with meanings. The determinate practice is not just determinate but an *expression*, and we must recognize it as such and turn to its agents for aid in its interpretation.

If worlds are the grounds in terms of which people find mechanisms and resources for the meaningful filling out of their own freedom, then they demand respect and protection—though they can also of course suppress their members' attempts to engage in these practices (we will address this issue later). If a free, meaningful life depends on environmental determinacies, on what other people have produced, on a richly filled out world, then it is this world, not simply individuals as such, that needs protection, as does access to such worlds (see Hoff [2014b]).

Abu-Lughod is relevant here again, as she reveals the violence at work in the attempt to strip people of world (2002). One of the factors invoked to motivate the illegal US war in Afghanistan in purported response to the attacks of September 11, 2001, was the Taliban's mistreatment of women. In Abu-Lughod's analysis, the US highlighted the unacceptable determinacy of the world from which it would be saving these women without noticing its own determinacy. Abu-Lughod challenges the violence entailed in this "saving to": The women "to be saved" would not experience this foreign place as a home, with readily circulating meaning, value, and avenues for their experience of freedom. In fact, the women she spoke with reflected critically on the isolation and loneliness they imagined women in the West would experience, alienated as they were perceived to be in their private domains, with space and the border between home and world established at a different point in each world. If what is to be human is to be inside of a way of life, and to borrow from that way of life to be oneself, it is not a solution to the problems inside of that way of life to offer the terms of a different way of life as a replacement.

The deeper problem here is that the phenomenon of ethical life—the singularity of worlds and cultures and the experience of belonging they offer—is simply not adequately noticed and described; it is not taken, as Hegel takes it, to be an important priority (among others). The phenomenon of ethical life is self-concealing, particularly in and by individualist cultures, but also because it is a matter of deep habituation. And it is not a neutral or indifferent matter to take someone away from this way of life, demanding that they live in the terms of another.

If we are alive to the reality of ethical life, then we can be mobilized to ask better questions. What does one's mode of ethical living empower one to notice, and what does it conceal? As Abu-Lughod argues, it stages voices like that of then First Lady Laura Bush, and silences, for instance,

Palestinian women, which shows that it is important to be particularly "suspicious" of one's "bedfellows."[21] This kind of ethical life conceals the advantages one accrues due to exploitation, to which the solution is a global redistribution of wealth (2002, 787). Wealth is a shared product: Colonial, Western wealth is built on exploitation; it does not simply come from morally respectable ingenuity but from the mobilization and theft of the labor of others, upon which ingenuity itself is built. This way of life relies on exploitation and the appropriation by the West of the world's resources. This mode of ethical life is very good at concealing that from itself—particularly, again, through its overemphasis on the importance of individual self-making. Here the model of freedom as individual is again complicit in oppression rather than liberatory.

If we really recognized the significance of belonging to a world, then we might be more just and curious in our attitudes toward other worlds, wondering what rich experiences of belonging could be unfolding there, how these experiences would "feel," and how the "they" living there would perceive "us." If we take Hegel and Mahmood seriously, recognizing the significance to us of the shared world in which we enact freedom, then Muslim women (and other "others") have something to teach "Western" feminists about freedom, about what they need in order to be themselves. Similarly, the profound inadequacies of the colonial world could be clearer—how the focus on individual self-making cuts people off from sharing, access, and the transmission of cultural values, how it can lead to the degradation through neglect of shared goods, how it can manifest "ethical barbarism and... crude arbitrariness (*PR/GPR* §359). To protect individuality and autonomy requires protection of the conditions under which it develops, which is access to a world and its riches, and the virtues (to use Hegel's various terms, "honour," "loyalty," and "companionship") required to prevent it from becoming a "crude self-interest" that would endanger these conditions (§359).

Since self-consciousness exists only in being recognized, we are beings of ethical life. This is a universal structure of experience, the way it unfolds for everyone, everywhere. This claim regarding a universal structure is not a claim regarding a universal *content*, which would always be produced inside of an ethical life and could in its attempt to be universal suppress claims on the part of other ethical worlds to be more or less coherent in their own right. We share a universal—that we are beings of ethical life—but it manifests itself in different kinds of content. We may share more, but asking about the possibility of sharing must engage with the reality of ethical life. We will always come to insight about universals via the determinate avenues of a specific way of life, developing the capacity to think in principled ways by *these* people in *these* situations. We should think about how these principles reflect the determinate context through which we grasped them.

To be clear, we have not abandoned here the possibility of critically engaging with practices that are violent, oppressive, and exclusionary. As we have said, this discussion of ethical life is intended to establish the condition under which that critical engagement can occur: acknowledgment of ethical life in oneself and respect for it in another. Only on that basis can we begin to think about what it would mean to critically engage with practices of oppression, exploitation, and violence.

Let us discuss one final point in this chapter, in the name of discerning grounds for the critique of oppression, exploitation, and violence in the very universality of ethical life. Most of us are aware of the fact that others live according to different modes of ethical life, and our recognition of the significance of our own determinacy should also lead us to recognize the significance to others of their determinacy. That is, the very existence of ethical life leads us to the discernment of a universal, "we are all beings of ethical life." If this is a universal structure of experience, it would imply a norm: something like "people should be more or less supported in their status as such beings and in their practices of ethical homemaking."

In this "anyone is to be supported in their homemaking, no matter their home," there is a recognition of "people as such." On the other side of this recognition of the importance of home, that is, we have affirmation of the universality of the human: The human always makes a home, and in so doing projects the familiar and the unfamiliar; human projects of homemaking must be respected as such. Russon makes this point, arguing that the meaning "no culture is privileged" lies in the fact that all cultures are engaged in the significant practice of determinate homemaking. He calls this an expression of the stance of "indifference," involving recognition of a general standard, beyond any specific cultural difference (2017, 78).

To recognize that one is implicated in a domain governed by the familiar is simultaneously to recognize that the other side of the practice of homemaking is the unfamiliar—namely, where and how others live. My homemaking is responsible, so to speak, for the constitution of an outside where I am not at home; the I/we is not neutral with regard to the construction of the unfamiliar. The unfamiliar is perceived simultaneously and inseparably with the familiar (Russon 2017, 61).

But there is a limit to the stance of indifference. There is no complete departure from ethical life; or, what is beyond homemaking is never purely beyond homemaking. The stance of indifference, the idea of a universal humanity in every human, *is itself expressed only in determinate, one-sided, cultural practices*. This is Russon's next point, which I take to be fundamentally Hegelian in spirit: As Hegel writes, "everything that forces its way into real objectivity is subject... to the principle of particularization" (A.II 1195/VA.III 522; see also Russon [2016, 176–91]). Insistence on the importance of recognizing the humanity in human beings is always itself only expressed in determinate practices and codes and enacted by determinate forms of ethical life with all of their privileging of familiarity and projection of unfamiliarity. For instance, the idea of universal human rights is expressed in the UN Declaration of Human Rights, a production of a particularly one-sided institution (the UN) often mobilized for the advancement of particular societies; in the democratic ideal of the fair distribution of political power, which is expressed one-sidedly in practices such as equal voting rights yet not typically expressed by setting limits on capital-advancing lobbyists; in the ideal of procedural impartiality in assessing matters of injustice, which is enacted in capitalist economies where more money buys better legal representation.

In the very fact that the stance of indifference must be expressed, we should notice that it can never be purely indifferent. The institutionalized practices of recognizing indifference—as Russon argues, economically in capitalism (2017, 87ff), scientifically in the Scientific Revolution (89ff), and politically in liberal, representative democracy (88–92)—*necessarily* fail to uphold the indifference to which they are committed in principle. The operation of capitalism empowers the already powerful, creating intense social division, and motivates colonialism (93–95); modern science produces an instrumental conception of truth that drives an invasive relationship with nature and normless technological development that undermines human inhabitation of the planet (96–99); and the political idea of individual rights fails to protect the necessarily exclusionary needs of "belonging" and can easily be made to work against the redressing of injustice in the context of historically established situations of inequality (96–99). All of these practices and institutions can be criticized in the name of the very principle that inspired them, such that supporting the principle may require opposing these practices and institutions that, while they once ushered that principle into being, now *betray and jeopardize* it.

Further, one of the central ways in which these practices and institutions betray and jeopardize the stance of indifference is precisely by transgressing the norm associated with ethical life—to care for the practices of homemaking—insofar as the stance of indifference has been abused and taken to justify colonial imposition of the stance of indifference. Its one-sided character—its status as "not the whole story"—is suppressed, and the colonial powers who wield it employ it to justify their sense of righteousness as liberators, when through its suppression of determinacy in the form of ethical life it in fact becomes a force of oppression.

Thus it is imperative that our particular modes of expression of the stance of indifference be held open to the possibility that they are not in fact indifferent, and that they be revised in the name of the very principle by which they were purportedly motivated, or with reference to which they are often justified, as well as in the name of ethical life.

In Hegel's discussion of conscience—itself, as we will see, demanded by the stance of indifference—we witness his account of how this stance must be reconciled with the ever-present demand that it be actualized and expressed in determinacy. The necessity of determinacy as the home for our ideals means that there will always be an unfamiliar outside, and how we conduct ourselves there, in interaction with that outside, will be the measure of how well we are mobilizing the stance of indifference. In other words, the stance of indifference propels us to ethical engagement with the unfamiliar, because it is there that we can perceive and be held to account for the non-indifferent ways in which we enact it.

Hegel treats conscience in its embeddedness in a historical form of life. In the *Phenomenology*, it occurs in a discussion of spirit, which "is the ethical life of a people... the individual who is a world," and which comprises "a series of shapes" that are "shapes of a world," not only shapes of consciousness (*PS* §440/*PG* 240). Thus, here we have Hegel's discussion of conscience-in-the-world, so to speak. This is not an abstract individual, but an individual who inhabits a world and enacts their answerability to it. As I will use Hegel to argue, the ultimate ethical commitment is to the norm of conscientious communication.

With the appearance of conscience on the scene we reach a kind of conclusion regarding the real phenomenon of individuality or selfhood, but in light of all the other aspects of experience in which it is embedded and by which it is shaped. The phenomenon of the individual self, in relation to which conscience is a kind of norm (as we shall see), was reflected in the stance of indifference discussed in the previous chapter, historically discerned and developed in determinate historical practices of art, religion, and philosophy, and implicitly reflected in revolutions of various kinds—political, economic, and scientific. This is then what conscience is: Hegel's conclusions regarding the very real phenomenon of singular selfhood that was being worked out historically, in a way that at the same time coexists with the other very real things that were historically developed and discerned, such as the irreducible dimensions of interpersonal life and the situatedness of individuals in history. Here again we see the importance of being able to hold onto multiple truths at once, which Hegel trains us to do, and of bringing to reality not simply one principle of observation, evaluation, and assessment but multiple. "There is also conscience": This will be an important supplement to the political issues addressed above. It too will have an interpersonal slant, as we shall see; with Hegel, nothing ever gets away from that.

CHAPTER FOUR

Conscience

Given that I am pulling out only a few sections of Hegel's philosophy in this book, so as to show how they can operate in contemporary discussions, let us make time here for a brief note of orientation. Hegel discusses conscience in both the *Phenomenology* and the *Philosophy of Right*. I will focus on the *Phenomenology*'s discussion, because I am interested here in the *world* around conscience: conscience not considered logically, in the abstract, but conscience considered in the "shape of a world" (PS §440/PG 240). Conscience is included in the section on "Spirit," in which Hegel discusses periods in the actual history of the West, or the history it has assumed as its heritage. (The discussion of conscience in the *Philosophy of Right* is found in the analysis of "Morality," just prior to the section on "Ethical Life.") We have skipped over many parts of the *Phenomenology* here: the "legal condition" (*der Rechtzustand*)[1] that immediately follows ethical life; "Self-Alienated Spirit: Culture," which includes discussions of faith and the Enlightenment (as well as of the French Revolution with which the book began); and much of the final section of spirit, "Spirit Certain of Itself: Morality."

The human being takes what it "receives" and interprets it "as" something, and thereby manifests itself as not simply passive but self-making, but it always does this more or less as a member of a collective. The sections of the *Phenomenology* called "Culture" and "Morality" track the self-making of specific, historical forms of life, specific instances of "the *I* that is *we* and the *we* that is *I*" (PS §177/PG 108). The actions and self-descriptions of any "we" are a matter of transformative self-making: thought and development in thought are never merely abstract matters, but shape the world; they are expressed and "tried out" in practical structures. "What does this mean?" is a question that is answered by the world, by "how this works out here, if we make it real." Tracking the development of ideas is a matter of tracking the practical worlds in which they have been born, to whose limitations they are presented as a solution, which they have thereby transformed, and in which the limitations of these very ideas themselves have been demonstrated—the ways in which the worlds they entail do not quite work well enough. The practical is not simply an afterthought or a shadow of ideas; it is where and how ideas get their genuine working-through. As Hegel observes, and as we cited earlier, a principle is developed in a determinate way of life, by being clothed

> with all the wealth of its existence; the shape in which it exists is a people into whose morality, constitution, domestic, civil, and public life, arts, international relations, etc. this principle is built, and the wholly specific form of concrete history is stamped on every aspect of the people's external life. This is the material which the principle of a people has to work through, and this is not the business of one day; on the contrary, there are all the needs, skill, relations, laws, constitution, arts, sciences which this material has to develop in accordance with this principle. (*LHP*, 44)

In "Culture" and "Morality," Hegel tracks the formation of particular versions of human collectives, showing the gradual discernment that demanded changes to how the human world was organized. All of us live in some sense in the terms of that history, and those for whom it counts as "our heritage" no longer relate to it as an answer to a pressing question or as a genuinely new insight; rather, they assume, sometimes consciously but more often not, the historically discerned insights that have endured.

In the section on conscience, we will find Hegel's treatment of the historical emergence of the centrality of the I. This is an I that knows that human beings are also self-making, even though they are so only ever within situations they inherit and by which they have already been made. It is an I that knows it makes itself with existent tools that inevitably guide this making. It is the I that has taken to heart its status both as a self and as a sociohistorical being. While there are historical conditions of its emergence—actual human beings discern the reality of conscience and work on producing a world in which this is officially acknowledged—it is not something that all human beings automatically assume. It is an immanent norm, one that emerges to clarity for us if we perceive our own situations well. And even while conscience and the demand for it exists, the possibility of it was not always politically recognized, because that required historical work. Let us turn to the details of Hegel's description.

The Determinacies and Relations of Conscience

To illuminate the nature of and the need for conscience, Hegel considers the simple phenomenon of finding oneself in a situation in which "a case calling for action is present" (*PS* §635/*PG* 342). What is this like, and what happens when such a case presents itself? Our answers here will illuminate something very important: namely, the nature of the existing and acting I. Who is that I? What is it like to grapple with a situation with an accurate and honest sense of what one's powers and responsibilities are? This section is in fact, like many others, dizzyingly complex, with significant twists and turns. We will only pull out some of the details of the determinate conditions faced by the I in action, after which we will focus in particular on its relations.

THE DETERMINACIES OF CONSCIENTIOUS ACTION

First, Hegel calls the "case calling for action... an objective actuality for the knowing consciousness. As conscience, it knows the case in an immediately concrete manner, and at the same time the case is only as conscience knows it." That is, we already see the case *as* a specific kind of case—we see it in a particular way—and the way it appears to us reflects who *we* are. Our sense of the case calling for action says as much about ourselves as it says about itself: "It is the mere reversal of actuality as a case *which exists* into an actuality which *has been done*" (*PS* §635/*PG* 342). In perceiving a situation *as* something, we do not simply passively receive it but assist in producing it. If what is, in addition to bringing something of itself to the scene, is also *how we see it*, and if we act on the basis of how we see it, then reality is going to take the shape of how we see things. In other words, we cannot simply distinguish between "objective actuality" and "how we see things," because we transform objective actuality on the basis of how we see things, and so it will become (and has become) how we see it. Perceiving is making. The determinacy a "case" has is co-made by it and by the way of grasping it that belongs to the I. While we can name each, we could never sort out which piece of reality belongs to which; they appear always as a pair. I see myself in the way I see the factical world, such that the way I act within and thus transform the world is the way I make it into myself, and the fact that it takes the shape of me, so to speak, means that my view of it will likely be confirmed in its ongoing unfolding. As we know by now, however, we never simply have an I here, and so we do not simply see an I in seeing its interpreting perception: The I is always also a we. Thus we see the history of its formation by others in the I's interpreting perception; it carries their "eyes" along and sees through them; *our* perception is a making.

A second determinacy of conscience's perspective here is that, through it, "the good" becomes determinate. I feel called to action and compelled by a standard I experience as not-me, but it must also travel through the gauntlet of my perspective. Hegel observes, for instance, that "I fulfill a *Determinate* duty" (*PS* §637/*PG* 343): My action "buries" "conflicting duties," "diverse moral substances," or the "variety of moral relations" (§635/343). The good as such is specified as the duty, for instance, to care for others (which is in turn specified as this action, our third determinacy). A sense of responsibility to do the right thing will always be manifest or experienced as this value, this obligation.

The third form of determinacy in a "case calling for action" is the action itself. Situations effectively require us to engage in determinate action: writing an email to a business partner, fixing the fence, making Tuesday's supper. "Whatever the content may be, each content bears the *flaw of determinateness*"—designated as "flaw" only from the perspective of a disdainful knowing that imagines itself to be pure (*PS* §645/*PG* 348). Determinate action, further, closes us off from other such action; actions are exclusive of other actions, using up resources that can no longer be spent elsewhere. This determinacy is a determinacy also of materiality, with which comes the insight that conscientious action is never simply principled but material and requiring resources.

Finally, a fourth form of determinacy, related to the determinacy of the situation in which we find ourselves, has to do with others. Acting in a way that strives to be good is acting in a way that has others on the horizon, because the good is something that in principle includes their welfare and well-being. When I act, I affect them and inevitably take a stand on their behalf, because I am changing a world we share; I am making an assertion of a "should" that claims recognition as a purpose to be valued as such. What I do makes a difference in principle to them; they have a "take" on it in principle, if not in every situation. Thus Hegel's descriptions of these scenarios always involve others looking on.

What do these four determinacies mean for action, when what is on our minds is the issue particularly of acting well, or rightly? With each, we should witness how the experience of conscience is more complex than the simple ideal of acting dutifully initially reflects. The situation needs to be interpreted, the good needs to be concrete, an action needs to be done, and all in the company of non-indifferent others.

Conscience has to respond, judge, and act, but it is cut off from definite guidance and asked to be specific. Conscience is the mode of singular selfhood in the form of "I will assume this responsibility for determination, with all of its temptations and dangers."

The first determinacy suggests that our knowledge of the situation is already conviction, that perception is morally charged, that in the way in which we grasp the situation we have already asserted our own sense of what is proper. We bring our perception and singularity to the situation; they act as though they were an "ought." Thus Hegel says that the law exists for the self and not vice versa (*PS* §639/*PG* 344); any duty or good submits as it were to our perspective. In saying, "this is what I see," conscience inadvertently says, "I am the law." And we cannot know if our already existent way of perceiving already reflects answerability to duty. Further, our perception operates on the basis of inadequate knowledge; we cannot know all the relevant factors or even what would need to be known.

This of course is related to the second determinacy: that a situation perceived a certain way will call for a specific kind of ought; the genuine diversity of duties as though vanishes as *this* duty or good becomes salient. Situations demand this kind of specification of us, even when doing something specific in the here and now may jeopardize our capacity to answer to the good as such, whatever that might be. Values and obligations are always specific inside of actual moral situations, to the extent that the existence of these moral situations and their urgent demands exist in tension with the idea of the good as such.

The third determinacy, that of the specific action we resolve to do, also separates us from the law or duty, in two ways: First, the universal could be expressed in a possibly infinite number of specific ways (just how do I "love my neighbor," for instance?), and we can choose only one. Second, this choice could make us less capable of answering to duty differently, because in acting we use up finite resources—our energy, resources, time. Further, we build specific kinds of lives through our actions, and as our lives become more determinate the possibility of living differently becomes more remote.

The fourth determinacy also separates us from "duty" and "law" by rendering us answerable to others, which is itself not simply a matter of fulfilment of duty or law. In demanding our care and concern, so to speak, others can be the occasion through which "dutifulness" is turned into "how we serve them in their specificity." In other words, even as duty or good or morality would in principle be consistent with care for others, and the opposite would be destructive for them, others are always also specific, and a good that takes its measure from them might be incompatible with the measure of other others.

Notwithstanding all of these determinacies, action is *demanded*. It is the "the essence of conscience to *cut itself off* from this *calculating* and balancing of duties and to come to a decision solely on its own" (*PS* §645/*PG* 349). Inaction in the face of a demand to act is resolution and action as well, a refusal to respond to "a case calling for action."

Given these necessary determinacies, however, any action one takes will always be judged critically. One already grasps the situation in a specific and potentially selfish and ignorant way. As Hegel notes, if action were accompanied by fame it could be construed as a craving for such, or if it were connected to one's status it could be an ambition for honor. One could arrive "at a feeling for [one's] own self in [one's] existence and thus obtain enjoyment," in which case one could be acting for the sake of one's "inner moral vanity, in the enjoyment of a consciousness of [one's] own excellence, and in the foretaste of a hope for a future happiness" (*PS* §665/*PG* 358).

But Hegel criticizes this kind of judgment for putting "the action outside of its existence," whereas existence is the only place where abstractions such as duty and purpose can be expressed. The existential specificity that attaches to action is ineliminable, and so the demand that action be pure is itself a wrongheaded demand that would oppose any action at all, and thus oppose the possibility of the good becoming actual in the world. It is only as a "trace" that the good comes to exist, and thus this "trace" accrues for action a dignity that can seem to be "above its station," as it were. If conscience is genuine, then it is not trying to make itself the authority or enact its own will, but express its answerability to the good. It is *answering*; it is acting in the name of something that it takes to be other than itself. Conscience takes the good to be something other than itself, independent of its contingent insight and desires and having its own demands. When we ask ourselves what the right thing to do is and try to do it, we are not simply being ourselves; we are doing something not simply on our own behalf, but on behalf of something we take to be irreducible to ourselves (though we attest to all this only, as we shall see, in submitting to dialogue with other finite beings like us). We find that acting for the sake of ourselves and acting for the sake of the good come into being together.

Along with the trace of the good, others are here as well. When we perceive a situation as calling for action, we are not simply being ourselves as individuals, but ourselves as universal, aiming not at the answer we might arbitrarily give but at the right answer. In this way, we are also "for others," insofar as they live under the umbrella of the good as well, so to speak—desiring, needing, and answering to it. We see situations not simply in terms of our concern for ourselves but, through a concern for the good, in terms of a concern for others—or, through a concern for others, in terms of the good.

No action, however, can escape the possibility that it is "self-worship" (*PS* §655/*PG* 353) rather than service of the good. "No action can escape being judged in such a way, for duty for duty's sake, this pure purpose, is the non-actual" (§665/358). We would oppose the appearance of even a trace of goodness if we demanded purity in action. In action persists a tension between goodness and self-assertion or self-worship, between determinate actuality and the indeterminacy of the good.

CONSCIENCE AS INTERPERSONAL: THE ACTOR AND THE JUDGE

So far, I have spoken about conscience while only implying the context to which Hegel ultimately brings it, which is interaction between two people, an actor and a judge. Human conscience is always inside of a human situation, and others are always inside this situation with and beside it. The fact that there are two is an implicit claim related to the fourth determinacy, regarding others: Moral action, in its answerability to the idea of the right or good, is being for others, implying the affectability of others and their implied participation. The duality also illuminates the fact that we engage in two basic kinds of moral action: judging and acting (though judging is also an action). And so we have one figure portrayed as acting, and the other portrayed as critically judging the action, on the basis of the various reasons we have explored: The actor is not answering to the good but to herself; she is not doing "this good thing" but being selfish; she is concealing her self-interest by saying she is motivated by the good, and so she is a hypocrite, putting herself in the place of the law, asserting that her interest is more important than the good. In short, she is judged to be evil.

In judging, the judge reveals the real ways in which action is open to criticism on all sides. The actor, however, who has been portrayed as aiming at the good, is sufficiently morally engaged to see the reasonableness of this judgment, and so confesses that yes, she is guilty (*PS* §662/*PG* 356), because she is in fact likely getting in the way of the good and inadequate to it in the multiple ways that the judgment exposes. In her expectation of understanding from the judge, however, she projects the sense that this problem is shared (§666/359): that the good is not capable of enacting itself, as it were, and both action and judgment on its behalf are transgressive—I am expressing and answering to myself when I do what I think is a good thing and when I judge actions.

The judge, however, rebuffs the actor's expectation of commiseration, holding themself above the actor (*PS* §667/*PG* 359). In their judgment, they reiterate the action of the one they accused: answering to themselves and not the good, placing their own judgment at the level of the universal, disavowing the way their own interpretive specificity is mobilized in judgment. The judge falls prey to their own judgment. And even worse, the judge has rebuffed the actor's anticipation of solidarity—a solidarity that, it will turn out, is the quintessential position for a being of conscience. Hegel's judgment here is especially harsh: The "hard heart" of the judge is "forsaken by spirit" (§667/360).

We can see here that the only way in which good comes into existence is through these "uncertain creatures," to use de Beauvoir's term (1976, 39). The good requires the finite in order to make its way into the world, and thus is finitude thereby redeemed, at least in principle. But it is also raw, imperfect, misguided, and errant. Is there anything beyond this, then, by which individual action can be guided? There is no perfect answer here, but there is, or so we will find, *an* answer, and it lies in the relation between actor and judge, which will allow us to develop further this fourth determinacy, regarding others.

We have seen how principle, duty, and law lie fundamentally at a distance from the specificity of knowing, of the situation, and of action, such that actors have little support in discerning the moral quality of their actions. Principle does not speak clearly at the level of detail, and actions rebound in ways that exceed our predictions. But there is something here that *can* help us—namely, other people and the world. When we do something, it has effects, and so we find out what it is and means on the basis of what it sets in motion. In externalizing ourselves in action, we allot to the world the possibility of showing us what the action means, whereupon we can find out whether it was good or not. This is not a version of moral consequentialism, but simply how the finitude of insight is expanded by actuality. In that world there are also other actors—themselves bearing a universal orientation, being for others, and grappling with possible actions—who can show us a different view of the action, one that we may not ourselves have seen because of the determinacy of our perspective. Another person and the world offer us the possibility of seeing aspects of the meaning of action that we did not see, and therefore the possibility that we may act better next time. The shame and noncommunity the hard heart potentially inspires is an obstacle to that solidarity and to the assumption of vulnerability to others, and this is the reason Hegel condemns it.

One cannot erase the finitude of perspective, and one cannot aspire to do so, if only because it prevents and immobilizes action. One must act, and thus act in a finite way. But one is not simply condemned to act poorly, for action is potentially the site of development, if we can remain open to the witness of others and the world about its meaning. One must act—the good "needs" our action—but action is not simply itself; it is itself *and* it is the dialogue that it launches between me and the other, me and the world, which potentially allows the good to become clearer.

Our own interpretations—of ourselves, our situations, and others—are limited. We operate inside of a specific way of life that has developed in us a general form of orientation to our situations. We live on the basis of assumptions that certain behavior is "normal" and "abnormal." With another person, however, we have someone who came to be a different self in a different way, who may be able to shed light on one's action, who can add their power of interpretation to one's own. In being interpreted, in opening oneself up for interpretation, one has the added orientation of that person, potentially empowering one to act from an expanded perspective in the future. Principles, laws, and ideals are not responsive in the way that people are; they cannot provide meaningful, intelligent, and responsive interpretations of our action, or have the power to disarm us by captivating us with their perspectives and restructuring the way we see things.

We are not automatically good, and we do not become good in a vacuum. The most fundamental thing we require in order to act well, given the silence of principle within determinate situations, and given that we are determinate creatures, is the opportunity to inhabit a condition in which, over time, we can hone our capacity for moral action. This condition is the open availability of others who have perspectives on our action that we cannot have. What allows their interpretation to have bearing upon ours is their proximity to us in communicative contexts and the cultivation of good communicative practices, which means that this most fundamental condition requires that we break down obstacles in the way of such practices and contexts and build such communicative contexts. This is not simply to insist that people talk with each other, for this could simply mean extending frameworks of domination by which communication is currently structured.

From this perspective, the ultimate moral commitment may be a commitment to the cultivation of communicative, conscientious communities, structured by a couple of basic principles: namely, those of confession and forgiveness. That is, it would be a community of confession on the part of actors: "I did this, because I felt the call of the good, but I may have been kidding myself, and I may have acted poorly, with insufficient information and insight; what does my action mean?" And then the interpreter could also say: "I respect that you felt answerable and that you did something, and I know that your action must be specific. The thing you did seems flawed in this particular way, but I may be kidding myself, and may have judged poorly, with insufficient information, insight, and experience." This, I would argue, is Hegel's "reconciling yes" (*PS* §671/*PG* 362). The most important thing, from the point of view of the nature of action, is to cultivate that context of communication that permits and affirms action as such while at the same time critically reviewing it, but in a way that recognizes that finite action is needed and understands that judgment is itself finite action. What we need in our efforts at action are recognition—confession and forgiveness—of the necessity of our determinacy, whether in ourselves or others, in action or judgment. We need action (and thus we need to not be defensive about its inadequate character, so that we can be open to seeing the meaning of our action through the eyes of others), and we need non-righteous criticism (see Hoff [2018b]).

Before we move to discuss the relevance of Hegel's account of conscience to specific tensions and issues operative in liberal universalism and colonialism, I want to underline a significant point that emerges here: that our discussion *began* in the interpersonal and it has *concluded* (so far) in the interpersonal. Recognition and ethical life allow us to perceive that we develop out of specific relations, such that those relations will always bear a trace in us. Conscience—and ultimately exposure to conscientious communication—allows us to perceive that answerability to ongoing relations is how we learn what is morally needed. Relation seems to be the "alpha and omega" for Hegel, the beginning and the end, though not "end" in the sense of "finished"; it is where we are now and how we discern how to live well in this now. Relatedly, I am confident that the flaws of this book are due to failures on the part of history, social institutions, and myself to constitute relations of communicative answerability (as well as due to the impossibility that a book could be written after it has been taken up by others). It would be better if I were in better relations, and yet we must do the work of building them and finding out who we are through them.

The model of conscience and conscientious communication is not the model of individuality that circulates in basically liberal, individualistic societies. Conscience is not self-possessed, self-protective insistence upon itself, but the experience of answerability and of the importance of others. Now, with the help of Fanon and Merleau-Ponty, let us explore how this account of individuality we find in Hegel's account of conscience resounds in contemporary political life, particularly in relation to the problem of the relation between so-called Western ideals and modern Western colonialism. I will show the relevance here of the themes that Hegel raises in his analysis of conscience: the difficulty of action in the face of the distance between principle and situation; the status of conscience as the ethically relevant site; the ambiguity of conscience as an expression of principle; and the relevance of communicative relations. The model of individuality Hegel offers with his account of conscience brings with it many threads of attachment—to others, to determinacy, to the situation, and to its own growth, learning, and transformation thereby—and the "evangelical" practices of the liberal West in relation to its others suppress the significance of these threads of attachment. This critique should aid in efforts at grappling, as Fanon does vividly in *Black Skin, White Masks*, with the psychical and political challenge that the West presents in its self-view as the incubator and proselytizer of superior ideals of individual freedom. That model, as we shall see, disavows the determinate reality of conscience.

Fanon, Merleau-Ponty, and Liberalism

Gayatri Chakravorty Spivak famously wrote that rights are what "we cannot not want" (1999, 110). While this seems true, what it really raises is the need for a broader description of what lies around them, of how they are an all-too-basic part of a larger story, and with some parts of which they conflict. As a narrator of that larger story, in which what rights pinpoint is put in its place, Hegel is helpful here. From the point of view of what we have said here so far, we should be able to recognize that the ideals mobilized to protect individuals are but a small part of a much larger picture, and prone to be wielded deceptively and destructively. Part of the work they require, as we will see in the analysis of conscience, is that of figuring out how to actualize them and what they mean for beings who are always specific. How do we make the principles of individual freedom, equality, dignity, and so on, actual in the world and inside of concrete situations; how do we do the difficult work of conscience? What does the "principle of subjectivity" and its protection require, in determinate contexts? It would be an error to hold ourselves simply accountable to this basic paradigm, since "the devil is in the details."

Let us begin with the problems with actual, historical efforts on the part of the so-called West to purportedly "bring its principles" to intercultural encounters. We will then move to the thematization of determinacy at the level of content and the question of how it would change our practices and our ideals if we were to take determinacy seriously. If the question of how ideals meet the world is made central, as it should be, we see justification for different practices. To prioritize the ideal is to begin the conversation in the wrong spot, as Claudia Rankine and Beth Loffreda argue about conversations among white artists about rights and freedoms (2015); or, to use Maggie Nelson's paraphrase, to "set up shop in the wrong spot" (2021, 42). Once we shift focus to the assemblage of ideal and actuality, the ambiguity of their realization takes center stage.

PRINCIPLE AS FALSE ALIBI

Merleau-Ponty argues, following Marx, that "there is a mystification in liberalism"; it conceals the fact that "liberal ideas belong to a system of violence" (1969, xiii). He writes:

> in refusing to judge liberalism in terms of the ideas it espouses and inscribes in constitutions and in demanding that these ideas be compared with the prevailing relations between [people] in a liberal state, Marx... is providing a formula for the concrete study of society which cannot be refuted by idealist arguments.... It is not just a question of knowing what the liberals have in mind but what in reality is done by the liberal state within and beyond its frontiers. (xiv)

What "they" have in mind, the "principles and the inner life" in which they are conceptualized, become "alibis the moment they cease to animate external and everyday life" (xiv–xv).

It is this idea of an alibi that I want to track here, in light of Hegel's focus on the determinate and the concrete, the situation, the fact that "truth is simply the unity of concept and existence" (*PR/GPR* §280), neither solely thought nor solely materiality considered dualistically. With Fanon and Merleau-Ponty, I will argue that we must look not simply at what liberal theorists have written and argued but also at what has been done in the name of liberalism, which exposes its principles as false alibis. "This Europe," as Fanon writes,

> which never stopped talking of [the human], which never stopped proclaiming its sole concern was [the human], ... massacres [them] at every one of its street corners, at every corner of the world. For centuries, Europe has brought the progress of other [people] to a halt and enslaved them for its own purposes and glory; for centuries it has stifled virtually the whole of humanity in the name of a so-called "spiritual adventure." (2008, 235–36)

The human being "as a living, working, self-made being is replaced by words, assemblages of words and the tensions generated by their meanings" (2004, 237); a masquerade of words replaces the beings they are supposed to defend.

What are the practices of the West within and beyond its frontiers? How does it treat its "insiders" and "outsiders"? Fanon offers one answer: It massacres, enslaves, and stifles almost the whole of humanity, those outside Europe but also those within. In its actions, liberalism is global, colonial, European empire. It is expendable soldiers in trenches, mobilized to secure a globe organized to benefit Europe and "America." It is the accrual through theft and exploitation of massive wealth for powerful, mostly white people. It is the displacement and elimination of entire peoples. It is the exploitation of wage laborers by wealthy capitalists, the alienation of meaning from body. It is the harnessing of sexist expectations to perpetuate the exploitation of women's labor for the propping up of other forms of labor exploitation. It is the infrastructure of dehumanization: The human, its individuality celebrated in words, has its power harnessed for profit-making. It is the suppression of other human priorities and the disavowal of any claim to existence on the part of nonhuman.

In this context, individualism, the attestation of individual freedom, and dignity are alibis, concealing the material systems that shape human life, that exploit the vulnerable within and those beyond the borders of liberal states for the production of wealth for liberal societies, that allot meager possibilities: Do you "want" to work for Amazon or for Uber; do you "want" to accept Western garbage in your country's borders; do you "want" to manufacture plastic in a factory that will suffocate your oceans and accelerate the process of global extinction; do you "want" to aid in the increasing expansion of Google and Amazon, their suppression of other practices of communication and consumption, their channeling of global wealth? It is easy to promise individual choice when the terrain of that choice is already structured in a certain way; the message of freedom conceals the diminishment of possibility it brings with it. The claim that human beings are free and equal can be very effective at concealing exploitation and suppression.

Fanon clearly exposes the mystification operative in the colonial situation with his evocative description of the material encounter of colonized peoples with so-called Western ideals on colonized land. Whenever Western values are invoked, he says, the colonized make sure their machetes are close by, because values mean violence. What is equality? A contemporary, Fanonian answer would be that equality is expressed by "all lives matter," the reactionary response to the Black Lives Matter movement; the ideal of "equality" is mobilized to oppose the work required in order to accomplish it. As Hegel writes, "the defect of these determinations" of freedom and equality is "that they are entirely abstract: ... they are what prevents the concrete, i.e. an articulation of the state, i.e. a *constitution* and a government, from arising at all, or else destroys them" (*PM/E* §539R). What is individualism? Individualism opposes the solidarity that would stand against colonial oppression; it prevents access to comrades in struggle. Fanon writes:

> The colonialist bourgeoisie hammered into the colonized mind the notion of a society of individuals where each is locked in his subjectivity, where wealth lies in thought.... Involvement in the organization of the struggle will already introduce [the colonized intellectual] to a different vocabulary. "Brother," "sister," "comrade." (2004, 11)

What is truth? Truth is required of the colonized subject by those who refuse the relation of accountability with her but have the power to demand truth from her, disavowing the alienation that undergirds that relationship, to which falsity is a more truthful response (see Bonhoeffer's similar discussion of truth [1995, 358–67]). What is nonviolence? "At the critical, deciding moment the colonialist bourgeoisie, which had remained silent up till then, enters the fray. They introduce a new notion, in actual fact a creation of the colonial situation: nonviolence" (Fanon 2004, 23). The colonized bourgeoisie announce that it is "a matter of urgency to reach an agreement for the common good. Nonviolence is an attempt to settle the colonial problem around the negotiating table before the irreparable is done, before any bloodshed or regrettable act is committed" (23). But the idea of a negotiating table conceals the fact of who governs it—who decides upon the participants, the agenda, the content of negotiations—and the violence required for the situation to already have been constituted in this way. Equality, individualism, truth, nonviolence, democratic negotiation: These ideals are all undermined by power, operating as support for the interests of the colonizer in the colonial situation. In this situation, it is incumbent upon people to ask how these ideals are mobilized, construed, and enacted, in what violence they are complicit, and what structures they uphold and perpetuate.

The appropriation of these ideas for oppression and exploitation is due to the severing of ideal and existence, which are in fact interdependent. Hegel's analysis of conscience illuminates the fact that principles are only ever expressed determinately in situations. If determinacy is animated by principles and principles are expressed in determinacy, then insiders to a situation potentially have the best insight into the translation from principle to determinacy. Here, the relation between colonizer and colonized that Fanon portrays seems nonconscientious; the colonizer, like the judge, refuses solidarity in the shared and necessarily one-sided condition of existence, where we are supposed to be doing the difficult work of discerning how to make the good actual. The colonizer is "forsaken by spirit" (*PS* §667/*PG* 360).

When Merleau-Ponty asks that we look not at what liberalism says about itself but what it has *done*, he is homing in on the precise location at which we try to express in action what lies behind and moves us, that to which we attest and are committed. He insists that this is the location at which inquiry and discussion must begin. We need to "set up shop" (Nelson 2021, 42) at the point of the alchemy between principle and actuality.

This general call to "set up shop in a different spot" shares a justification with that of phenomenological and Hegelian method. That justification runs as follows. Experience has always already been underway when we begin to think about it, when we reflect on the question of what is real. Philosophy always already borrows its insights from experience. The first philosophical project that needs to be attended to, therefore, prior to jumping into the deep end of thinking about the nature of reality and knowledge, for instance, is the specific interpersonal condition in which our thoughts and ideas germinate. If experience is fundamentally shaped by the perspectives of concrete others upon us, a central point of philosophical interest is to investigate the historical and cultural character of those specific others. This is the reason behind the centrality of spirit in ethical life and in Hegel's philosophy. The case phenomenology makes to philosophy as such, and that history and spirit present to the operationally abstract understanding, is that our principles are generated in disavowed determinacy, and that the character of that determinacy must be investigated. In conscience, the phenomenological circle comes round to itself: Principles emerge from this determinacy, and they are also *expressed* in that determinacy. Universals are always the universals *of* something, having their roots in this determinate life; and they are the universals *to* or *for* something, returning to and existing for this determinate life.

The centrality of determinacy here relates to the material of the previous chapter on ethical life—that we draw upon our existing worlds to enact individual agency, that we rely on these worlds for the content of freedom, the experience of dignity, and so on. When these ideals are reduced to their individual expression, or mobilized to protect individuals, then the social conditions of their actualization become undermined. If our possibilities are sculpted from the determinate systems we inhabit and the relations that have shaped us, then we have one significant clue about ourselves — that our freedom, our rights, our dignity, depend on the world around us, on *its* resources and possibilities. Persistent focus on "individual" dignity, freedom, equality, and so on conceals our dependence upon that developed, determinate world. If in the name of the support of agency we take the primary political task to be the protection of human beings from each other, then we undermine agency, because the possibility of meaningful and free action exists only on the condition that we have access to each other and to the rich resources we have collectively and historically developed. Other people, society, tradition, culture, and materiality are not the enemies of freedom but its conditions. Fanon thereby interprets dignity as "bread and land" (2008, 9), and names relations: "brother, sister, comrade" (2004, 11). This is the dignity of material bodies in situations and relations. Ideals must be articulated in and through the terms of actual experience, which is that of determinate beings in determinate, historical situations and relations.

We have now discussed the historical problem with liberal ideals: that they have operated as alibis, concealing what liberal regimes have done. A second issue emerges from philosophical consideration of the necessary relation between ideal and practice. At the beginning of this chapter we discussed the multiple determinacies at play in conscientious action, the threads that attach conscience to what is other to it. Let us go through these forms of determinacy again, but with the purpose of exposing the flaws of an approach that would think ideals without reference to determinacy. To respect ideals, as I will argue through both Fanon and Hegel, is to respect the time, effort, insight, and experience needed to fill them out, the conditions in which they are actualized, and the world and the agents of their actualization.

WHAT DETERMINACY DOES TO PRINCIPLE

Hegel's discussion of conscience identifies four forms of determinacy implicit in conscientious action. There is the determinacy of (1) the situation as conscience takes it, which therefore appears in terms of its perspective; (2) the specific duty, which will always be one duty and not all, or this good and not good as such; (3) the action, done so as to answer the call; and (4) the specific others informing and affected by the action whose welfare is subsumed under the umbrella of the good. These are all threads of attachment between conscience and (1) a situation, in which it is *responsible* for how it takes the situation; (2) a call, in which context its attachment takes the form of *responsiveness* or *answerability*; (3) an action, in which it takes the form of *resolve*; and (4) others, in which context attachment takes the form of *accountability*.

This is what it is to be an individual: to be responsible, answerable, resolving, and accountable, attached to the world by multiple threads. These threads of attachment projected by the individual point to the fact that her interests are elsewhere, and that to protect her is to protect this elsewhere—not simply to protect her as such in her abstract singularity. Hegel effectively shows that the ideals that express the privileging of subjectivity must be thought in terms of an "ideal/determinacy" relation. The description of what is actually involved in the experience of selfhood exposes the abstraction of the ideals that are typically attached to it, and Fanon's and Merleau-Ponty's descriptions of colonialism will expose what damage these ideals can do *to it* in its own name.

First, there is the determinacy of the situation and conscience's own grasp of it. The singular self is never separate from a situation, which is always culturally, historically, geographically, and so on, determinate. For it to be itself is for it to inhabit and navigate *these* situations, in a tangle of determinate involvements. The I and the situation co-occur, each asserting itself within the other. Thus, supporting the experience of conscientious individuality requires protecting the determinate contexts of its action. The diversity, multiplicity, and affordances of situations, and their dignity, so to speak, is the dignity of conscience.[2]

In due fashion, Fanon interprets dignity as given, with "bread," by "land" (2004, 9): Individual dignity is afforded by the material conditions of singular selves. Dignity is the dignity of bodies in situations— material, extended, and engaged. To care for conscience is to care for it as a situated being, as its "who" is substantially its situation and its "take" on it. To do justice to conscience is to do justice to its situation and its determinate grasp thereof: "This is what I take to be salient here." The conditions of this action are many: home, a meaningful context, literacy, things to do, the cultivated ability to do them. To protect this self is not to condemn its world and reject the legitimacy of its situations and its take on them on the basis of its difference from one's own, but to support and build up the world of its action, as action is always a matter of pairing with a world and with things.

Now to the second and third determinacies, regarding conscience's answerability and resolve. Conscientious action, in Hegel, is action on behalf of what conscience experiences as good and as compelling: It acts on behalf of its felt answerability to something it takes to be not itself. In acting, then, conscience affirms the existence of that "not-self" that moves it. However, it also translates the ideal to which it feels answerable into "this thing that I do." The ideal to which it is committed is expressed in a *this*, in a specific action. Any given principle is quiet about the specific action it requires, and so the question of what action will express it in a given situation is a question requiring judgment. The single individual must always accompany principle: Principle cannot stand on its own, but always comes with the claim that *this* action reflects and expresses it.

There are many implications to notice here, in relation specifically to others who would act differently. For one, the specificity of conscientious action should be avowed as specific, not simply paraded as "the good." Further, conscience should keep open the possibility that specific, unfamiliar actions are also expressions of ideals, commitments, and a sense of answerability to them. Finally, the non-transparency of other determinate modes of expression of ideality should be taken not as an indication that what is appearing is something alien and to be opposed, but rather as a meaning that could potentially be understood through communication. In each of these domains, liberal colonialism can be said to have fallen short, operating on the basis of what Fanon calls a "Manicheanism" in which good is simply the colonist and bad the colonized. It construes "good" not as that which motivates determinate action but as these actions themselves, taking difference at the level of action to be definitive of difference at the level of the good. Colonial agency disavows the determinacy of its expression and the existence for itself (and everyone) of an "expressive palette" of determinate means by which commitments are manifested. It imposes the "how" of its expression upon others. Freedom, to invoke a contrast that has become cliché, is expressed by being able to wear revealing clothes or to vote, not by participating in discussion of the Qur'an. The necessary entanglement between indeterminate principle and its expression in determinate action is disavowed; the "how" of determinate expression is construed as universal and imposed upon others; other forms of expression of the universal are concealed as such; and relations of communication that would allow the meaning of "other" forms of determinacy to come to light are suppressed, often violently. Think again of Mahmood's argument that Western feminism implicitly construes freedom as resistance or rebellion, rather than, for instance, freedom as taking up for oneself the rich meanings of a tradition. In some sense these modes of expression belong to the principle itself, such that we would even understand it differently if we could encounter different modes of its expression.

This structural relation between principle and determinacy encourages a kind of hesitation in the face of alterity. I think, for instance, of encountering in India a particular gesture of the head—a kind of wobble or tilt. Talking to a rickshaw driver about whether he could take my friend and me somewhere, I received that gesture in response, and turned to my friend and reported, "he said no." But that is not what he "said" with his head; what he actually communicated was something more like "sure." The differences between his habits and cultural context and my own required hesitation on my part, a moment in which a question could emerge—namely, what legible meaning is being expressed here, in this unfamiliar mode of expression?

There is another point to notice here regarding conscientious answerability to the good. Because there exists a class of action that is not just self-expression but also receptivity or the experience of a call, we can see that it dignifies beings capable of receptivity to have protected our status as circuits through which the good enters into the world, as sites of its appearance. This means sustaining the material conditions of existence, for without them we cannot operate as such circuits, and without a world for us on the other end of our action we cannot develop and express ideals. Fanon's words resonate again here: The colonized "have not yet had time to elaborate a society or build and ascertain values"; a "threatening atmosphere of violence and missiles" is far from the right context for the "citizen and individual [to] develop and mature" (2004, 40; 2002, 78).

The fourth determinacy of conscience emphasizes the importance to individual action of its links with others. In assuming the necessity of determination, conscience had inevitably made the law exist for the sake of the self, instead of vice versa (PS §639/PG 344). But in confessing its one-sidedness and reaching for solidarity with the other, as the actor does, its knowing can become more than *its* knowing: The knowing and judgment of the other may now be included; inwardness is expanded and made existent in relation to another inwardness, and they are mutually guiding. Externality here is another inward being. As Hegel says, language (§652/351) and "the word of reconciliation is the *existing* spirit" (§670/361), constituted by two selves who have let go of their opposition and been "extended into two-ness" (§671/362). The good requires actors, but actors require communicative contexts peopled by beings similarly attuned to the call of the good and to the infinite determinacies of ethical situations. This is a *live* universality, because it can aid in discernment of the virtually unmanageable diversity of situated existence. What we have in each other is the remarkable capacity of externality to *speak of itself*. The "reconciling yes"—that is, conscientious communicative practice—is the proper home of conscience.

In seeing the threads of attachment that link the agent with others (4), we see ethical life emerge again here in connection with conscience. These threads are many: others of the past, who have cultivated the agent as one who can act and the world as calling for action; others of the present, who can potentially interpret its action and give it a better sense of what this action means; and others of the future, who may make something of it. We are all potentially conscience; thus we have reason to support activity that recognizes and affirms the activity of conscientious others, and to critique activity that does not do this. We are made inside of relationships and have ourselves because of others, and we have the world we do because of their independent activity. There is an immanent norm here: If we depend on the freedom of others, then being free should be construed as a matter of inserting ourselves and our freedom into the web of the freedom of others, not of opposing it. Hegel's account of conscientious communication reveals the significance, to our capacity to act, of fostering relations of accountability, such that the question for free action is not simply, how shall I be me, but also, how can I honor my relations and our interdependence in my individual action? We must act in such a way that does not disavow the fact that our free action happens on the ground of the free action of others, and that their freedom, if it affirms the interdependence of freedoms, is the occasion for our own.

To care for a human being, then, in their rights and freedom, is to care for their *relations*. Here is where Fanon's critique of liberal colonialism is most cutting. He condemns colonial Europe particularly for its crimes against relations, for attacking "the heart of the human" by eroding its unity, by suppressing, dominating, and eliminating others in the name of "humanity." He argues that it has fed stratification and bloody tensions by class, with the demands of the productive machine determining our relations with each other, rather than vice versa (2004, 238). On the immense level of humanity, Europe has promulgated "racial hatred, slavery, exploitation and, above all, the bloodless genocide whereby one and a half billion [people] have been written off." These are crimes against the capacity for togetherness with other human lives, for shared, interdependent becoming, for the opportunity, as Fanon writes, "to walk in the company of [human beings], every [human being], night and day, for all times" (238). Fanon opposes the "individualism" of colonizers and their colonized bourgeois "servants" in favor of the solidarity and resistance captured in "brother, sister, comrade" (11). Merleau-Ponty similarly condemns liberalism for its failure to support relations among people that are human, which, in his view, is the key question to ask of any paradigm, since "we are through and through what we are for others and in our relations to them" (1969, 28). The focus here is, again, determinacy. Hegel's account of conscience reveals where the challenge of action lies: not in the formulation of principles, but in the translation they must undergo to become real in the world. In that translation, it is the reflective, historically developed insight of other human beings—who are, as we are, stuck between principle and practice—that can shed light on the meaning of our actions in a way that principles never could.

While it may be that the principle of singular subjectivity was explored in its complex intricacies particularly in the modern, Western, liberal tradition, that tradition has had a poor track record in fostering its conditions: protecting the determinate situations and worldly conditions of action; supporting the human capacity, propped up by material conditions, to answer to ideals; giving room to interpret one-sided actions as the expression of ideals; and fostering social conditions that would put us in contact with each other and encourage the live universality of conscientious communication. These conditions are what we see when we follow free, individual action into reality and observe it there, and it is a human responsibility to cultivate them.

To cultivate these conditions, further, we need the capacity to interpret the world well, so that we do not fundamentally err in the way we take the situation and do not continue to build the world on the basis of such errors. Most basically, the capacity to answer to ideals requires protection, which means that the exigencies of bodily life must be supported, since without that support answerability to ideals is difficult or impossible to sustain. Further, as action is always a matter of pairing with a world, and worlds are always local and specific, the support of conscience requires support of sometimes unfamiliar ethical worlds. This in turn requires working on the capacity to understand what is being expressed in determinacies that are unfamiliar to us, which means building up contexts of communication in which these determinacies can be explained and discerned. This is at least relevant to places where there is already interaction and this interaction is done poorly, which is almost everywhere; for the most part, even against our will, we are irretrievably implicated in each other, and the imperative of communication accompanies this mutual implication. Mutual curiosity and openness have been significantly hampered by a history of relational violence, which understandably fosters an unwillingness to engage; addressing this problem is a piece of cultivating conditions of communication. Insofar as others are omnipresent mediators of action and judgment, we must support each other, which means supporting each other's capacity to interpret reality well, to determine the ideal, and to act, and supporting the flourishing of the worlds we inhabit and the social conditions by which we are put in healthy contact with each other.

What must also be opposed, in this work of cultivating the conditions of action, is an expectation of and desire for purity. Conscientious action will always be ambivalent, as Hegel argues: simultaneously a fulfillment and transgression of its ideal and its answerability. Conscientious action is always also a transgression of the very ideas that it is trying to actualize because it requires a determinate person with imperfect knowledge who must fall back on their own interpretation of what the good requires. What an action will be and mean is not up to us—it will redound upon others, sometimes negatively—but the good only comes into being through these finite, uncertain creatures. Properly conscientious action is thus done in fear and trembling, taking guidance *from* determinacy and not imagining it can take refuge in the abstract principles from which it extends. We must follow such action out into the world and see what it becomes, in communicative interaction with others, in awareness of the ideal that it both answers to and betrays, in the assumption of conscientious responsibility. This is where the work is done—not in the abstract textbooks of liberalism.

THE OBJECTION FROM "URGENCY"

I want to wrap up here by entertaining an objection stemming from the claim of urgency, since it seems so common. What if, as this objection goes, a particularly destructive practice is unfolding in another place? A Western feminist might invoke, for instance, the example of "honor killing," "dowry-murder," the practice of *sati* (the ritual suicide of widows), or what is called "female genital mutilation."[3] The objection runs something like: Shouldn't one consider jettisoning respect for determinacy and for "ethical life" in the name of opposition to these practices? Beyond following Uma Narayan's (1997) diagnosis of a failure to perceive the "colonial representation" of such practices and Western versions of "death by culture," we could take guidance from Abu-Lughod's analysis of honor killing (2013): There is a complexity to the situation and to the culture in which such a situation *may* occur that is just not understood, probably because of a general, racist refusal to consider that there could be a layered complexity to perceive in alien determinacy. Meaningful engagement would demand a willingness to consider the possibility of this complexity in another world and a sense of how immense the project of interpretation would be. This fact demands a refusal to truck with "decontextualized information" (Narayan 1997) and a hesitation to reach conclusions about what one is seeing (Al-Saji 2014)—especially because what we are seeing might be the long-term destructive consequences of the policies of our own world in that one (Abu-Lughod 2002). Narayan makes this latter point too, asking Western subjects to consider how Western aid organizations might impact democratic self-governance of state operations in non-Western countries (2019, 11) and operate as an "ideological smoke screen" allowing "problematic Western economic and geopolitical agendas to continue" (13). The appropriate target for such Western subjects would be their home ground, which is responsible for global structural inequity that exacerbates local problems (15).

Again, what we see here is that it is above all conscientious communication that is required. Claims to urgency can inadvertently be assertions that we should be able to bring our prejudices to bear upon situations, that there is no complexity to be understood here, that that world has no discerning agents of its own that could take and have taken leadership in this situation (and also no history of discernment). Without engagement, we would have no way of realizing, for instance, that other things may be more urgent: Opposition to Western imperialism or a reorganization of the global distribution of wealth are a couple of candidates. As Abu-Lughod asks,

> how many feminists who felt good about saving Afghan women from the Taliban are also asking for a global redistribution of wealth or contemplating sacrificing their own consumption radically so that African or Afghan women could have some chance of having... the right to freedom from the structural violence of global inequality and from the ravages of war, the everyday rights of having enough to eat, having homes for their families in which to live and thrive, having ways to make decent livings so their children can grow, and having the strength and security to work out... how to live a good life, which might very well include changing the ways those communities are organized[?] (2002, 787)

In the absence of engagement, there is a strong temptation to see things in a way that is disconnected from the larger picture, and little capacity to discern and judge what the underlying causes of suffering are.

I am not claiming here that there should and can be no engagement between and among worlds, that they are necessarily opaque to each other, that there is no sharing at the level of principle. Conscientious communication is not the same as throwing up one's hands or committing to a thoroughgoing cultural relativism; it recognizes that we are already imbricated in each other (Abu-Lughod 2002), such that "leaving each other well enough alone" is no longer possible for us, and it works on freeing the present from the racist past without any illusions about its own freedom from that past. I am arguing that engagement should happen at the level of conscientious communication, which recognizes the need for determinate, transgressive action and the force of ethical life. We are not independent moral subjectivities encountering each other as abstract moral agents, rationality confronting rationality; we come with layers of history and culture that operate inside of consciousness, informing our orientation to each other behind our backs. The insistence on transparency and rationality is in fact an expression of a particular form of ethical life that denies the operation of ethical life.

What we have in each other is remarkable: the capacity of worlds to speak of themselves, to be not simply submerged in mystery, but to be self-articulating, self-interpreting. In human individuals, worlds become discerning and articulate. Do we encounter other beings as these powers of expression? Do we build up our capacity to be self-interpreting forces for each other, by working on the material conditions that build us up as interpreting beings, the communicative contexts that allow us to be available to each other in our interpretive power? Do we own up, as in Hegel's scene of reconciliation with the judge and the actor, to the other's authority to interpret the meaning of the things we have done; do we cultivate contexts in which they have that authority? Or, conversely, do we cultivate contexts in which it is always a certain class of humanity that gets to define how things are done, that never has to answer to another, and that shuts off for itself the possibility of experiencing this other's interpretive power?

Absolute Spirit

Conscience sheds light on both the import and the limits of ethical life as such, because while it finds its orientation and content within these forms of life, these forms in turn do not make themselves but are enacted by simultaneously "faithful" and transgressive beings. In dependence on these beings, forms of life are susceptible to change. Absolute spirit also holds ethical life open, insofar as the activities of absolute spirit—which are, for Hegel, art, religion, and philosophy—involve conscientious reflection on who "we" are, a reflection that is never "harmless" with regard to that which it grasps. To arrive at an insight about oneself is generative, setting the stage for new insight and comprehension and changing one's relation to materiality, which also means changing materiality. Human existence is thus essentially embedded *and* historical. To be beings of ethical life is to be empowered to engage with these absolute pursuits, which rely on the concrete ethical specificity of the domains we experience as home, but to be beings "of the absolute" is to open the practice of "homemaking" to contact with the absolute. We will see in what follows that Hegel's account of absolute spirit also offers an orientation to the phenomenon of ethical life, the modern priority of subjectivity, the character of intercultural interaction and cultural transformation, and the logic of world history.

Not much of Hegel's published writings are dedicated to discussion of absolute spirit, with the exception of significant early work on religion and Christianity. The *Encyclopaedia* concludes with a brief discussion of art (§§556–63), revealed religion (§§564–71), and philosophy (§§572–77). The *Phenomenology* contains of course an extended discussion of religion, in which is included treatment of Greek classical art. *PR/GPR* §§341–60 is a discussion of world history, with which the text concludes, and which is connected to absolute spirit: that is, Hegel claims that "the *element* of the *universal spirit's* existence is intuition and image in art, feeling and presentational in religion, and pure and free thought in philosophy. In *world history*, it is spiritual actuality in its entire range of inwardness and externality" (§341). But most of what Hegel says systematically about religion, art, and philosophy is contained in recorded lectures, so scholarship in these areas is based largely on transcriptions.

As Hegel observes in his lectures on aesthetics in the 1820s, we are not the kind of beings who relate to the finitude around us as if it were all there was: "ensnared in finitude on all sides, the human being seeks the region of a higher truth" (A.I 99/VA.I 137). We are not simply determinate beings of this way of life and these relations, as conscience has revealed, in its sense of answerability to the principles it seeks to actualize and to the future of its action in a shared domain with others. Human beings and cultures also engage in practices by which they make the facticity of determinate life an object of reflection and thereby propel it in new directions.

Such practices, as Hegel notes, are practices of creative expression, by which we bring into being new meanings and experience our character as creators (art); practices of elaborating a domain of meaning that we take to be the imperceptible depth of the finite world and by which it is interpreted and held to account (religion); and practices of comprehension by which we grasp the nature of reality (philosophy). As noted above, the practice of world history is also ambiguously included here. These are all practices by which human beings grapple with their status as beings who live in *this* way, whatever it is—in this here and now, but also in imaginative, reverential, and intellectual contact with what lies at the basis of this finite context as its interpretive key, contact with what is other and elsewhere, or with the idea of meaning, value, and truth beyond this finite context.

The questions for this kind of being are, How do we answer to our status as elsewhere? How do we live our lives and inhabit our situations and forms of life in a way that does them and ourselves justice? How does our relation to the indeterminate, to the question of who we are and what might be, shape and change us? Hegel describes human beings as ethically specific and embedded in one-sided forms of life, but also as capable of relating to our own determinacy, particularly with conscience. What does it mean for us that we are two-sided in this way? The practices of absolute spirit do not explicitly work to serve or sustain the "we" or the "I" as it happens to be, but in them we follow what we experience as the call to comprehend what is real and to make something real. Our stories about ourselves resituate our relation to the world and to ourselves, transforming that of which they tell.

As I have noted, Hegel observes that human beings turn to the practices of absolute spirit in part out of a sense of the limitations of the finite: He thinks we want the distinctive satisfaction that comes with being involved with more than just the local and determinate, or that comes from finding meaning in its very contingent forms. As he says, we experience the dissatisfaction of being "ensnared in finitude on all sides" and seek "the region of a higher, more substantial, truth" (A.I 99/ VA.I 137). The specific rituals, texts, artifacts, practices, and insights of cultures are that in and through which human beings have expressed or discerned something *true*. This discernment and expression, however, does not leave things as they are; rather, it is transformative. When the "thing," the "true," and the "human" come into contact, none leaves the encounter unchanged. If engagement in absolute spirit is transformative, then it is not that the "me" or "we" *sustains* itself as it already is in these practices, even though it seeks to understand or express itself in these practices. Also changed is that which we "look at" or engage with—namely, the real—which in turn then demands of us new thought, new comprehension.

This connection between grasping and transformation is due to what Hegel flags as the distinctive character of selfhood. As Hegel writes, "thinking is spirit's descent into itself and therefore what it is as perceptive it makes objective to itself; it collects itself together within itself and therefore separates itself from itself" (*LHP* 42). When I try to understand myself, I separate myself from myself; I do not inhabit my perspective in the ordinary way but look upon it, and that "looking upon perspective" is distinct from the simple inhabitation of perspective and takes me away from it, even though it is still nothing other than a way of living my perspective. We carry out this self-reflection via the terms that are inherited from our self-reflecting human communities—"I am this kind of person, who does this kind of thing in this kind of world"; "it is my destiny to grow up, find a spouse, become a parent," and so on—but these terms can themselves become objects of reflection; the assumptions implicit in our reflective self-interpretation can be considered. Capable of self-separation, we can in principle scrutinize every sedimentation of meaning. As Russon writes, "our perspective is... inherently open to the question of itself qua perspective, and to recognizing itself as answerable to what is in principle non-perspectival" (2020, 24). This is key to the intertwining of ethical life and absolute spirit: One can never let go of the distinction, *intrinsic to having a perspective*, between what appears within that perspective and the idea of the "truth of the matter" to which that perspective must answer.

This capacity for self-separation and the experience of dissatisfaction with the finite support us in the ability to appreciate other responses to the experience of the true. Inasmuch as any work of absolute spirit is in principle expressing a perspective of answerability to truth (A.I 101/ VA.I 139), it is potentially a *human* lesson, meaningful as such for all those whose intellectual and imaginative powers allow them to relate to meaning and to imagine the conditions of that experience of discovery. Indeed, dissatisfaction with the finite can even be inspired by those human lessons, those works that, though produced in and as the life of another culture, can by their alienness expose and address the limitations of one's own familiar world.

We misunderstand the aesthetic, religious, and philosophical practices of other cultures—other modes of ethical life—if we see them as simply determinate and simply historical. They are indeed the specific practices of a particular culture, but it is intrinsic to them to speak to that which is universal and therefore potentially to the needs of others who do not share that cultural specificity. At the same time, we also misunderstand them if we see them as indifferent to specificity, for the specificities of a culture are precisely the terms in and through which those principles have been allowed to gain entry into our human world. In short, the practices of absolute spirit are always embedded in a specific form of ethical life, but they do not merely serve it; while it is true that these are the practices by which a culture expresses and explores itself, they are simultaneously the practices by which that culture, in the mode of conscience, answers to something. It is this answerability—this universality—that precludes the practices from being defined by what Sylvia Wynter (2003) calls the "adaptive knowing" of that culture.[4]

In art, religion, and philosophy, there is thus a particular kind of relation at play between entanglement and transcendence—a relation characterized, as Russon notes, by the tension between idolatry and non-idolatry (2015, 233). Art makes determinacy expressive of meaning, showing the explosive, universal significance that materiality can have, but it does so by embracing the expressive object in its singularity. Art is historically situated, embedded in ethical life, because it is only effective as expression if it uses living, existent terms that are capable of communicating, and this requires beings who can understand those terms. But it does not secure unchanging reality for those terms and those beings; it does not make them into idols, declaring them the absolute itself, but makes them point to something else. Religion, similarly, employs and develops determinate means by which to honor the absolute—ritual, doctrine, ceremony—relating to the absolute through these media, but it implies too that they must not be made into idols. And philosophy is the practice of discerning in the determinacy in front of us the meanings that show through it. As Merleau-Ponty writes, philosophy is "consciousness of rationality in contingency" (1964, 111)—indeed, it is also, as Hegel might add, consciousness of the rationality and necessity of contingency. But, precisely because of this constitutive commitment to the historically specific and determinate, each of these domains of absolute spirit risks falling into idolatry by treating the specific contingencies with which it works as if they, qua contingent and specific, simply were "the absolute."

There is, however, a converse danger, which is that of disdaining determinacy. The play of entanglement and transcendence that characterizes all the works of absolute spirit entails that the universal is never experienced "by itself." As aforementioned, a principle is revealed "in history *in the relations of that existence*"; it is clothed "with all the wealth of [that] existence"; it works through a people's "morality, constitution, domestic, civil, and public life, arts, international relations"; it advances through "concrete life" (*LHP* 44). The human experience of answering to the pull of truth will always be the work of ethical life's "wealth of . . . existence," the rich diversity of finite reality. As Hegel is reported to have said, "everything that forces itself out into real objectivity is subject . . . to the principle of particularization" (*A.II* 1195/*VA.III* 522). The question is thus whether we one-sidedly treat either the determinate or the universal as having its authority solely on its own terms, or whether we relate to the determinate as authoritative only insofar as it expresses or grasps meaning, and relate to the meaning or principle as authoritative only under the condition that it expresses itself in and respects the determinate. Thus, in addition to acknowledging the significance of ethical life and the significance of absolute spirit, we can note the significance of inhabiting and enacting each in light of the accompanying existence of the other.

We can fail to perceive determinacy as that through which we aim for a kind of answerability to truth: This would be to absolutize the determinate, rendering it an idol—indeed, rendering the current form of the "I" or the "we" as set, inert. But we can also fail to grasp that the absolute needs the historical and determinate. The terms of experience that assert themselves as absolute require, as we have seen, an entire existence, social reality, era: They take time to be seen in their fuller (though never full) meaning. Hence the philosophical significance and moral weight of exposure to other forms of life—and here also lies the significance of Hegel's ambiguous inclusion of world history in absolute spirit. In world history, we see different principles in their rich determinate concrete significance, in their homes, which fill out these principles insofar as they are worked on through so many different aspects of the concrete. It is philosophically incumbent upon us to work to perceive the meaningfulness of the determinacies of the practices of other cultures as the home of another principle or other principles, as a mode of expression of the absolute. "The element of the existence of *universal spirit*, which in art is intuition and image, in religion is feeling and presentation [*Vorstellung*], and in philosophy is pure, free thought, is, in world history, spiritual actuality in its entire range of inwardness and externality" (*PR/GPR* §341). This connection makes intuitive sense: Getting to a broader perspective is supported by observation of differences between different modes of ethical life. Hegel's analysis thus lays the groundwork here for intercultural practices that can only develop after him, when the concrete determinacies of intercultural interaction have led us there.

Ethical life and absolute spirit are perspectives on the relation between action and its context, and they are also effectively perspectives on two different ways of relating to stories and accounts—in the form of "the story tells me/us" and in the form of "I/we tell a story." Hegel's description of the art of storytelling, or dramatic poetry and specifically tragedy, is particularly helpful for illuminating these issues, and so we will turn to it as a kind of case study for seeing how the story of who we ultimately are is always one that remains to be told. We are beings of both ethical life and conscience, of ethical life and absolute spirit; our stories precede us, and we make them and thus ourselves anew.

DRAMATIC POETRY

Dramatic poetry, says Hegel, "displays a complete action as actually taking place before our eyes; the action originates in the minds of the characters who bring it about, but at the same time its outcome is decided by the really substantive nature of the aims, individuals, and collisions involved." Dramatic poetry presents a picture of human reality, of individual action in the world with others, "uniting the objectivity of epic with the subjective character of lyric" (A.II 1158/VA.III 474). Action is preceded by the story of ethical life, which "tells it"; action expresses our possession by the substantial. But action is also a potentially transformative, disruptive telling that brings about a transformation in that world, changing the stage. Dramatic poetry, in other words, presents the human being precisely as a being both of ethical life and of absolute spirit.

Hegel's discussion of tragedy, the form of dramatic poetry upon which I will focus, itself focuses on ancient Greek and modern tragic drama. Tragedy, in his account, portrays the collision of the human agent with reality, and with it the very multiplicity and complexity of reality. Greek and modern tragedy differ in where they locate the site of collision, but they share the presentation of human action as a transformative transgression of the existing situation, an expressive act that could make sense only in a world that does not or not yet exist.

Greek tragedy is particularly powerful in displaying the ethical powers by which individuals are moved—the "substantive spheres of life" (A.II 1195/VA.III 522), "the universal and essential element in the aim which the characters are realizing" (1206/535). Commitment to the formative dimensions of ethical life is experienced as passion, which spurs action. Agents bring about effects in the world that sustain substantive universal elements or realize ethical principles, but, in the context of an ethical life defined by conflicting imperatives, actions have meanings and sources other than that which the actor honors. In answering to one imperative, we can transgress another, and the tragedy of our condition is displayed in the collision of ethical powers incapable of co-manifestation in the finite specificities of action. Greek tragedy shows the divine to be plural and infinite, while action must be individual and finite. What is tragic here is that in the situation as it appears in this form of life, there is no action that could answer to all of the substantive values or forces by which the lives of its members are grounded and oriented. Greek tragedy portrays the complexity of that by which the lives of its members (and our own) are written, to which these (and our) lives are a response, indebted and obligated. It portrays the trial of action: How can what is of utmost significance be compressed into and expressed in this one, single act?[5] There is a mismatch between the true and the act: The act cannot do the true justice, and yet there is no alternative to acting.[6]

The substantive powers expressed in the action of ancient tragedy (as well as the objectivity of epic) express one side of who we are: We are as though vessels for meanings that outstrip us, by which our lives are made worthwhile; we are possessed by the substantial. The "greatness of soul" portrayed in modern tragedy (as well as the subjective character of lyric) express another side: we are "natality," to put it in Hannah Arendt's (1998) terms, and our action can disrupt and transform reality; it can change the stage.

Modern tragedy is the reflection of subjectivity and its irreducibility to the world of objectivity: "The principal topic is provided by an individual's passion, which is satisfied in the pursuit of a purely subjective end... the poetic interest here lies in the greatness of the characters who by their imagination or disposition and aptitude display the full wealth of their heart, and their elevation over their situations and actions, as a real possibility" (A.II 1206–7/VA.III 533). Subjectivity collides tragically with the world that does not take its form, that does not necessarily cooperate, because it is of a different substance. The agents of modern tragedy are "great souls" (1230/564) who adhere to something in their passion, because of who they are, "once and for all." Hegel calls these agents "free artists of their own selves" (1228/562); this form of tragedy presents to us a being that "goes beyond," whose gestures would bring into being a new home. But externality here refuses to take shape around the agent's singularity. In modern tragedy, it is not the action that falls short of the true, but the finitude and multiplicity of the world that falls short of the infinitude and singularity (and sometimes destructive voraciousness) of subjectivity.

The contrast of ancient and modern tragedy thus puts on display precisely the two-sided character of our condition as human: We live by the stories we tell about ourselves, but we also have the capacity to write new stories, and doing so is in fact incumbent upon us because of our felt experience of answerability to truth. It is precisely both answerability as well as the attendant "unsettled" character of human reality that is expressed in stories.

Art, as well as religion and philosophy, is ultimately how we apprehend reality as something that resonates with our own character as "becoming": reality that beckons to us in our potentiality rather than our actuality, that does not allow itself to be appropriated as detached object, inert stuff, secure possession. In the experience of aesthetic expression, religious worship, and philosophical comprehension, we experience ourselves as grasping something about ourselves, which in turn has the power to change how we live. The activities of absolute spirit are efforts at comprehension and expression of the real, but they are efforts that turn around and look back at us, so to speak, presenting us with an ongoing demand for redescription, for retelling, for changing the terms of our lives to suit our transformation.

In Hegel's understanding, absolute spirit outstrips the objective forms of life we develop for ourselves, in relation to which we must concern ourselves with finite preoccupations: this law, this piece of property, this capacity to freely walk down the sidewalk, this need, this body. These preoccupations are necessary and important, but they are always finite matters relative to a specific, finite world. The works of absolute spirit illuminate the human as unsettled, dispossessed, and open to reinterpretation. Through art, religion, and philosophy, we foster the conditions for our transformation; we bring into being the possibility that we will be changed by what is outside of us. The human is that which tells a story that in turn sees and tells it. Hegel's human is not settled; it is a storytelling that has always happened but that also always begins again.

As we have noted, art, religion, and philosophy are paired with world history in Hegel's philosophy, which is another way in which we experience the eyes of an external reality upon us. World history is "spiritual actuality in its entire range of inwardness and externality" (*PR/GPR* §341). The "judgement of the world" that grasps "the dialectic of the particular spirits of peoples" (*PM/E* §548) is, I believe, the context that allows a given "we" to see itself as finite, as a determinate "spirit." Having the eyes of world history upon ourselves is again a matter of being positioned by another view not our own, in relation to which we can find ourselves challenged. But to see history this way, we must recognize in another culture the same "self-referring negativity" (*PR/GPR* §278), the same complexity of grappling with the terms that make our lives meaningful, that we recognize in ourselves. And that means that history, like art, is neither simple nor transparent in its meaning, and our reading of it will always be open, because it is a reading of cultures who engage in absolute spirit and who have the capacity to see us and thereby get inside of our own transformative self-understanding.

Our challenges are these: to inhabit our cultures, whatever they might be, in a way that honors their status as that relatively closed reality that is needed for any opening to the experience of meaning and significance; and to relate to other cultures as the home of the absolute, whatever that might be. It is to embrace our two-sidedness, our character as ethical and absolute, in ourselves and others; it is to see and to let ourselves be seen.

By now, we have looked at three ingredients of a critical response to the revolutionary abstraction, three phenomena that can be critically brought to bear upon our contemporary situation: recognition, ethical life, and conscience. In this final section, we will turn to objective spirit and to the significance of materiality, as a fourth ingredient. However, this section also operates differently than the others, insofar as it also offers a vision of what kind of government and social organization we require as beings of recognition, ethical life, and conscience. I take seriously Hegel's proposal regarding what concrete institutions free beings require, and present them as the finite, material embodiment of the vision of the human as recognized, ethical, and conscientious.[7]

CHAPTER FIVE

Objective Spirit

One might say that Hegel does not thematize materiality much. One might not notice in his philosophy an explicit focus on the body, for instance, as in Merleau-Ponty, or a category such as being-in-the-world or the "I-can," as in Heidegger or Husserl, or a systematic analysis of the pervasive influence of the economic domain in which the satisfaction of need is pursued, as Marx provides. These are valuable and transformative ideas supporting an explicit and self-conscious philosophical turn to the basic category of materiality. However, because of their very efficacy and power in setting the philosophical stage, these ideas may also have had the indirect effect of concealing the extent to which Hegel was in fact preoccupied with materiality. The fact that he is not particularly known for his work on the body and materiality might also reflect a lack in the scholarship on him as well as the preoccupations of the tradition in which he emerges.

I will argue here that there are significant and numerous reasons to go to Hegel for consideration of materiality. The methodology of the *Phenomenology* is to look at how hypotheses are lived or imagined as lived, or what happens to them in their enactment in the concrete world with others; it is a catalog of a being's experiential interactions with *its world*. In the *Philosophy of Right*, Hegel, like Locke, begins with the immediate materiality of the will: The most immediate appearance of freedom, or freedom considered in its most abstract form, is the upsurge of free initiative in the human being, but this upsurge is always a doing, or this doing always involves material things or material space. Freedom is thingly and worldly. Finally, one can find a non-dualistic account of the relation between the soul and body, between body and consciousness, in his discussion of "Anthropology" in the *Encyclopaedia*. In registering materiality as meaning, natural data as experience, the body appears as the fold between the natural and ideal, and it is its nature to be this fold; in it, material nature is ideal and immaterial.

As the discussions of recognition, ethical life, conscience, and absolute spirit have shown, Hegel's focus is persistently the finite, determinate, actual, existent, and historical. To use the term "idealism" in Hegel can be quite misleading unless we understand it in a way that thematizes the intimacy of the ideal and the material, the *link* between what is internal and external to consciousness, simplistically construed. Idealism names the fact that there is no easy way to make a hard distinction between what is "out there" and what is "in here" or in my mind, or between my mind and the minds of others. The world is charged with, calls for, and supports human expression. Thought, desire, love, urge, and feeling circulate, emerge in action, weave in and out of bodies, others, and world. They are inspired by materiality and they are expressed; they do not maintain purely ideational form but are materialized. Recognition, ethical life, and conscience have pointed us to the concrete and to how philosophy must answer to the determinate, historical, and local reality of interpersonal life. This discussion too will open up another dimension of the concrete that philosophy must grapple with—that of the concretely material.

The Dimensions of Materiality

A central aspect of the materiality of existing and doing is *body*. Activity in the world is bodily activity, involving individual abilities. It is a body that "can," a body that "does," a body that walks, grabs, reads, talks, sits, or does some version of these things. Everything that unfolds inside of our experience relies on this body as its medium, but in a way that discourages us from using the terms "relies on" and "medium," since the body is better captured by the idea that it conducts our experience. The body's "know-how" typically operates independently of reflection, which is more intermittent than this know-how. The body is intelligent, a materiality that grasps both literally and figuratively.

Let's say I go to a music show. I walk, or manipulate a car that will move me, or go to the subway, or get on a bicycle, and the coupling of my body and the vehicle or sidewalk gets me there. I enter the space of the show. I put myself in proximity to the instruments so that I can hear them; I bring my ears to the event, so to speak. I must *be there*, in sensory, bodily proximity, in order to experience anything. It is the body and its capacity to be sensorily open to music, its capacity for movement, its capacity to attach to things that move—car, subway, bicycle, its, and so on—that allow me to experience a musical event, which itself is "intertwinedly" both material and meaningful.

A different kind of thingliness or materiality we rely upon is that of determinate objects. To write this book, I pair up with pen and paper; computer and outlet; food and drink; chair, desk, kitchen, and bathroom: My experience of writing is a matter of mixing with material. If the body is always doing, it is always mixing with these objects. And if the body is always a capacity for doing, then its environment is filled with objects that are as if suspended and available, as though ready for its action with and on them. It is as though the I is (and needs) a steady, harmonious ecosystem of body, things, space, and movement or mechanisms for movement in space and to and around things.

Determinate objects, however, bring me into contact with dimensions of materiality that exist far beyond this place in the world and this site of our pairing. Beyond the immediate scene extends the electrical grid, the sewage system, systems of food production and distribution, economic systems of exchange. These are materially organized *systems* that support both objects and bodies, delivering things to us, supporting the readiness of things for our doing. They support the ongoing sustenance of bodies.

Beyond these systems contextualizing the immediate scene, there are the rules and regulations by which they are sustained, and by which human beings attend to the precarity of the body's situation as needy. Without rules and regulations governing the organization of space, the meeting of people and things, the delivery of electricity, water, and sewage drainage to the spaces we occupy, our bodies could not trust the meeting with the world upon which they depend. Regulations pervade our existing and doing: regulations ensuring the security of space—for instance, that people will more or less obey traffic rules and that buildings will not collapse or set on fire; regulations regarding the safety of the food we eat, and the security of electrical, water, and sewage systems; regulations against, for instance, theft, which fosters the expectation that our stuff is available for us and that there will be recourse if it is taken. Because of them, the body can respond unreflectively and unconcernedly to the world's many invitations.

These regulations are themselves deeply historical, and reveal another dimension behind the scenes of immediate pairing with the world, materially organized systems, and rules or regulations: the history of other human beings having discovered the need for and having developed these systems and rules. The history of their work and their pairing is as it were captured in all of the dimensions of materiality. The systems of electricity, water, sewage, and roads have developed through the labor of others mixing with the world. The sounds, music, and instruments that we hear in going to a music show are different than they were centuries ago. It is as though we contact the bodies of others—the discerning that was done by their bodies—in handling things ourselves. This historical and interpersonal dimension makes itself manifest also in the fact that any pairing with the world that we do depends on an earlier guidance: To write this book I needed to learn how to move my limbs, read and write, make letters, mobilize grammar, interpret. Activity makes reference to the phenomena of care and transmission, to the passing down of human activity through educational processes and institutions, familial and social. These institutions are in turn material insofar as they involve buildings, books, water, sewage, electricity, and words.

All of these dimensions—the intelligent body, body-object pairings, organized systems, rules and regulations, historical inventiveness, transmission—are given their due in Hegel's philosophy. We will go to various sites to see these various dimensions: to the "Anthropology" to look at the body; to the *Phenomenology*'s discussion of the servant to look at bodies, objects, and activity; and to the practical philosophy to look at the built, historical world with its systems, regulations, and operation in time. First, to the "Anthropology."

THE BODY

Hegel's treatment of the body in the *Encyclopaedia*'s "Anthropology" begins with the basic phenomenon of natural determinacy.[1] While Hegel uses the term "soul" here, discerning distinct functions in it such as the "natural soul" and the "feeling soul," I will use the term "soul-body" to reflect the fact that, as he argues, the immaterial and the material are originally a unity (and to adapt to our changed context, in which we tend not to have a living sense of the traditional meaning of "soul"). To ask how the material and immaterial could possibly be related, as he remarks in an Addition, is "impossible to answer," because "this way of posing [the question] ... is inadmissible; ... the separation of the material and the immaterial can be explained only on the basis of the original unity of both" (*PM/E* §389A).[2]

Sensation is the simple matter of the soul-body's receptivity to external reality, in which context it has the wondrous capacity to register external data as internal experience. Hegel calls attention here to the fact that this is nature's own ideality: In sensation, what is external is converted into experience. The natural soul "finds within itself... the natural and immediate, as within the soul ideally and made its own" (*PM/E*

§401). The soul-body registers this datum not solely as a datum but also as an ideal *meaning* beyond its materiality:

> Nowhere else is it of such essential importance for our understanding to keep hold of the determination of *ideality* as it is in the case of the soul and still more of the mind. Ideality is the *negation* of the real, but the real is also *stored up*, virtually retained, although it does not *exist*. It is this determination that we have before us in respect of presentations, memory. (§403R)

The soul-body retains the sensory experience of, for instance, hardness as "ideal" or meaningful, as information about possibility, and remembers and develops habits around this information.

Hegel continues: "Yet *I* am for all that an entirely *simple* entity,—a cavern without determinations, in which all this is stored up, without existing.... The individuality is and remains this *simple inwardness*, amidst all the determinacy and mediation of consciousness that is later installed in it" (*PM/E* §403R). This second point—"I am for all that an entirely *simple* entity"—is a further manifestation of ideality in nature. The soul-body is a *one*, a naturally occurring form in which parts that lie asunder spatially speaking are in fact one. Being physically impacted by external reality affects the soul-body as a one.[3] This unity is a phenomenon of nature; nature in the soul-body is not a matter of parts that lie asunder or side by side. As Hegel says, in soul we witness nature's own "universal immateriality ... its simple ideal life" (§389).[4] This is "nature in its own self sublat[ing] itself as what is untrue," its "self-externality," since soul is a universality that is "*simple* in its concretion and totality" (§388).

Insofar as experience takes shape around sensing, the soul-body as a one and the status of what is externally received as data are intrinsically related. The soul-body develops as a oneness or whole on the basis of these data, such that its existence is a function or product of them. Hegel calls this emergence of oneness in these two ways the "feeling soul" (*PM/E* §§403–10).

To summarize, there are three basic points to notice about the soul-body in sensation: First, it is not simply the hand, let's say, as a part of the body that registers the contact, but the soul-body as a whole; second, the soul-body retains the experience as information; and third, the soul-body takes shape around it, becoming competent, developing physically and psychically in relation to materiality registered as meaningful.

What is evident here is a kind of "fold" between materiality and meaning. When materiality comes into contact with the material soul-body, it is registered as meaning; hardness, for instance, is not materially transported inside the soul-body. This determinacy is "held" even after it disappears: "Being is contained as an ideal moment in the being-for-self of the waking soul" (*PM/E* §399). This is the power of the soul-body: to take the material within itself ideally. To be the soul-body is to connect and suspend in itself the history of material contact as moments of *its own experience*.

The power of the soul-body to idealize matter is a power of the soul-*body*; body is not grasped as body if it is not grasped as idealizing. Hegel warns against input from consciousness and the intellect here, which propel us toward dualism, taking over the agency of other elements of the experiencing being: "We must resist the idea suggested by consciousness and the intellect, that this bodiliness is a materiality outside the soul and with its parts external to each other. Just as the *variety* of the many *presentations* does not establish an asunderness and real plurality in the *I*, so the real asunderness of bodiliness has no truth for the feeling soul" (*PM/E* §403R). Bodiliness is not materiality outside of the soul; body is ensouled; body is one because it is soul, not a collection of pieces lying beside each other in the world.

Just as the apparent externality of the body is untrue, so also is the externality of the world untrue, and here Hegel subtly and without significant emphasis makes a further dramatic point. The soul "is itself the posited totality of its *particular* world, so that this world is included in it, its fulfilment; in relating to this world it relates only to itself" (*PM/E* §403R). As the alchemy that converts the external into the internal, that retains the real even though it no longer exists, the soul-body also internalizes a world; its "who" is inseparable from that world. This point is rather understated in the actual text and only developed significantly in the Addition to *PM/E* §402.[5] It follows, however, from the argument so far: The soul-body's contact with materiality is contact with a specific external domain to which it is exposed—its world—such that the soul-body is a soul-body *of* this world. To the concrete being of the individual belong the empirical relationships in which she stands in relation to others and the world, because soul-body is the conversion of outer to inner.

Habit is another important site of relation between materiality and ideality, another way in which something in nature shows that bodiliness is not a materiality outside of soul (*PM/E* §403). In habit, the soul-body is construed as its own intelligence, not driven by consciousness: Hegel says that the soul has these determinations "in itself and moves in them, without sensation or consciousness" (§410). In habit, "bodiliness" is "thoroughly trained and made its own," and "the subject is related only to itself" (§411). Here again we see the wondrous alchemy in terms of which bodily determinations are turned into the "who" of the human being: The "soul exists as substance in its bodiliness" (§410R). Habit shows the expression of the internal in bodiliness and in the world, the intertwining of bodiliness and ideality.

Hegel hereby argues that materiality is ideal and ideality is material. In the very basic character of the human body, we have externality internalized and internality externalizing and extending its "who" into materiality. The more complex dimensions of human existence as it is externalized in materiality emerge from this foundation; let us turn to these sites now, beginning with the *Phenomenology*'s analysis of the work of the servant.

WORK

Chapter 2's examination of recognition focused on the interpersonal dimensions of Hegel's discussion of mastery and servitude, but here we will turn to the servant's work. First and foremost, we should note the framing: Work is instituted by a command and taken up as a consequence of a relationship, that between the servant and the master. This should briefly alert us to the fact that relations with other people are always implicit in our relationship with materiality; we never get pure materiality or pure relations. But let us turn to the specificity of work.

The very fact that a person in Hegel's scenario feels compelled to accept the condition of submission says something important about materiality. As noted above, at stake in the struggle to the death is the assertion that perspective is not reducible to materiality, and I can stake my life for the sake of a meaning or purpose. By this I declare that, as perspective, I am beyond materiality insofar as I am a manner of taking up material reality in the mode of an "as-structure": I see x "as" meaningful in this or that way; I relate to y "as" demanding this kind of action or response; I bring a comportment to things that is not dictated by materiality but by me. The difference between perspective and materiality also makes itself manifest insofar as I experience myself and my experience as irreducible to physical terms: It typically does not particularly matter to my self-conception that my behavior could be explicable in terms of neurological and hormonal activity and so on. I simply do not "take it to be decisive," and *I am the kind of being whose life is made out of how I take things to be.* My experience has a meaningful character that is not translatable into the terms of physical reality; how my life unfolds depends on what I take to be important and neurological activity is not that; we could not even take it to be anything because we cannot sense it.

However—and here we return to the question of why the servant feels compelled to work—there is no perspective without materiality. As Butler notes, "the human dependency on the object is insuperable" (2021, 29). To face death and choose servitude over death displays something else that is true: Life is essential to consciousness; consciousness operates inside of and through life and nature; perspective is a phenomenon of nature. In the duality of the master and servant, however, the duality of consciousness and life is divided into two different persons: The master is "pure self-consciousness," and the servant is "existing consciousness" or "consciousness in the shape of thinghood" (*PS* §189/*PG* 112). Hegel will show that this severance does not stand up to critical scrutiny, but in the meantime we get a meditation on the idea that thinghood or materiality is an aspect of our reality, even if not the whole story.

The world rises up to match the master's desire through the servant. The servant transforms the world into what the master wants. The master experiences almost absolutely how her perspective is beyond things: It dictates how things will appear to it, and they comply (because of the servant). The master's perspective is not typically forced to grapple with the recalcitrance of things (with the exception of needing to ongoingly threaten the servant materially), and so the master can largely experience herself as "pure consciousness." The servant, however, must turn himself into a kind of thing in order to be able to obey the master's commands. The servant's body has to become a tool, a mediation between the master's will and the world.[6] He has to "be thing" to act *upon* things, to shape the world in ways that fulfill the master's desires. The servant has to answer both to the will of the master and to the recalcitrance of the object, to figure out what action the object requires in order to become satisfaction for the master. He becomes a thing to work on things; his hand becomes the tool of tools; he holds the hammer, the wood, fixes the nails in place in response to the master's command, "house."

Hegel says that the servant has "felt the fear of death, the absolute master" (*PS* §194/*PG* 114). Confrontation with the possibility of death—with dependence on materiality—propels a specific kind of transformation. In response to this confrontation, the servant suppresses desire and sets himself to work; this confrontation completely transforms his situation. He has given up the possibility of answering to his own desire because he has had to sacrifice that to satisfy his most basic desire, to stay alive. Because of this conversion, he learns how to deal with the object, since the master and the object (in its independence) demand it. The recalcitrance presented by the wood—it is not going to turn itself into a chair—then becomes the very occasion through which his working hands develop powers and insight into the character of wood and of tool, into the effects of tools, into the workings of reality; hands learn to hold wood, hammer nails. The servant develops physical and mental competencies by obeying the demands implicit in the nature of the thing, by answering to it rather than to his own self.

Further, he learns how to turn reality into something that "endures"; the servant's activity or "formative *doing*... enters into the element of lasting." It is the servant who gives the objective world lasting "form," such that he intuits his "own self" in the object, the "self-sufficient being." While work, therefore, is "desire *held in check*, vanishing *staved off*" (*PS* §195/*PG* 115), its consequence is to stave off the fleetingness of satisfaction. The worker knows how to make the world satisfy desire in a predictable way, how to make the world for the temporality of human desire. While seeking to satisfy the master, he has given and learned how to give the object form.

The experience of the servant shows that, far from being ourselves on our own, we—our consciousness, our agency—depend upon interaction with a world, where exposure to the object and its nature is the occasion for development. The servant retrieves himself in this object; "through this retrieval, he comes to acquire through himself a *mind of his own*, and he does this precisely in the work in which there had seemed to be only some *alien mind*" (*PS* §196/*PG* 116). While the master's mind dictated the work, what comes to be developed is the servant's mind, because the servant can look at an object and understand it. The formed object confirms the servant's and not the master's activity.

Here Hegel makes a profound point: "Through work this servile consciousness comes round to itself" (*PS* §195/*PG* 115). We are selves, but this is something we "come round to" through a detour through the world and things and by answering to them. Development and capacity depend on subjection to external, material reality, on mixing with the world. I subject myself to the piano, and it makes my body, my mind, me. But subordination to the object is not the end of the story: The object takes the form it is given; the self and the object are collaborators. The piano sings *my* melody; it develops and gives expression to my feeling.

This is not, again, an affirmation of the institution of servitude. It shows the contradiction inherent to the institution of servitude; it affirms the irrepressible character of human freedom, while also affirming the interdependence of materiality and consciousness and, with it, the collaboration with things and the development of skillful activity that is requisite for becoming a competent self.

OBJECTIVE SPIRIT

The servant's work shows that selfhood is "thinghood" integrated with "pure consciousness"; selfhood is accomplished through collaboration between the self and the object. The object, however, is not one or simple, but a complex of objects embedded in a built, historical, human context, where it plays a role in relation to other objects, and where each admits of being defined in a vague sense by the whole. Thus we go now from the *Phenomenology*'s abstract discussion of work to the *Philosophy of Right*'s and the *Encyclopaedia*'s concrete discussions of objective spirit. While I will not get into the details of the relations between Hegel's various texts, suffice it to say for now that we move here from a piece of Hegel's analysis of the nature and structure of self-consciousness to insight into how that world and those things must be organized so as to be available for self-object collaboration, on the basis of a fundamental conception of free activity as involving a world and things. As finite, material, living, needy beings, beings who are material and formed by materiality, we must take pains on behalf of materiality. We have to work in order to make the world a home for ourselves; we must satisfy the needs of our bodies; inwardness needs a world. We must answer to necessity, since the world does not offer itself to us in the form of immediate satisfaction. We must become thing, as the servant does, so as to work the world and satisfy our needs. But our way of "making the world" is to give it organization, to turn it into a life-sustaining environment, and so materiality will implicate us in historically shaped, human systems. Let us explore this dimension now. What is it, what are its terms, and how is it itself contextualized by other aspects of human life and the dimensions they project?

Hegel captures the idea of "objective spirit" in the aspects of external objectivity described here:

> The free will initially has these distinctions in it immediately: freedom is its *inner* determination and aim and it enters into relation with an *external* objectivity that it finds before it, an objectivity that splits up into the anthropological factor of particular needs, external things of nature which are for consciousness, and the relationship of single wills to single wills [*von einzelnen zu einzelnen Willen*], which are a self-consciousness of themselves in their diversity and particularity; this aspect makes up the external material for the embodiment of the will. (*PM/E* §483)

The free will is not simply itself—it has within it "immediately" this reference to external objectivity, which includes others. Freedom is always a matter of things, not just the will. Freedom is action, action is pairing, and every pairing is mediated by others. The piano is not my invention but bespeaks a history of human insight and labor, as does the rice I have for lunch and the bowl and fork, spoon, or chopsticks with which I eat it, and each comes along with myriad cultural meanings.

If the "free will" always has to do with things and nature and others, that means that it depends on things that are potentially recalcitrant and that do not necessarily cooperate. For freedom to exist, objects and nature and the wills of others need to somehow be organized. If free agency is always in, of, and with things, they have to somehow suit it, which means that they will be different from the way that it is. For objectivity to be a place for freedom, it has to be predictable; its pieces have to fit together; they have to operate in an anticipatable way. Objectivity becomes a place or a house for freedom by being stable and regulated. Freedom requires houses, money, streets, traffic regulations, food, and systems of food distribution, and while the free will is initiative, perspective, they are not; they are recalcitrant and passive. Somehow this recalcitrance and passivity must be channeled for freedom, rather than standing against it (see Saner [2025]).

This is why Hegel writes, "freedom, shaped into the actuality of a world, acquires the *form of necessity*" (PM/E §484). One makes recalcitrant and passive things and other people into a place or home for freedom by organizing them in such a way that they are available and predictable, by opposing their capacity for oppositional force and channeling their capacity for collaborative force. At the level of objects, this will happen through their induction into systems of production and regulation. At the level of people, it will happen in terms of the regulation of behavior. One cannot do just anything in shared space, for instance, but must behave in such a way that allows for the presence of others in that space: One may be able to dance on the sidewalk, for instance, but one should not block the sidewalk. The human is free in a different way in which the world becomes a place for freedom. Freedom is unpredictable; objectivity becomes a place for it by being stable, regulated, and predictable: Red light means stop, period. It will just not work to switch the meaning of the red and green lights at whim; it will not work to switch the street and the sidewalk.

With this regularity or predictability must come a kind of coherence; things have to hang together. The water system has to be compatible with the sewage system, so that each can operate in the way that it is supposed to, and they must fit and be consistent with food production and food distribution—alive, so to speak, to each other's demands. The pieces of external life have to be connected with each other and fit into a more or less coherent system.

This can all seem very different from the self as perspective. For it to be supported in its freedom is for it to be allowed to be unpredictable, creative, and new, to turn aside from any specific thing it has done and go in a different direction; it is recognition of the will's "element of *pure indeterminacy*" in which any limitation can be dissolved (*PR/GPR* §5), or of the moment of "transcendence" in the existential sense (de Beauvoir 1976, 2009; Sartre 2018). For objectivity to be a place for a being capable of transcendence, transformation, and expression is for objectivity to be regular. We should notice that there are two further points that emerge here, on the basis of this relationship between freedom and necessity.

First, and most briefly, the capacity for transcendence on the part of perspective may at times illuminate about objectivity that it is not adequate and must be different. Objectivity must have therefore a further characteristic in order to be a place for freedom: It has to be open to being transformed by the being capable of transcendence. The institutions of objectivity must therefore contain stable mechanisms allowing for transformation of objectivity.

A second point to notice here, in the fact that freedom is dynamism of perspective sheltered by the regularity of objectivity, is that a significant part of this objectivity is actually subjectivity, but that of others. We operate differently in relation to ourselves and others: for ourselves, as free perspective, and for others, as difference that appears in their perspectives. There are, further, two different ways in which we operate as difference for the perspectives of others: first, as materially relevant, and second, as perspectivally relevant—or, to borrow the evocative language Sartre uses, as "eye" and as "look" (2018, 354). Each of these operates in a limiting and an expanding way. Materially, we take up space, get in the way of others, use resources that they also like to use, and can turn externality into a hostile force mobilized against others. In that sense we operate as a kind of material limit for each other. But it is more noteworthy how much we enrich each other's experience by producing goods and interacting with materiality in productive ways, thus expanding their material reality; without the engagement of others with materiality we would find the world a wasteland. Perspectivally, we are vulnerable to other perspectives as well, as we have explored already in the discussion of recognition. To be a perspective is to be open to the influence of the regard of others, or the lack of it. Others are an externality that has internal effect, debilitating or building our capacity to take up reality and ourselves productively. The circulation of hatred and disgust or love and respect cultivates beings who bring that interpersonal dynamic to interaction with others. Further, however, materiality and perspective are also muddled together, since the perspectives of others are not simply perspectival but operate inside of and as materiality: Another's learning and insight takes the form, for instance, of a developed object, and I interact with that object, not specifically with the other, and develop on the basis of that interaction. The influence of the perspectives of others upon our own perspectives is typically materially mediated.

Far from being something I exercise on my own in abstraction from others, freedom is meaningful and rich insofar as I have the existence and action of others, expressed both perspectivally and materially, as the basis, source, and resource for my own existence and action. Thus Hegel derides what he takes to be the fact that "nothing has become more common than the idea that each of us must restrict our freedom in relation to the freedom of others, and the state is the condition in which this reciprocal condition occurs, and the laws are the restrictions. In ideas of this sort freedom is conceived only as contingent preference and wilfulness" (*PM/E* §539R).

Insofar as we are other to others—insofar as for others we take the form of potentially recalcitrant and potentially supportive externality—we ourselves have to submit to the demand to regulate our behavior in relation to others. But again, the potential for another's freedom to interfere with ours, like the idea of objects as recalcitrant and nature as indifferent, is relatively superficial compared to the mutual cultivation. Things, as we said earlier, cultivate agency in us. It is through engagement with determinate objects that we develop. It is on the basis of the existence of nature and my existence as a natural being that I have life, and that the very possibility of nature as obstruction can arise. This is similarly true of others. The others who distributed this book, who made water appear in my apartment, who met my needs as a baby, who developed regulations governing the stability of buildings, who invented electricity and the wheel—all of these others are the well of my action and existence. I find myself inside of a world that is their handiwork, with initiative in myself that they cultivated, with possibilities they provided that I now call "mine." We also see here again the profound connection between "materiality" and "ideality": The stuff of the world is not simply inert, material, fixed, or finite; it is the trace of dynamic, living freedoms making the world suit their thoughts and desires and pursuit of meaning.

It is important to note here that a certain contingency is intrinsic to the external nature of freedom. Hegel writes that "the objective spirit is the absolute Idea, but it is only so *in itself*; since it is thus on the terrain of finitude, its actual rationality retains in it the aspect of external appearance" (*PM/E* §483). Freedom unfolds in finitude, and so its rationality has the aspect of "external appearance": I may satisfy my thirst with a glass of water, but I could drink another liquid or use a different container. While my freedom requires some one thing (I require a container, even if just my hand, and I require liquid), it could be this thing or that thing; I do not need this container and this liquid in particular. I might prefer water but accept lemonade; I may like the tall green glass but use the stout translucent glass. My green glass might break. The book I read in order to try to understand Hegel may be missing a few pages, so I may turn to a digital copy. That I have an object is necessary, but which object is typically not. The free will requires externality, stuff, and space, and interaction with specific others, but not these in particular. That there is a something—the structures and institutions of one's time, living under shelter, drinking fluids—is necessary. Specificity as such is necessary, without the specific something being so.

In this domain, in other words, the rational and the necessary never come apart from the contingent; there is always contingency at the heart of this kind of necessity. Freedom always has a kind of specificity as its expression; the individual operates always inside of a specific kind of domain or element. Freedom is concrete, never abstract, and so the determinacy of its existence requires a certain kind of care, but also the awareness that this determinacy need not absolutely be the way that it is. We must care for this determinacy in the sense that determinacy is necessary, but without necessarily exalting this specific version of it above all other forms.

Similarly, we must recognize that it is freedom that expresses itself in contingent determinacy, and thus that determinacy is not simply contingent but the expression of a freedom. An artwork, for instance, is not simply a thing, but a new meaning that stems from a specific insight on someone's part and the capacity to render materiality an expression of that insight. A plate of cookies is not typically just a matter of food, the determinate means for enjoyment or the satisfaction of need; it is also potentially an expression of care, manipulation, a desire for community, and so on.

To make specific things and people into a place or home for freedom in turn requires mechanisms that support our availability to each other, and our minimal awareness of how others and things work and of our interdependence and our dependence upon things. That is, freedom depends on organization and on recognition, as we have said, but also on our insight about it. If I am wrong about the character of externality, then my efforts to enact my freedom, which requires a coupling with it, will not be very effective. I may not understand that a glass needs to be free of holes in order to be effective as a vessel, and thus will be ineffective in my effort to drink. I may not understand that it is the efforts of other people that make my experience of artistic productions moving to me, and oppose their capacity to develop it, in which case I find my own free engagement with such productions jeopardized. For the single will to be actually free, to execute its intentions, it has to have insight into how things work. This is what Hegel means when he writes that "the unity of the rational will with the single will constitutes the simple actuality of freedom" (*PM/E* §485): We can live in the world effectively if we are more or less capable of grasping its sense.

But this is not just a matter of conforming to the way the world happens to be: By rational will, Hegel does not simply mean the will that has insight into what merely is, but the will that has insight into what makes sense and wills that. I can fit the way the world is, working for management in a publicly traded company that advances the interests of shareholders over workers and consumers, eliminating the competition, foreclosing the emergence of everyday entrepreneurship, and crushing unionization efforts, but a world that permits this is not a world that supports freedom, given the fact of interdependence. In other words, we could say that Hegel's infamous equating of the rational and the actual (*PR* 20/*GPR* 14) cannot be said to simply uphold existing forms of practical life, because they may suppress the real freedom of real beings; one of these "actualities" would have to make way for the other. In his editorial notes to the *Philosophy of Right*, Wood points to *EL/E* §6, in which Hegel notes that when the "ought" of the understanding

> is directed against trivial, superficial and transitory objects, arrangements, situations, and so forth..., then this understanding may indeed be right to find many things that are not in accord with universal and correct standards. Who would not have enough good sense to see much around him that is indeed not as it should be? But this cleverness is in the wrong when it fancies itself to have the interest of the philosophical science at heart with such objects and their "ought." Philosophical science deals solely with the idea which is not so impotent as to demand that it merely ought to be actual without being so and, hence, it deals with an actuality of which those objects, arrangements, situations, etc., are only the superficial exterior. (*EL/E* §6; *PR* 390)

The unity of the rational and single will is accomplished if the single will is educated about the world of its actualization and of the freedom of others, and actual possibilities for freedom will be richer the more freedom that understands itself properly operates in the world.

The general framework here is that it is proper to the human being that its world be organized for freedom, and that materiality needs to be and has been relatively intentionally shaped. This should draw our attention immediately to the question of how that world is built and organized, what kinds of activities it supports, and whether or not it is just in its support: Does it serve all bodies? Is it universal? There are many directions in which to go from here, including toward the issue of government, but let us first turn to a context in which the importance of fit and the problem of misfitting between human beings and their world is deeply felt: the issue of disability. I believe that here Hegel again provides interesting and valuable resources, most basically in terms of framing. I will not do this issue justice, but my aim is simply to show once more here how we could use Hegel both to reorient scholarship on Hegel and to emphasize the import and philosophical foundations of anti-ableist politics.

Canguilhem, Garland-Thomson, and Ableism

Hegel's notion of objective spirit underlines freedom's objective and worldly conditions; it is accomplished in space, things, practices, others, and institutions. These are humanly produced material systems, and they reflect the concerns of those human beings who have struggled to make, refine, and understand them. We have an organized, material world that has established systems for action and interaction, that supports specific kinds of activities (like driving, online shopping, and eating), and that has developed infrastructures and specific kinds of instituted relations in connection with those activities (for example, electrical grid, traffic regulations, boss, worker, consumer, service provider). Whether we can be free in that world depends on whether we can insert ourselves into its existing systems, whether our bodies can interact with it, and whether its systems suit our needs and our self-conceptions. Hegel's discussion of the servant, similarly, highlights the way in which pairing with the object and answering to its demands is the occasion for developing "a mind of one's own," and so, rather than simply subordinating it to our own ends, we develop by answering to the object, allowing it to "insist upon" itself.

Interaction with objects, with these systems, and with these relations, however, depends on whether we, in our bodily character, can approach and contact them; it depends on whether objects and systems, as well as the expectations that welcome us or not into the world, are suited to our bodies and their capacities. Hegel's analysis highlights the significance of what Garland-Thomson (2011) calls *"fit"*—between self and object, self and world, self and others—for human development. We see the importance of this fit in very basic ways: Learning how to walk is typically a matter of a particular operation of young legs upon flat, smooth, and unobstructed surfaces, and of the availability of caring hands that support the child and beckon to it. Learning to read is typically a matter of a particular kind of operation of the eye upon offered letters and paper appropriate to their sensitivity, a particular kind of operation of the fingers upon the material appropriate to them, and the care taken to bring this materiality and its meanings to the child. The development of agency requires this mélange of elements: a *care* that places the body in a *context* or brings *materiality* to the body, arranges that context and materiality to *suit* that body, and *communicates* meanings that guide it. These careful arrangements accomplish for that body a *fit* of materiality and body that supports the development of its capacities. That is, on the basis of this dynamic, interpersonal, and temporal "fitting," the body develops abilities.[7]

But the shape of the objective world, to which care helps accommodate us, has already been defined, historically and collectively; it preexists us. The shape it has, as Hegel tries to show, is due to the past of freedom, which means it is due to the exercise of a certain *kind* of care for the fit of certain *kinds* of bodies, the development of certain kinds of capacities, and the accomplishment of certain kinds of abilities. The human being has projected the demand to be accommodated. Hegel's interest is in the ongoing ways in which this demand makes itself known and reshapes the world to suit it: and in the context of increasing awareness of existent and nonexistent accommodations, of how freedom is manifested in materiality, we see freedom making new demands.

Disability is a phenomenon in which the lack of "fit" between world and body is manifest (Garland-Thomson 2011). Ability, conversely, is socially accomplished, as we have so far seen, by the world's accommodation and assistance; it is a product of fit between body and the shaped objective world. It is the result of ongoing, historically voiced demands that the world be organized to suit the body's capacities. We should notice that these demands have not always been voiced and have not always been effective, but their efficacy in the past, for some people, and the world's revision in response, is a testament to the answerability of the existing world to *all* such demands. By their very reshaping of the world to fit their freedom, "accommodated" human beings project a norm: that the world be reshaped to accommodate the "non-accommodated" as well.

The very powers of the bodies for whom fit has been accomplished, however, conceal the external conditions of that fit. We can turn again to Hegel's observations about the objective accomplishment of freedom and the way it conceals itself, as they fit well here:

> The more we reinforce freedom, as security of property, as the possibility of developing and exercising, etc., one's talents and good qualities, the more it appears *to become a matter of course*; then the consciousness and estimation of freedom especially turns towards the *subjective* sense of freedom.... But... this very freedom... only arises under conditions of objective freedom. (*PM/E* §539)

Because freedom is objective—because being at home and being ourselves depend on the world being constructed to be that home—the one who is at home is empowered to occupy herself with her own inward experience and to take herself to be independent. The very success of fit brings about its concealment: Rather than highlighted as an accomplishment, it recedes to the level of a "matter of course," leading the self to thematize its own terms and attribute to them its feeling of its own agency.

Disability may seem like it occurs in the discrete body of a disabled person, but it is a product, rather, of the historical construction of a world that has disdained the responsibility of fitting itself to the capacities of the bodies of the nondominant. Accomplished but disavowed "fit" lends itself to "ableism," which we could define in this way: It implies a division of the world into two types—those who fit the existing world and have thereby developed abilities are called "normal," and those who do not fit and thus have been disabled by the world are called "abnormal." It privileges the development of the body that the world has been built to accommodate and devalues the body that the world has not been built to accommodate.

In teaching, I sometimes ask students what their bodies are for them, what their bodies do, and they typically say things like this: "With my body I move from place to place. I communicate, I speak with others, with my body. I grab things with my body. Through my body I exist. I support my body's survival by feeding it. I get sensory information through my body and that allows me to engage with what is around me. My body perceives, and then my body acts in response to what it perceives. My body expresses care and love; it touches and speaks and cultivates relationships and meaningful contact with other people." Evident in all of these descriptions is the fact that the human body is a linking body; its basic "doing" is contact. It is never simply itself, discrete, separate from things, objects, others, and the world. It is not its own thing, lived in relation solely to the norms projected by its own discrete parts, but it is a pairing, a "being-with." It is lived in a way that is caught up in materiality, relations, cultural life, and meaning. The world outside of it—a world of objects, spaces, customary practices, and expectations—has a particular kind of shape and supports and calls for particular kinds of activities. The shape the world has and the activities it calls for shape the bodies that inhabit it, their capacities and powers. This means that bodies, oddly enough, *are not what they are*; they are defined by what extends far beyond their own physiological qualities.

De Beauvoir makes a similar point in "Biological Data," the powerful first chapter of *The Second Sex*. She begins her discussion of the biological body by exploring the experience of reproduction in bodies, in a broad range from the smallest, simplest of organisms to human organisms. But the human body also takes up its situation, and the human female's relation to the fact that the body has the capacity to participate in reproduction of the species, de Beauvoir says, is the most deeply alienated of such relations among all the female mammals: "In no other [animal] is the subordination of the organism to the reproductive function more imperious nor accepted with greater difficulty" (2009, 44). This "taking up" is always a social matter or a matter of meaning: De Beauvoir argues that the human female is what humanity has made of it. That is, a world that reduces women to reproductive and domestic roles, that produces cultural narratives encouraging girls to dream of one day being able to fulfill such roles, and that offers them little support in those roles and little support in evading reproduction: This kind of world will make female bodies into reproducing bodies. A world in which women and men were not opposed to each other and restricted to specific heterosexualized roles, in which inarticulate dominance was not presented as the developmental aim for boys and passive receptivity was not presented as the developmental aim for girls, but in which cultural narratives were framed around self-invention, in which technologies supported creativity and freedom regarding the possibilities nature "gives" and "withholds," and in which nature's possibilities were simultaneously respected: This world would make female bodies into many kinds of bodies. The world, in other words, has everything to do with the kinds of bodies that we have and with what activities of pairing with the world that they enact. The body is not simply itself but what it does with what is available to it; or, it is a result of its pairing with what it is not, such that it is always other than what it is considered discretely. What it is depends on the character of what it pairs with, and on the demands and expectations coming from the world with which it pairs.

Merleau-Ponty, one of the most astute observers of the nature of the body, notices that it is not an object like other objects, but "that by which there are objects" (2012, 94)—not "an object of the world but... our means of communication with it" (95). The body is not (simply) its physiological reality, is not simply the body considered from a biological point of view, because it immediately expands beyond itself into that with which it communicates. Further, the "it" with which it communicates will shape the communication: or, as Merleau-Ponty writes, it cannot simply be determined "if it is the look or the things that command" (1968, 133). The body takes shape around the existing world, in response to it; it does not precede that world's invocation of it. Through their thematization of the entanglement of materiality and objectivity with subjectivity, Hegel, de Beauvoir, and Merleau-Ponty challenge our sense of ourselves as subjects, of world as objectivity, and of things as objects. Given the ongoing pairing of selves, worlds, and things, we must resist the ordinary sense that they are fundamentally discrete. Experience shows us their mutual complicity, their entanglement with each other.

The objects, others, and world with which the body is in relation, however, have been established prior to its existence, as though on its behalf, not by it, such that its possibilities are dictated by past modes of inhabitation of the world. Freedom, as Hegel writes, is "shaped into the actuality of a world," where it "acquires the *form of necessity*" (*PM/E* §484). Our materiality implicates us in historically shaped, human systems. These potentially recalcitrant and passive things, these potentially hostile and potentially welcoming others, have been organized to make them available for certain kinds of collaborations with body.

In this context, it would be fundamentally inaccurate to insist that the measure and projection of what an organism can do lies simply in its own body discretely or biologically considered, and it would be wrong to deny that the shape of our lives is defined by how effective our bodies are as powers for linking with the world around them in the form of objects, others, situations, and spaces. Human beings have always been bodies in meaningful-material environments, and have always had to reckon with the issue of fit. As we discussed above in relation to Hegel's "Anthropology," the soul-body "is itself the posited totality of its *particular* world, so that this world is included in it, its fulfilment; in relating to this world it relates only to itself" (*PM/E* §403R). The soul-body converts the external into the internal, internalizing a world; its "who" is inseparable from that world. Lack of fit with that world makes of the body a "misfitting" body. Human history, which is a history of objectively supported freedom making ongoing demands of objectivity, is long and complex, and it has resulted in a complex, built world.

Further, however, while we are material and the condition of existence is interaction with things, whether and how our lives work is not determined by how effectively bodies "compete" with each other at the level of pure physiology or the body objectively considered, because the world is not merely material, and objects and bodies are never "merely objects." We are material, yet the materiality that we are is meaningful, is constructed to answer to what is "beyond" material; materiality and meaning never come separately in human existence. And the material world is already not simply material but meaning-bearing.

The measure of what an organism can do comes not simply from it and the idea of a telos projected by it or its parts considered discretely, but from the historically shaped construction of an amalgamation of care, materiality, and bodies, which makes possible different constructions of their amalgamation in the future. Experience is a matter of integration of body and world, body and objects, and these bodies live in and with determinate worlds and objects, with the capacity for adaptation and innovation that could take infinitely different directions.

If freedom is a matter of materiality, projection into a material-meaningful world, and engagement with that world, then engagement and projection must be able to occur for freedom to exist. If material bodies are always specific and not generic, then the accommodation that would allow for engagement and projection cannot simply take its lead from the idea of a generic body. If the "I can" of the body is not simply a matter of its own projection but of how the world is built to accommodate it through the activity of care, then we must be oriented toward the specific mode of adaptation among these three elements—world, care, and body—and not simply take our directives from what has been historically and prejudicially presented as a generic conception of the body or the world or care.

In his influential *The Normal and the Pathological*, Canguilhem observes, similarly, that experience is always going to be a matter of "qualified living beings" living among a world of "qualified objects and thus possible accidents," not a matter of living among laws: "The creature does not live among laws but among creatures and events that vary these laws, such that the bird is not held up by the law but by the branch and not the laws of elasticity" (1991, 197). He argues that health, normality, and pathology cannot be determined for the individual by means of a "supra-individual norm" (181) and that "the abnormal can be evaluated only in terms of a relationship," since the person "must always be judged in terms of the situation to which he is reacting and the instruments of action which the environment itself offers him" (188). A statistically obtained average does not allow us to decide whether an individual is normal (181). For beings who pair with their situation, the norm is open to being "transformed in its relation to individual conditions" (182). Canguilhem discerns here a definition of health that is appropriate to a being whose being it is to be in a situation, in a world: It is a matter of being adapted to the environment and its given demands but also, beyond adaptation, a matter of being versatile, capable of projecting new norms (200), tolerating infractions of the norm, and instituting new norms in new situations (197). This is a powerful expression of how—if we take seriously the specificity of material bodies and of their accommodation, and the fact that health is an expression of how a situation is inhabited and not simply of how a body "is"—health is a characteristic not of an organism but of an *adaptive relationship*. If accommodation is suited to the body, it can support what to the perspective of a nondisabled person might seem like an "atypical" definition of health, through an "atypical" version of accommodation and, inside of that accommodation, the empowerment of the body toward a versatility that is specific to its situation.

If health is a matter not simply of the body but of accommodation, relationship, and versatility within a situation, then, as Canguilhem argues, the pathological and the normal are not related to each other as points at the opposed ends of a shared trajectory, but occupy different trajectories entirely. The pathological "cannot be linearly deduced from the normal" (1991, 190) but entails "a new dimension of life" (186) that brings with it a new "normal." The pathological is pathological only according to the terms of the previous situation, not intrinsically, and we are led to re-envision its situation so as to allow it to project a new normal—or make available, through care, a new context for new behavior. If this is true, then "cure" as repair or restoration of the former condition—to follow Eli Clare's (2017), Garland-Thomson's (2011), and others' critique thereof—is ill-conceived. Rather than directed toward the idea of a retrievable past, we should think in terms of innovation and transformation. In Canguilhem's terms, we should take as our norm innovation rather than cure. What new dimension of life, projected by this new body, is possible? What new normality could be launched from this position? To what situation can *this* body adapt, and what situation could support in it a new versatility by which it could discern new norms? Or, as Sara Hendren asks, what can this body do here, in this space, with this ingenuity in design (2020)? What health can we accomplish as we are, not as generic but as qualified living beings existing among qualified objects? How can we redirect care and materiality to be responsive to the health of specific bodies, to cultivate our capacities for answerability to the specific situations our contemporary condition projects?

Ableism rests, it seems, on a fundamental disavowal of the role that the material-meaningful dimensions of externality play in developing the body's capacities and agency. Capacities and agency do not develop simply due to the body but because of the availability of a world to pair with, and thus depend on care for the conditions of pairing and on the cultivation of "qualified" objects. At the core of ableism is an abstract conception of agency, an insufficient sense of the body's dependence on the accommodation of it by the world and objects, and a dualistic separation of materiality and meaning. Ableism rests on a refusal to see that certain bodies, rather than being generically powerful in themselves, are generally assisted, both meaningfully and materially; the objective world is constituted to rise up to meet them, both in its ideal encouragement and in its material structures, aimed at their potential and their powers. The ableist world does not adequately see how objects and others' perspectives make people, as Hegel's reading of self-consciousness shows; how people need to be able to be in relation with objects and perspectives in order to become themselves; and that this pairing can take different forms. And these causal elements of materiality and meaning "crisscross" each other, as Young has shown (1980); encouragement has material effects. Just as the single being of civil society, while it may believe that it operates in terms of a fully independent pursuit of self-interest, is really entangled already in a materially and meaningfully organized world and must slot itself into this world's existing terms so as to support its single existence, so also can the able body believe in its independence even as it became such because the world was made to assist it. Again, "the more we reinforce freedom ... as the possibility of developing and exercising, etc., one's talents and good qualities, the more it appears *to become a matter of course*" (PM/E §539).

Oblivious to its own dependence and interdependence and seeing only its own strength, ableism implicitly allies human value with strength. In its disavowal of dependence on the objective world, the ableist world reflects a discomfort with dependence and interdependence. It is indeed unsurprising that ableism would come hand in hand with sexism and heterosexism, given the traditionally masculine degradation of the labor of care and the condition of vulnerability. The ableist world is also a world that sequesters vulnerability at home, building the world beyond the home to fit a profoundly assisted, falsely independent body. It disdains human multiplicity, the many possible body-world pairings that exist in potential, which means that even their protest is disabled, insofar as they are prevented by the world from taking up space, developing voice, and exercising opposition.

It is not capacity and development as such that are being challenged here, for human beings themselves express an orientation toward doing, which is a matter of expanding into the world, learning, and changing. What is being challenged is, first, the presupposition that there is a shared telos for such development across all bodies, implied in the telos of their parts and construed merely in terms of what they are as organisms considered discretely from the world of their pairing; and second, the disavowal of the way the world has been historically built to accommodate and assist bodies that have what are construed to be generic capacities.[8] The philosophical emphasis on materiality reminds us again of the significance of the concrete—this body, this capacity, this space—and the fact that our ideals are always of and for concrete bodies, which require determinate acts of caring. Thus we ask, what are the developmental capacities a body *does* have and project; what is the plasticity suitable to *it*; how can the world be brought *to it*? The body projects plasticity, versatility, development, and dynamic, potentially transformative engagement as a norm, but this is therefore not a norm of a particular kind, and the kind it is must be discerned through attention and caring perception. Speaking of development, growth, and accomplishment as though they could be measured by one trajectory having its origin in one kind of body in abstraction from a world—this, and not the idea of development as such, is the ableist culprit. Taking care to find out where, for specific bodies, the hinge between them and the world can be installed and fortified—this is the task for we who have inherited this objective world and its homogeneous approach to hinge construction. With this discussion of doing and its projection into the objective world, we are ready to turn to our final discussion on Hegel's conception of the state.

Hegel on Civil Society, State, Constitution, and Government

To launch this discussion of the state, we will first do two different things: turn briefly to the theme of counterfinality in Sartre, which puts in relief the need for the various institutions of civil society and for the state and its institutions, and then turn once more to the idea of civil society, to track how the mechanisms by which we engage in singular pursuits side by side themselves produce the demand for institutions that ensure our availability to each other and that themselves depend upon our awareness of the need for them. All of these ideas are particularly relevant for those of us who live in capitalist societies in which the argument for individual enterprise has led to the dismantling of the institutions, practices, and perspectives that are acquired required for the support of individual enterprise. As Michael J. Thompson argues, capitalism deforms the recognitive relations that make free, rational agency possible (Buchwalter 2015, 122).[9] I will not present a thoroughgoing critique of capitalism or an assessment of Hegel's relation thereto, but will try to show the rich phenomena that Hegel has available for such a discussion, regarding both how to frame the issue of the relationship between the political and the economic as well as what kind of institutions are required for their flourishing. We will show that, like ableism, capitalism rests on a denial of dependence, on the fact that whether the human being can exist and develop depends on whether its body has available to it a system organized in a particular way. Hegel and Sartre attend to the material, worldly conditions that need to be in place if we are really committed to the support of free, individual action. Both capitalism and ableism are disabling, and we need the world to be shaped differently to accommodate specific and specifically *human* beings.

SARTRE AND COUNTERFINALITY

Sartre claims that over the past four thousand years, "Chinese peasants" have been engaged in the activity of removing trees in order to plant crops, "appropriating arable land on the frontiers of their territory" (2004, 161). They act, as Sartre says, in response to what he calls the condition, structure, or relation of "scarcity"[10]—the fact that they do not immediately have what they need and must work to bring it about. Their action, for them, is that of cultivating land in order to live: the removal of an obstacle so as to enlarge the arable sector (162). This activity rebounds upon them, however, in a way that could not be identified as their action but is linked to it. Because many have engaged in this action and over a long period of time, the overall outcome is widespread, systematic deforestation, and the outcome of deforestation is flooding: "Since the loess of the mountains and peneplains is no longer retained by trees, it congests the rivers, raising them higher than the plains and bottling them up in their lower reaches, and forcing them to overflow their banks" (162).

This example is not being invoked for its scientific accuracy, nor with any conviction that Sartre's perspective is innocent of imperial arrogance. I believe it is nonetheless a powerful example for discussion of a particular point. As we have seen with Hegel, there is a kind of system on the other side of action that is not explicitly "done" by the action, grasped by its agent, or reflected in the intention lying behind it. In this example, Sartre shows that action is always action in a context to which it belongs and in which it resonates. Here we see in particular two clear, contextual phenomena emerging—two "trajectories of generality," so to speak—that lie implicit in the action of individual farmers: one related to the character of interiority (i.e., human thought) and the other to externality (matter).

First, according to Sartre, these farmers, on the basis of a shared capacity for thought and insight, are joined with each other in construing the trees as something to be removed for the sake of life. That is, these human beings are "organisms whose deep bonds of interiority cannot be masked by their dispersal" (2004, 122): Their dispersed, separate pursuit of individual life conceal a sharing at the level of interiority. Through their action they show themselves to be a group or a unit linked internally, by thought; their action is such that they turn themselves into a body or a collective through it. This is not something they do consciously or choose to do; it is simply produced by their shared capacity for thought. This activity is "carried on *elsewhere*: peasants *everywhere* must burn or uproot the scrub" (2004, 163) in order to farm and thus to exist.

Second, their individual action on *this* piece of matter turns into collective action on "the land as such." It is not simply the case that "I farm here" but that "we farm this area." Action is interaction with materiality ("signification takes on the character of materiality"), and as such it potentially "enters into relation with the entire universe" (2004, 161). In other words, materiality itself has a logic, operation, and extension, such that action does not stop or stop resonating where we want or intend it to. One eliminates these trees here, alongside others who are eliminating other trees elsewhere. Together, they are unintentionally enacting widespread deforestation, producing one deforested mass, which raises rivers and causes them to flood. The area is turned into one region that operates "in a flooded way." Even though a single farmer's action is not a force upon this one field, the materiality upon which they act *is* unified, and their actions thus become a unity: Their actions "are united by the matter they unify." *En masse*, they constitute themselves into one seal impressed upon one piece of wax, "just one seal impressed on just one land" (163), because the matter upon which they act is itself unified.

Sartre notes that this action turns both nature and socioeconomic conditions against the farmers. In working to mobilize nature for their survival, the farmers have inadvertently unleashed its force against them. Their actions' more or less unintended passage through each other and through materiality has the effect that these actions undermine the survival they were intended to accomplish. And flooding, while a "single danger" inspiring "universal solidarity," also "aggravates antagonisms"; "peasants" and "land-owners" jostle with each other to adjust to the new situation, which inevitably brings "renewed inequality" (2004, 164). The negative effects of this natural problem are exacerbated for some due to prevailing socioeconomic conditions.

"Counterfinality" is the term that Sartre gives to the effect produced by actions that undermine the possibility of action. In this case, a "counterfinality" would be the flooding produced by the farmers' actions. Action is not simply defined by actors, since the matter we act upon and in has its own mode of operation, and since our action unfolds alongside the action of others. What action is and means is determined by what happens when it goes into the world and mingles with materiality and others.

"In being realised, human ends define a field of counter-finality around themselves" (2004, 164). Action, in other words, is never really our own; this thing that we do is always also alien, because it is necessarily material, exterior, and happening with the action of others. We may insist that we define the meaning of our action, but that insistence means little in the face of materiality, a world, and others, and it can be fatal to action and to life when we do not perceive how the meaning of our action is defined. If our action is always material, exteriorized, and linked to the actions of others and to the world, then to act effectively, in a way that does not rebound destructively upon that very action, we must also somehow think *from the perspective of this externality*. What is the exteriority of my action; what is my action as it links up with the action of others; how does the whole operate; if I were looking at my action from that point of view, would I act differently? This is a profound challenge: to see beyond the thing we are explicitly doing to the web that absorbs the thing we are doing—a web that could be a counterfinality, opposed to our action. What are we inadvertently doing to ourselves when we act "freely"? What kind of forces are we mobilizing against ourselves?

Sartre's work here expresses in vivid color the point that Hegel's analysis of civil society also shows: There is a necessary perspective missing in individuals acting on their own behalf. Both Hegel and Sartre show the need for a perspective that would discern what it would take for free action to be sustained as such in its inevitable encounter with the world of materiality and the interiority of others. We can insist that we be able to act on our own terms, but insistence cannot actually make that happen if action has an inevitably material and a social character, which follows from, first, the unification of human beings in their capacity for thought, and second, the unification of matter. The demand for various kinds of discernment is projected here: a scientific discernment that would look at the operation of the matter that is unified through action; a theoretical discernment, like that of Sartre and Hegel and this work here, that would grapple with the nature of action; various kinds of political and economic discernment that would find a way of facilitating individual action so that it avoids the production of counterfinalities—discernment that one could imagine happening at a governmental level or in a labor union or Hegel's corporation, bodies that would have some insight regarding the larger context by which action is inevitably "interpreted."

I invoke Sartre's example here because it so clearly shows how free individual action itself projects, by virtue of the united forces it implicitly invokes, the need for a perspective that could never be simply individual, which is the matter of the self-organization of a "we." Let us turn now to Hegel's account of civil society, which includes duties of support for individual action; of the state and the constitution, as organized externality and responsive subjectivity that allows freedoms to resonate "within" each other and in the world; and of government, as the body tasked with being the perspective of the whole and sustaining it as such. We will not be able to sort out the rich details of Hegel's analyses—particularly given that it also requires exploring the political context that may have restricted what Hegel could say (see D'Hondt [1988])—but will remain, again, mostly at the level of framing. The point is to focus on the world projected by the material, thingly character of human existence, and to see through the material, external determinations of the world to the human agents who shaped it to suit their activity.

CIVIL SOCIETY

In the *Republic*, Socrates posits that the city comes into being because we are not self-sufficient but need much that we cannot acquire on our own (1968, 369b). Civil society also takes its justification from this, that we are material beings with material needs who pursue the satisfaction of those needs and can only do so with others: "The possibility of satisfying these needs is here situated in the social system, the general resources, from which all obtain their satisfaction" (*PM/E* §524). The existence of needs projects around itself a "system of needs." In other words, because the point of focus here is our own neediness, this mode of interaction is not explicitly oriented or committed to a "we," but the "we" is instrumental; it is "for" each I:

> The substance as spirit particularizes itself abstractly into many persons.... These persons have, in their consciousness and as their aim, not the absolute unity, but their own particularity and their own being-for-self, the system of atomism. In this way the substance becomes only a universal mediating interconnection of independent extremes and their particular interests. The internally developed totality of this interconnection is the state as civil society, or as *external state*. (§523)

Civil society is one mode of being a "we," the interconnection of human beings in their mode of having their own being as their aim, engaging in self-satisfaction and self-pursuit. But there is necessarily a "we" here: Self-pursuit is a matter of integration into a world that is organized in a particular way, with which we collaborate to meet our needs. One does not have the capacity to procure satisfaction of one's needs on one's own, but must integrate oneself into a system available for the satisfaction of need. Because a particular being has needs, its activity is "conditioned and mediated by the ever-renewed production of exchangeable means" that are produced by labor (*PM/E* §524). And satisfaction is mediated "by the labour of all," which essentially offers to individuals "the general resources" (§524). In order to meet our needs, we produce something through labor that will fit into this system of general resources. We essentially "become a *being* for *others*" because our satisfaction "is mutually conditioned" by each other's "needs and work." Needs and means come to have the quality of "abstraction" because the context in which they are met and developed is much vaster than they are: Rather than "isolated," they are "social" (*PR/GPR* §192).

On the one side, we see individual activity engaging in its own thing; on the other side, we see its dependence on all who do this or on the "general resources." This is key to what Hegel means when he says that "universality shines into the particularity of needs" (*PM/E* §525). My very needs project the existence of a system of organized means production, and my labor (partly inspired by need) reflects the character of that system. As needy beings, we cannot and do not engage in just any activity; the decision about what we will do to produce exchangeable means is itself made or guided by the operation of the whole. I must in some sense observe, interpret, and answer to the system of production already in existence. For instance, as a twenty-first-century person, if I am passionate about cars, it is unlikely that I will choose to build cars for a living and likely that I will take a different route: working in a factory with machines that build cars, becoming an engineer, generally adapting to the terms presented by the means of production in place. As a mechanic,

I would probably need to learn how to deal with computer systems and fix specific kinds of cars like Hondas and Kias; as a designer, I would likely build websites rather than design posters or storefronts; as a factory worker, my work would change after the invention of the assembly line. The activity demanded by the need to satisfy needs is a piece of an immensely complex, divided, and articulated system that extends far beyond both that activity and individual know-how. Because we have needs (or, as Sartre says, because we exist in a condition of "scarcity" [2004, 125]), we are more or less required to produce exchangeable means in response to existing technologies circulating in contemporary economic and social life, to labor in ways they determine, to answer to the division of labor, and to take into account the activity of others. Our materiality forces us to discern the character of this abstract, material "machine" and make ourselves a piece of it. What we do is not merely decided or chosen by us but "decided" and "chosen" by this machinic system; we must slot ourselves into it somehow. Thus the concealed side of this domain of apparently self-defined activity that Hegel aims to reveal is the determination of this activity by the contemporary state of production and technology and *its* priorities and mode of operation.

Further, as Hegel notes, the fact that "the intellect draws distinctions among needs... making the needs and the means ever more abstract" converts labor in turn "to restriction to *one* skill, and thus to a more unconditional dependence on the social system" (*PM/E* §526). The development of the system of production, the increasing sophistication of the division of labor by which a "we" as a whole becomes more productive and powerful, increases workers' dependence upon it and makes them less powerful as individuals. Think, for instance, of a factory worker who now shuttles metal to a machine instead of building a car, or a software engineer who writes code for Amazon. As labor becomes a smaller and smaller piece of a more and more complex system, the autonomy and power of major players in that system of production increases, our dependence upon the system of labor as it is presently organized becomes more severe, our vulnerability to changes in that system of labor becomes more extreme, and our importance as single parts of that complex machine and those in charge of it is minimized; skills are hardly transportable beyond the specific arrangement of labor that exists in a specific context, and workers have less power to make demands upon their employers.

Hegel names many vulnerabilities here. The process of abstraction and the intellect's capacity to break down processes of production into simpler parts makes workers more dependent upon the social system because it restricts their labor "to one skill," because it becomes possible to replace the labor of human beings with machines, and because it makes employers less dependent on them (*PM/E* §526; *PR/GPR* §198). Further, there is no limit in principle on the kinds of "needs," means, and pleasures we may develop, which Hegel calls a tendency toward "luxury" and which is accompanied by "an increase in dependence and want" (*PR/GPR* §195). Presumably the problem with luxury that Hegel has in mind here is that the desire for it necessarily requires wealth and thus encourages in some the desire to construct situations of advantage and exploitation and the capacity to suppress the sense of answerability to and solidarity with other human beings. Finally, whether we can participate in this system of need satisfaction depends on our basic skills, and Hegel remarks that the development of skills depends upon assets. Thus are we dependent in multiple ways on a system we cannot control, in which contingencies define our fate as participants and the nature and degree of our participation.

The development of modern civil society is based, for Hegel, on the historical emergence of the priority of individual self-determination. The productive and needy individual cannot, however, protect herself as such and ensure her own ongoing success, because the system in which she participates has its own logic and trajectory, and she does not define or control that system. As a perspective within the system, acting for the sake of itself as a piece of it, she is not a perspective *on* the whole as such. The system with its division of labor affects my activity, yet I cannot assume responsibility for it and my perspective is developed within it, not upon it. I must go through it to become myself.

The free pursuit of independent activity, however, amounts to nothing much if that existing system and division of labor imposes upon it a wretched existence, if it means that contingency takes over independent activity as its ruling principle, if the only option for independent activity is to accept the exigencies presented by a machine that disables independent activity. This is what Sartre means by the "practico-inert" (2004, 67): It is the result of human action, but its inertia potentially turns it into a force against human action.[11] The fact that our labor is linked with and dependent on the labor of others and on the logic of the system produced by that labor means that much can go wrong here for individuals engaged in self-pursuit: Their activity can result in counterfinality; the practico-inert world can become hostile to the specifically human. My apparently independent activity takes place within a system with its own logic, which needs to be perceived and understood for the sake of the humans within it. This is how the logic of civil society itself reveals the need for perspectives upon it—one a perspective that it has upon itself, and another associated with the state and government.

On its own terms, the self-interested action to which civil society is committed has the tendency to produce a practico-inert materiality that holds the human hostage, so to speak, making us the tool of it as tool, rather than vice versa, and threatening the very existence of materiality as the ground of action. Insofar as the human is material—made by objects and the economy, by material circumstances, by the demand that it slot itself into a system of material production and exchange—it faces the challenge of coexistence with materiality. The interdependence between objectivity and perspective can be underthought particularly in a world in which the "triumph" of individual subjectivity conceals its material conditions. Because civil society "tears the individual away from family ties, alienates the members of the family from one another, and recognizes them as self-sufficient persons," because "it substitutes its own soil for the external inorganic nature and paternal soil from which the individual gained his livelihood, and subjects the existence of the whole family itself to dependence on civil society and to contingency," it must take responsibility for the individual as a child "*of civil society*, which has as many claims upon him as he has rights in relation to it" (*PR/GPR* §238). As a "universal family," civil society has duties, partly because of the vulnerabilities it itself creates: "to supervise and influence the *education* of children" (§239), "to act as guardian on behalf of those who destroy the security of their own and their family's livelihood by their extravagance" (§240), to address the wrong of poverty (§241). Because civil society is actually a system, and not simply individuals side by side, to serve its own ends it must produce its own way of mitigating these problems: law and the administration of justice, the police, and the corporation. They are the institutions that follow from civil society's own commitment to individual pursuits. Law and the courts protect against the infringement of individuals by each other; the police protect against contingency; and corporations protect against alienation and the degradation of human beings associated with it—degradation either through poverty or greed.

The institutions of civil society—the administration of justice, the police, and the corporations—are addressed to the human being as an individual, which will differentiate them from the institutions of the state, which are different in spirit. We will not talk about the administration of justice at any length here, because my point of focus is the vulnerability we encounter not in relation to conflicts with others and bad human behavior, but in relation to the economic system, in which context the police and corporations are relevant.

The function that Hegel allots to the police is different from what most people now think of as the work of the police. In Hegel's conception, the police is more like a public authority that protects against the contingent things that could happen to us that would put us in need of welfare and support, the possibility that we can be harmed by noncriminal actions of others and by the interpersonal, intermaterial system, so it takes care of us if we get in trouble and arranges for the provision of common goods, providing public utilities and ensuring the fulfillment of tasks necessary to maintenance of the system. It responds to the fact that industry is "dependent on external circumstances and remote combinations whose full implications cannot be grasped by the individuals who are tied to these spheres by their occupation" (*PR/GPR* §236). Civil society brings with it certain problems—increase in dependence and want, departure from the families that might otherwise be networks of support—and in its responsibility as a "universal family" (§239) it must address and ameliorate these problems.

A second institution here that is important from the point of view of taking care of the vulnerabilities that ensue from the operation of civil society, in which people pursue their own interests in ways that have the potential to become a counterfinality and turn back against their interest, is the corporation, discussed earlier in the context of ethical life. The corporation is the grouping together of people who engage in similar kinds of industry.

Since freedom projects its conditions, genuine freedom would entail, in Hegel's perspective, that free people involved in a shared form of industry would become members of a corporation. Hegel remarks that it is mostly the activity of trade and industry—the commercial estate, let's say—to which the corporation is especially suited (*PR/GPR* §250). Membership is based on the particular kind of skill that one has, as well as on "rectitude." Again, Hegel uses the metaphor of family, calling the corporation the "second family," and even says that the "first" family has its basis in the corporation, insofar as the corporation grants livelihood *and* recognition (§252).

The corporation is particularly interesting because it operates at two different levels: It protects against practical vulnerability but also against a kind of moral vulnerability. The corporation protects against practical vulnerability by supporting the development of expertise in its members and ensuring that the industry to which it is dedicated functions more or less smoothly in relation to material exigencies such as supply and demand and to the knowledge required for industry. It is civil society's own "internal regulative praxis," as Kohei Saito notes, fostering education and living dependence rather than an "abstract relation mediated by money" (Buchwalter 2015, 46, 48). But it plays an equally important role at the level of self-esteem and dignity. Membership in the corporation is membership in a group in which one is recognized for one's skill. We desire to have the worth of our activity affirmed, Hegel thinks, and without membership in the corporation, individuals will engage in a kind of endless seeking after affirmation from the external world gained mostly by "external manifestations of success," which are "without limit" (making a lot of money, living a way of life that manifests superiority over others, etc.) (*PR/GPR* §253R). The recognition provided by the corporation stands in the way of acquisition of recognition through external signs. With this, Hegel identifies what he sees to be at the heart of runaway possessive individualism—namely, a desire for recognition. In this way, the corporation indirectly addresses the issue of vulnerability particularly associated with the motivation toward luxury. Given the individual's care for this limited, determinate universal, wealth loses the power it otherwise has to provoke arrogance in its owner and envy in those without it (§253). The corporation expresses the fundamental reality of recognition at the economic level, reflecting, as Lisa Herzog argues, the fact that habits, preferences, and consumption patterns are not simply fixed but shaped by these social contexts (Buchwalter 2015, 154), and that this acknowledgment is an integral part of supporting satisfaction in labor—satisfaction that limits pursuit of external manifestations of success.

In addition to preventing economic conditions that would produce poverty, the corporation ameliorates the feeling that is associated with poverty, insofar as it takes away its humiliation. Any given individual could become vulnerable at any time, due perhaps to a poor business decision, unanticipated expenses, material exigencies, and unpredictable external factors of whatever form, and in providing recognition of the individual on the basis of their skill and rectitude, the corporation combats humiliation, coming to the aid of the individual and downplaying the shame of receiving aid. It combats this humiliation both practically by supporting them materially and psychologically by having already accorded them recognition for being competent in their domain.

Finally, the corporation opens the individual to an educative and transformative experience that resonates more broadly in social life in general. Simply by virtue of membership in this corporation, the individual's self-interested activity is inducted into a more universal context; it is brought in direct relation to concerns that exceed it. Thus Hegel calls the family and the corporation the first and second ethical roots of the state; in the corporation, "the moments of subjective particularity and objective universality are inevitably united"; "particular welfare is present as a right" (*PR/GPR* §255). Experiencing this belonging and this contextualization of one's activity in a greater whole will resonate with how Hegel describes the experience of belonging to a state (a parallel that is mentioned in an Addition).[12] "It is within the sphere of [her] corporation, community, etc. that the individual first attains [her] actual and living determination for the *universal*" (§308R).

The corporation gives individuals greater power in defining the scope of their work and the nature of their industry. It takes care of the vulnerability that we have as people who, because we do not necessarily have a perspective on the meaning of our action, and because we do not have insight into the entirety of the material and economic system and the thought of others, can produce counterfinality. Joining with others who are involved in the same sphere affords greater insight into the world that extends beyond that domain of activity and into how to operate in that domain of free activity in a way that is informed by reality. As Robert Pippin describes Hegel's ultimate conclusions here, "what is now not viable in Hegelian terms is a form of capitalism that works actively to suppress and distort what the requirements of labor, production and trade should have taught us: the depth of a mutual dependence that ought to be reflected in institutionalized forms of mutual respect and solidarity" (2020).

As we will see later in discussion of the state, expertise at the level of everyday activity is also respected in and relevant to government; it is allotted participation in legislative power. Noticing the significance of governmental connection with and accountability to *labor*, Hegel draws members of the legislature from the substantial, particular, and universal estates: from groups distinguished in terms of their industrious activity—farming, business and manufacturing, the civil service. Here Hegel is saying that freedom requires giving governmental voice to human beings in their character as active and as having dedicated their activity to become discerning experts in the domains in which they labor. In this way also do the corporations implicitly have a stake in how a society is structured and governed.

The corporation organizes labor, facilitates recognition of human activity and prevents the growth of luxury, and strips from poverty its contingent and unjustly humiliating character. Insofar as it opposes the acquisition of great wealth, it protects against the inequality that the tendency toward luxury tends to produce. The police redress contingent material factors and circumstances based on external conditions that may reduce individuals to poverty. Civil society in general, in outstripping the family, takes on its responsibilities for caring for individual people, particularly those impoverished by the structures of civil society, both with regard to their practical and their emotional and psychological needs (*PR/GPR* §§241–42). And the legislature is composed of representatives of the estates, which are organized in terms, again, of labor.

Butler notes that a political vision structured to answer to human interdependence, as Hegel's is, would oppose all forms of economic exploitation (2021, 51). Harris has argued that this arrangement would in fact preclude capitalist accumulation, significant economic inequality, and marketed labor (1983, 68). He presents several compelling observations about this structure: first, that it would have resolved "class" conflict, via the estates, even "before the political process can properly begin" (1983, 58); second, it would be "a world in which labor power itself would no longer be marketed" (66); and third, it involves a notion of freedom that "logically requires that every function in the economy should be *self*-governing," which means that "every effective member in the community is a *proprietor*" (69). It should be noted also that for Hegel it is a *right* and not a preference to be protected against poverty: "The right which is *actual in particularity* means not only that *contingencies* which interfere with this or that end should be *cancelled* and that the *undisturbed security* of *persons* and *property* should be guaranteed, but also that the subsistence and welfare of single individuals should be *secured*—i.e. that *particular welfare* should be *treated as a right* and duly actualized" (*PR/GPR* §230).

With the exception of the estates, the above mechanisms are all mechanisms of civil society, the body dedicated to the support of free individual action—that is, Hegel's vision of what it would look like and how we would fashion it if we and it were in fact committed to individual freedom. But there is more—another domain of mechanisms, institutions, and living together that is the actual state—because the external state is not adequate to human freedom. That is, the priority of individual freedom is not all there is, given our status as beings of recognition and ethical life; rather, an independent value accords to membership and the domain of which we are members.

THE STATE AND THE CONSTITUTION

I believe it is helpful to begin with Hegel's framing comments in the preface to the *Philosophy of Right* in order to understand his sense of what the state is and requires. There (in the disdainful tone he seems to sometimes allow himself when setting the stage for thought) he criticizes those who think that they can and should "invent and propound *yet another theory*" of the state, and those who "*think* and look for their freedom and the basis of ethics in thought." He characterizes them as imagining that their thought is free to "the extent to which it *diverges from what is universally acknowledged and valid* and manages to invent something *particular* for itself." They imply, he notes, "that no state or constitution had ever previously existed or were in existence today, but that we had *now*... to start right from the beginning, and that the ethical world had been waiting only for such intellectual constructions, discoveries, and proofs as are *now* available" (*PR* 12/*GPR* 8).

Because of the attention paid to ethical life in the above, we should know already why it is a problem to think one is especially insightful, as an individual independent of "what is": We live on the basis of what others have done, our own thinking produced and mobilized by what the world has managed to accomplish; our individual accomplishments are actually joint accomplishments—products of our jointure with history, nature, the world, and others. We can refer again to de Beauvoir and the contradiction we implicate ourselves in if we do not see the accomplishments of past freedoms as the condition of our own:

> I would distrust a humanism which was too indifferent to the efforts of the [people] of former times; if the disclosure of being achieved by our ancestors does not at all move us, why be so interested in that which is taking place today; why wish so ardently for future realizations?... If the world behind us were bare, we would hardly be able to see anything before us but an empty desert. (1976, 92–93)

Hegel perceives, in determinacy, the freedom that has made it, the ideality in the inert. Determinacy has already been made by and for freedom: "Spirit is objective and actual to itself not only as this necessity... but also as the *ideality* and inner dimension of this necessity" (*PR/GPR* §266). The reason we can develop a glorified sense of our own insight is because of what the insights of others have done in the actual world over time. This is not to say that all of the characteristics of existing worlds are the result of freedom fighting for itself, as we will explore in short order, but to say that we should *go through the existing world in order to learn what to look for*, in order to find our criteria, and that if all that freedom amounts to is the private functioning of inward subjectivity, it is not very substantial. In that spirit, Hegel castigates that "vainglorious," "superficial," "bad conscience" (16/10) that "identifies right with subjective conviction" and feels "the form of right as a duty and a law... to be a dead, cold letter and a shackle" (17/11); we require the determinate articulation of existing reality for the actual, determinate existence of freedom. Finally, one of the major things we notice if we turn to the accomplishments of the existing world is the fact that it has, over time, discerned the freedom of *all* rather than of some or one (*WH* 88). Thinking, in its embedded fashion, is now empowered to begin here, rather than argue to it.

The basic, historically accomplished recognition that all are free has given itself expression, Hegel notes, in law's *universality*; it is for all. In the following, he says that the form of rationality is both universality and determinacy: "Right and ethics, and the actual world of the right and the ethical ... give themselves the form of rationality—namely universality and determinacy—by means of thoughts," and this "is what constitutes *the law*" (*PR* 17/*GPR* 11). Focusing first on the idea that rationality is expressed in the fact that right and the actual world of right are "universal," the rule of law takes shape in and as the constitution, which is "the organization of the state and the process of its organic life *with reference to itself*, in which it differentiates its moments within itself and develops them to *established existence*" (§271). These constitutional forms have taken shape historically; they are existing political worlds that have taken the freedom of all to require the rule of law. Freedom as the rule of law shows its value, for instance, when we see democratically elected governments working to undermine it. In this vein Houlgate notes that the stability of a constitution can be better at protecting freedom than is democracy, which can tyrannize the minority (2024).[13] In Hegel, freedom must become *mundane*, or so I would argue: It exists with the support of a bureaucratic apparatus with the task of upholding the constitution that stabilizes its home and protects its everyday excursions out into the world with others, a constitution that tends to be relatively immune to political ebbs and flows and to whatever more or less democratically elected government comes to power.

In addition to universality, however, Hegel notes that "the form of rationality" is also *determinacy*. Insight regarding the freedom of all is expressed in action, in actuality; rationality is a phenomenon of the world, inscribing itself there, making itself determinate. Again (to return to Hegel's critique of the French Revolution), universality is genuinely fulfilled only in specificity: Because of our equality under law and our "differences under nature," for instance, different pieces of the world will need to be available to us in different ways if equality is to be respected (*PM/E* §539R).

Hegel notes that the "rational will" (which we should simply understand to mean something like "the will that understands the needs of freedom that we have articulated," or even just "the character of freedom") is both posited *and* found; in short, it is both constitution and constitutional government. The constitution, the "overall articulation of *state-power*," contains "the determinations by which the rational will... on the one hand comes to consciousness and understanding of itself and is *found*, and on the other hand is posited in actuality and therein maintained through the effectiveness of government and its particular branches, and protected just as much against the contingent subjectivity of government as against that of individuals" (*PM/E* §539).[14] This means both that the modern free state lives out of the historical inheritance of insight into freedom, but also that it needs to be sustained as such. We would have little guidance for what to posit if it did not in some partial way already exist, as the earlier discussion of ethical life should have made clear. The constitution is found, not made; we inherit and always already inhabit a more or less organized world that does a better or worse job supporting and mobilizing genuinely free human possibilities, and our own expectations are generated by it. Freedom is found in its regulations governing public space, building and development, property, contracts, the environment, arts funding, research funding, care for dependents, health, citizenship, agriculture, national borders, employment, industry, trade, labor, transportation, and revenue. *These are the state in its existence*. As Hegel says, "the truth concerning right, ethics, and the state is at any rate as old as its exposition and promulgation in public laws and in public morality and religion" (*PR* 11/*GPR* 7). It is already there, so to speak—we already live within a constitution, an articulation of external reality that has been accomplished by more or less by free beings. If we do not see freedom here, in the mechanisms of organization, we do not know what it is. Freedom is mundane, in both senses of the word: It is *of* the existing world, and it requires the relatively underwhelming articulation enacted by civil servants and bureaucratic systems and regulations. Government, then (which we will thematize below), would sustain the rational will in time, bringing the accomplishments of freedom into the future by grappling with emergent situations and the needs of freedom, because it is also in the character of human reality to continually produce unprecedented situations.

This is the objective side of freedom—the organized external world is "objective substantiality"—but there is also a "subjective substantiality" to freedom (*PR/GPR* §267). Freedom depends on a world that houses action but also a human being that acts in freedom. Regarding the subjective side, Hegel writes:

> *Concrete freedom* requires that personal singularity [*Einzelheit*] and its particular interests should reach their full development and gain

recognition of their right for itself (within the system of the family and civil society), and also that they should, on the one hand, *pass over* of their own accord into the interest of the universal, and on the other, knowingly and willingly acknowledge this universal interest even as their own *substantial spirit*, and *actively pursue it* as their *ultimate end*. The effect of this is that the universal does not attain validity or fulfilment without the interest, knowledge, and volition of the particular, and that individuals do not live as private persons merely for these particular interests without at the same time directing their will to a universal end and acting in conscious awareness of this end (§260).

The ongoing positing of freedom depends on people understanding and valuing it, not leaving them as they contingently happen to be. We cannot effectively develop or pursue particular, private interests if we are not generally aware and supportive of this universal end. This is where freedom gets complicated, because fostering it can look like disrespecting it. But we engage in freedom-respecting methods of freedom cultivation all the time (in education, in the fostering of associations that allow us to experience the good of membership, etc.), and (as we have already noted) Hegel observes that the very flourishing of this free world poses a danger that we will not recognize that our subjective freedom has objective conditions (*PM/E* §539). The better our societies are at circulating goods, empowering us, and giving us access to the riches and wealth of history, the less likely it may be that we can see that. As in the regulation of traffic, for instance, the effectiveness of regulation and of cultivated cooperation allows us to imagine that we are simply doing our own thing, and we do not have to notice others or the system of regulation. The fact that we are actually benefiting from a system is concealed in its effective operation.

Hegel calls the awareness that supports the existence of the state "patriotism" or "the political disposition" (*PR/GPR* §268). I will use the term "political disposition" rather than "patriotism," given the prevalent negative associations many may rightly have with the latter, used as it tends to be in the name of chauvinism and xenophobia. As Hegel observes, rationality is present in the institutions within the state, and the individual's habitual volition and political disposition are a consequence of these institutions (§268). Institutions precede the emergence of this volition and this disposition; who we are and how we act is indebted to them. This facilitates a disposition of trust (see Houlgate [2016]), which "habitually knows that the community is the substantial basis and end," but it also has to be grounded in "objective reality" (§268). If the political disposition exists and is justified by objective reality, then "this other immediately ceases to be an other for me"; I am conscious "that my substantial and particular interest is preserved and contained in the interest and end of an other (here, the state), and in the latter's relation to me as a single individual" (§268). Whether we will recognize or fight the determinations of freedom depends on whether we are educated into an awareness of how they function or into a denial of their significance; whether we can look under the surface of free subjectivity and see its conditions; whether we respect the freedom of others and their historical accomplishments; whether we understand that institutions, even though they are determinate, concrete, recalcitrant, and slow to move, have typically been constituted as they are through long, historical dialogue with free human beings—and indeed, in their very recalcitrance, are capable of weathering storms that can occasionally be caused by "the contingent subjectivity of government... and of individuals" (*PM/E* §539); and whether we do the political work we do with an awareness of the import of institutions, even in opposition to any actual, corrupt version of them. We foster the political disposition particularly through education and through the cultivation of interpersonal, communicative contexts in which we experience the goods of membership.

Of course, it is not always the case that the determinate world actually reflects the universality of freedom, that whatever happens to be is right and just, and that thinking beings need only accept the existing world. Hegel says that "the truth concerning *right, ethics, and the state*... needs... to be *comprehended* as well.... For such thinking does not stop at what is given, ... but starts out from itself and thereby demands to know itself as united in its innermost being with the truth" (*PR* 11/*GPR* 7). But one does not make much headway as a thinker if one does not live in terms of and notice what other thinking human beings have done; here we should remember the temptations of the self-aggrandizing moral stance. Civil rights legislation, universal public education, universal health care, safety regulations, and so on: These are accomplishments by which we can see that other free beings have effected something substantial in history, indirectly telling us what is needed by having struggled to make the world accommodate it. To initiate philosophical thinking in oneself requires discernment of the institutions of the actual world, noticing what freedom has made of itself. Freedom is not just that of the people of the present, but an accomplishment of the human beings of history and manifest in determinacy. Freedom, again, is mundane and determinate.

It is only in being *informed* by the actual world that such comprehension has a chance of being equipped to see, presumably, when irrationality has appropriated pieces of the public world and mobilized them for its own ends—that is, when there is a transgression of either the universal or the determinate aspects of rationality. We return again here to a point rehearsed in the context of ethical life: It is not the case that all things that unfold in the world are right and proper, but meaningful critical engagement can occur only on the basis of insight into freedom as a matter of objective and subjective substantiality, and only on the basis of understanding how it has made itself actual in the determinate materiality in which we live. If one does not perceive the ideal in the necessary—the existence of regulations governing space, for instance, as the condition of free movement—then one could hardly effectively discern between the oppressive and liberatory mobilization of materiality. If one does not perceive the need for determinacy and all of the ways in which the world is organized to care for different needs, then one could not easily perceive when formal universality is illegitimately mobilized to work against the actual accomplishment of universality: when, for instance, the ideal of equality is used to oppose the work that would actually accomplish it. If one does not perceive the demand for universality and how the determinate institutions of practical life accomplish it, then one could not easily see how determinacy is mobilized to undermine universality, as when particular powers appropriate the powers of interpersonal reality for their own private ends.

In fact, the simple coexistence of determinacy and universality lends itself well to the project of exposing injustice when it occurs. In the French Revolution, for instance, and in many expressions of liberal universalism, we can see the moment of determinacy underrecognized: As we have seen, Hegel's discussions of conscience and ethical life can be mobilized to critique the indeterminacy of universalism. There is also the possibility of an infidelity to universality, which is what we see when policies and institutions act on the basis of the presumption that not everyone is free, that not everyone deserves access to the external world and development of their internality. When we see determinacy or universality disrespected, we are seeing irrationality and injustice.

The proper character of the state is revealed historically by actually existing freedom manifesting itself and its demands, but this does not mean that any actual state is doing it well, and indeed, the state Hegel offers as a model is not the same as any actually existing state. As we have been emphasizing so far, our thinking about the state is historically mediated and accomplished, but the lessons of history also mean little if we do not recognize that *they empower critical orientations toward the existing world*. The structure here is similar to the relation between Athens and Socrates: it was precisely as a powerful, free culture that Athens could produce such a creature, but this was someone who would in turn bring his resources to bear critically upon it. Thinking, again, is both embedded and transcending. On the one hand, we have the existing, organized world that philosophy must probe in order to begin, and, on the other, we have the bodies of freedom that our character as free beings requires, that the existing world has discerned over time, and that could very well be opposed by the existing world.

These bodies of freedom are basically embedded in the structures and institutions Hegel has rehearsed: family, civil society, and state, with all of their articulated parts. Here he is simply arguing that we should recognize that we require interpersonal worlds in order to become and be ourselves—family and civil society—and that we require a place for ourselves as singular beings. And yet, second, the state "brings back both of them, the family and civil society, and the whole disposition and activity of the single individual—whose tendency is to become a centre for himself—into the life of the universal substance" (*PM/E* §537). It does this insofar as it offers something beyond them that we also require; it "apprehends and activates the universal aims of the whole which stand above the determination of the family and of civil society" (§541). That is, the state is that which is demanded, by the nature of freedom in its self-accomplishing reality, to be the organized, external reality in which the independent pursuits of others are made to resonate inside of our own. It is the preceding "living with" that generates resources and ourselves as individual agents and that facilitates the mutual resonating of freedom. If we look closely at our own activity, we do not see simply ourselves in it, but rather our social reality and all its power and capacity to sustain our singular action and to give it content. The state is a unity, like the family, but one that has "the form of conscious universality" (§535). Membership in a state registers the way our lives are conditioned and enriched by living together, and in it external reality is organized so as to facilitate interaction, participation, and membership. Because of this organized world, our lives can be meaningful and have significant content; the freedom of others can come to be operative within us, as our freedom; the mechanics of the outside world can allow us to make our way in it. In other words, the correct conception of freedom is one that allows one to "find one's way in actuality" (§539), not one that makes that impossible or is grounded in a fundamental opposition to actuality, and the best actuality for us is the one in which others are free and self-comprehending about the character of their freedom. Not simply their own business, or what people do away from us, the freedom of others resonates within our experience. It is for each and all of us.

This is a concrete universality: not just something of which we take a piece for ourselves, but the way that another's piece is also our own. We are not simply identical units existing alongside each other, to which the universal applies equally and indifferently; we are "inside of" each other, and the external world is inside of us, in and through the state, construed in ways that are consistent with the genuinely interpersonal character of freedom. This state would be the home of shared experience and freedom, of sustained practices of interaction, of experiences of resonance, of the transmission and sustenance of human goods over time. These are goods that increase when shared. This state would sustain communication, circulation, welfare, the sharing of goods, creativity, meaning, activity, and employment, making of our proximity mutual empowerment. Rather than restrictions, the laws would be the scaffolding, the mechanisms by which this circulation and empowerment are sustained. It is in this state that we would be near to each other, that we could become learned, insightful, and communicative in a way that supports the activities of absolute spirit, by which any existing state inevitably emerges from being the condition of our reflection into its object.

Yes, our proximity to each other also entails vulnerability, as we explored already in the chapter on recognition, particularly in relation to Fanon, and partly in our discussion of civil society. Civil society, the "external state," has mechanisms for protection, with its administration of justice, the police, and corporations. It is as though civil society were the "I" and the state were the "we," though each of course is a collective arrangement: civil society is the "we" oriented to the effective assertion and consolidation of the I and the state is the "we" oriented to care for the "we-world" that is the I's generative source. The state is ultimately the recognition that freedom always has a history, a past from which it has already inherited itself as desiring and imagining, and that it always has an external world in which it must make itself. Freedom requires an actuality that it can navigate. The constitution of a state is "the organization of [the] actualization" of freedoms (*PM/E* §539R).

GOVERNMENT

Now, government is the collective unity tasked with maintenance of the state, which means it must be the perspective of the state upon itself. The first point to make about government is a negative point, that it is fundamentally circumscribed by or embedded in the constitution or constitutional law. Government as Hegel describes it is

> the living totality, the preservation, i.e. the continual production of the state in general and of its constitution.... The government is the

universal part of the constitution, i.e. the part that has the preservation of those parts [family and civil society] as its intentional aim, but at the same time apprehends and activates the universal aims of the whole which stand above the determination of the family and of civil society. The organization of the government is likewise its differentiation into powers... [that] interpenetrate so as to form an *actual* unity. (*PM/E* §541)

Human beings require organized externality *and* its agent, one that manages and navigates the parts of this organized reality in relation to each other, one that does not take itself to be answerable to any single one of them but to their interaction as such, to their interdependence, to the job of cultivating the fertility of the freedom of each for all. Government is, from the point of view of the conditions of freedom, the perspective of the whole upon itself, an agent of the whole; it must not itself be a perspective shaped by its own private interests. It is intended to ensure that things are running smoothly from a systemic point of view, that the system as expressed in the constitution is operating, and it does so as itself a unity. To take "the relation of these powers to one another as negative, as one of mutual *limitation*," is to assume that "the reaction of each power to the others is one of hostility and fear, as if to an evil, and their determination is such that they oppose one another and produce, by means of this counterpose, a general equilibrium rather than a living unity" (*PR/GPR* §272). In their functions they are each a part of it as a whole and what freedom needs; this is not properly construed as a system of checks and balances between hostile, self-interested forces, though of course government requires also the conditions under which it can be what it is supposed to be.

So what are these conditions? To be a perspective on the whole, the government must be in relation with the parts, informed by their needs and expertise about the piece of the world they know and the methods they need to cultivate for dealing with it. Government, in other words, must be concrete, it must be engaged with the particular, for it is the organization of the particular dimensions of this world in relation to each other that it must care for. This contact, this concreteness, is accomplished in different ways by the executive, the legislature, and the monarch, each of whom stands for different aspects of "the form of rationality—namely universality and determinacy," which "is what constitutes *the law*" (*PR* 17/*GPR* 11).

The aspect of law that is "determinacy" (*PR* 17/*GPR* 11) belongs to each part of government: the executive, the monarch, and the legislature. While, again, we cannot get into detail here, the executive has the "task of subsumption in general..., which also includes the powers of the judiciary and the police; these have more immediate reference to the particular affairs of civil society, and they assert the universal interest within these [particular] ends" (§287). The good of the whole is brought, through the executive, to resonate within the care for singular beings that the police and judiciary are supposed to enact. This contact between the executive and the institutions of civil society is reiterated in the corporation, which "finds in the state," particularly in the executive, "the means of sustaining its particular ends" (§289). The executive functions as the fluid contact between the universal and the particular, answerable particularly to "the legal recognition accorded to communities and corporations," which "prevents subjective arbitrariness from interfering on its own account with the power entrusted to officials" in the executive (§295).

The monarch is perhaps the most difficult piece to comprehend here, since it is so alien to contemporary ears. It corresponds to the aspect of determinacy as well, since, as Alan Brudner notes, "Law would not be Law if thinking about what laws best realize equal freedom or about how such laws apply to cases did not end in *a decision having effective force in the world*" (2021).[15] Brudner's argument here is that it is impossible to exclude the moment of subjective arbitrariness from the law because of the need for decision, and the ground for a decision based on weighing different considerations lies in a "one."[16] Understanding the monarch also requires historical consideration of the context, which I must defer but for which I would refer the reader to Jacques D'Hondt (1988; see also Johnston [2021]). Beyond the *Philosophy of Right* (which he claims had difficulty penetrating the barricades of censorship), D'Hondt tries to discern Hegel's genuine orientation by exploring his letters, spoken comments, practical commitments, and actual situations, such as the tensions between Hegel and the court of Frederick III of Prussia around the time of Hegel's appointment in Berlin. As D'Hondt notes, "the Prussia of 1820 was under the controls and censorship of a feudal monarchy. A philosopher had to hold back from saying everything" (1988, 2). For our purposes, however, we should notice that Hegel invokes the idea of a constitutional monarchy, not the feudal monarchy operative in Prussia in his own time, and we could notice also that the monarch looks quite like the heads of state with which we are familiar, even though "he" is selected by heredity so as to preclude the "strife of factions round the throne" (*PR/GPR* §281). The monarch is the expression of the whole as a one in relation to itself and to other states, and it answers to the necessarily singular moment of decision.

The legislature is connected to the moment of determinacy because it comprises the monarch, the executive, and, perhaps most interestingly, the estates (*PR/GPR* §300). The estates are the way the social order is inevitably articulated into "particular systems of needs, with their corresponding means, varieties of work, modes of satisfaction, and theoretical and practical education... i.e. into different *estates*... the *substantial* or immediate estate, the reflecting or *formal* estate, and lastly, the *universal* estate" (§§201–2). These are diverse bodies unified not around geographical specificity, which is the mode of governmental organization with which contemporary democracies are typically more familiar, but around different forms of expertise—agriculture, industry and trade, and civil service. The estates are a "mediating organ" that stands between

> the government at large on the one hand and the people in their division into particular spheres and individuals [*Individuen*] on the other. Their determination requires that they should embody in equal measure both the *sense* and *disposition* of the *state* and *government* and the *interests* of *particular* circles and *single beings* [*Einzelnen*]... they share the mediating function of the organized power of the executive, ensuring on the one hand that the power of the sovereign does not appear as an isolated *extreme*—and hence simply as an arbitrary power of domination—and on the other, that the particular interests of communities, corporations and individuals [*Individuen*] do not become isolated either. (*PR/GPR* §302)

In other words, the legislature, as the body that has as its members experts in the specific kinds of industry and labor that make up the activities of citizens, is composed of people who have insight into the way a particular piece of human reality functions and the expertise and activity needed to navigate it.

The legislature is also associated with the aspect of law that is universality: It "has to do with the laws as such, insofar as they are in need of new and further determination, and with those internal concerns of the state whose content is wholly universal" (*PR/GPR* §298). Its members bring to the formulation, revision, and promulgation of law particular, important kinds of insight. With the estates in particular, Hegel introduces into the legislative body an expert perspective on the work and activity of everyday life, affording the government the building blocks by which to actually acquire an understanding perspective on the whole.

Again, while an in-depth analysis of Hegel's presentation of the structure of government is too much for this particular project, I take this framing to show the ongoing significance of Hegel's work: Government is, in principle, the perspective of the whole upon itself, which is ensured by the constitution—the work done by past human beings to produce, institute, and refine the various complex mechanisms of living together that have resulted in the regulations, institutions, ministries, and bureaucratic infrastructure of modern states, and the subjective awareness of what is needed for freedom that is partly the product of this work. It is this constitution, the mundanity of freedom, that keeps the thing running, and it is the links between the parts—their status as pieces of a whole—and their education and guidance by the different domains of free human activity and labor that holds in check the possible emergence of "contingent subjectivity" (*PM/E* §539) and "subjective arbitrariness" (*PR/GPR* §295) in government.

We are in the objective, material world, as Merleau-Ponty says, not in the way a thing is in a container (see, e.g., 2012, 103), but we take up that world and can reflect on and shape it. We have a strange dual character in relation to it: we are within it in a way that also can make it an object of our perspective. Hegel's practical philosophy takes up this duality—history has manifested the demands of freedom, inside of human societies, but this does not mean that everything that exists is good. "Philosophical science ... deals with an actuality of which those objects, arrangements, situations, etc., are only the superficial exterior" (*EL/E* §6). We are indebted to the material, actual world for insight into what freedom is and needs, but the lessons mean little if we cannot mobilize them to distinguish what is needed from what is destructive, what is rational from what is irrational. Freedom requires, Hegel argues, the kind of recognition afforded by corporations that protects us morally and practically from poverty and excessive wealth; the kind of connection that estates provide between everyday human activity and governance; care for the explicit (family) and implicit (civil society) communities upon which we rely and thus for the vulnerabilities they produce; and an existing constitution, with a government suited to its preservation. Hegel argues that these are the institutions that would house the beings we are, and, contra Pinkard, I am not confident that they "were not the right ones" (2021, 325). We have much here with which to critique the existing world that has nevertheless put freedom on our minds, particularly in its disavowal of our material vulnerability and its uninformed faith in an individual freedom that would never produce counterfinality.

Again, we end where we began: This is a political vision that centers *recognition*. We find our freedom mobilized by the ways in which it is outstripped by the perspectives of others, who can thereby give us a more expansive world, and we find it protected by perspectives committed to working to grasp the whole, from which perspective they can care for the inevitable counterfinalities produced by freedom, construct a world in which our free action will not typically rebound upon us destructively, and nourish the space for interaction that will allow the freedom of others to make its way to our own.

CONCLUSION

This book has explored the elements of our contextualization: others and their recognizing powers; social worlds and their constituting powers; the responsiveness implied in what we typically take to be most fundamentally singular, which is the experience of conscience and its experience of the absolutes that infiltrate the finite; and finally, externality, materiality, and objectivity. Each of these gives the lie to our sense that we make our own experience, even though each of them articulates what it means to be a participant in the dialogues with others, cultures, principles, and materiality in and through which we are made. I believe that these touchstones of human experience are the tools we require in order to approach independent issues that can otherwise be seductively deceptive. My aim has been to show that these ideas should be taken as fundamental points of guidance in thinking about human situations, and that we should not lose sight of any one of these touchstones in thinking through the various aspects of reality and experience.

However, we have used these touchstones also to discuss different forms of domination, each of which is a matter of severance and alienation. One can be alienated from one's own body and world by being made the object of racist perception, which converts body and world from the background of one's experience into objects. Sexist structures alienate us from the intertwining of dependence and independence. Capitalism and ableism alienate us from our activity and freedom by separating us from materiality and its trajectory. Coloniality separates the colonized from world and disavows worldedness in the colonizer. Domination operates through suppression of these touchstones, which are essentially relations: the interdependence reflected in recognition; the centrality of belonging; the answerability of conscience; the materiality of agency. Opposition to domination requires that we articulate *these relations,* honing our perception to see the complex webs of interdependence that surround existing objects of perception. Thinking well requires thinking this multiplicity of phenomena and the contexts of their appearance.

Hegel's method is precisely this: to allow things to show that to which they are connected and related, to allow them to guide us elsewhere in order to get a fuller account of what they are, to put them in communication with each other. This is what it is to be "dialectical." We build a concrete edifice of insight by going step-by-step through the individual things and seeing the realities in which they are embedded, the ternary relations by which they are contextualized, the elements that stand beside and supplement them. We develop a rich sense of the character of reality if we collect in our thoughts and practices, as he does, these various phenomena, coming to see the layers in their relation as reality, in the sense that "the true is the whole" (*PS* 20/*PG* 19). Each phenomenon announces, as it were: "I am not a whole on my own; you must look elsewhere to other elements to see what I am." The theoretical inclination to see the non-alienated, mutual embeddedness of things can support us in our practical work against the alienation produced by domination. Hegel's philosophy is a philosophy of belonging, of connection and relation, with the theoretical apparatus matching its practical intent: to bring us back to freedom as being at home in the world.

Hegel cannot, however, do all this work alone — bring us back to freedom as being at home in the world — because speaking of freedom also requires speaking of the concrete modes of domination and oppression operative in one's own time. Thus my project in this book has been to generate a conversation between his philosophy and more or less contemporary thinkers who have honed their capacity to think this domination and oppression. Insofar as Hegel, however, is a thinker of the concrete, the determinate, and the historical, with a method that is a matter of holding the ideal accountable to the real, his philosophy is a rich site for this kind of work. It is not the last word, as some have construed it, but a relational, interpersonal word that can enliven future conversations and worlds — that, in genuine Hegelian spirit, can be dispossessed of itself and live on in its others.

ACKNOWLEDGMENTS

Thinking about Hegel makes me think of the amazing quality another person's perspective has to turn things on their head and to show how wondrously vast reality is, extending indefinitely beyond one's sense of it. I wonder how my encounter with future others will make me say (and want to have said) things differently. I want better structures and more opportunities for finding out from people and other creatures, from places and situations, how to think, what needs to be thought, what I don't think fully enough. It is hard to see on one's own the onesidedness of the things one says, particularly when caught up in the enthusiasm of saying them. Nonetheless, there are many people, situations, and institutions that have given me opportunities for "thinking with":

The traditions of inquiry, the public universities, and the bureaucratic organizational forms that make it possible to live a life of thinking and talking and learning and writing, even when this kind of life is becoming endangered. This includes the Social Sciences and Humanities Research Council of Canada; the Centre for Ethics at the University of Toronto; the University of Chicago Press and its remarkable people, including its reviewers, who made this a better book than it would have been; and the press and journals who have worked with me on pieces of this material that were previously published: "White Gaze as a Concept in Phenomenology," in *Encyclopedia of Phenomenology*, ed. Nicholas de Warren and Ted Toadvine (Springer, 2025), which became a portion of chapter 2; "A Phenomenological Account of the Conditions of Transnational Feminism," *Symposium* 27, no. 2 (2023): 66–82, a portion of chapter 3; and "Hegel and Wynter on the Problem of Human Self-Interpretation," *Revue internationale de philosophie* 309, no. 3 (2024): 71–90, DOI: https://

doi.org/10.3917/rip.309.0071, URL: https://shs.cairn.info/journal-revue-internationale-de-philosophie-2024-3-page-71?lang=en, a portion of chapter 4. I am particularly grateful to Memorial University of Newfoundland and Labrador, including for its support of research and its provision of a Publication Subvention grant for this book. I am so fortunate to be able to work here in Newfoundland—in the ancestral, unceded territory of the Beothuk, the traditional gathering place for the Mi'kmaq, and the home of diverse Indigenous peoples, including First Nations, Inuit, and Métis—even as my own government is failing profoundly to join in on the responsibility of caretaking.

The people in St. John's who make it home: Luke Roman, in all of his wit and wisdom; the dear and singular Maria Mayr; colleagues and friends in the Philosophy Department and the Dean's Office, with whom I am happy to share the task of sustaining this inimitable place; and the undergraduate and graduate students whose buzz in the hallways helps make all the work seem worth something.

The alchemical combination of Rennie's River, an elegant boardroom, and a class on Hegel in the winter semester of 2022. Due to heavy administrative responsibilities, I had very little time for class preparation, so I decided to teach exactly what I was thinking about exactly in the way I think about it. In the morning I would walk to school along the river, figuring out what to say by saying it to myself. We would meet long after the sun had set, and, as Josephine so memorably observed, it felt like church. In this book is reflected the river, the room, and the efforts of those students who pulled thoughts from me, each other, and the text on those beautiful evenings: particularly Glenn Day, Antoine Gillett, Avo Broughton-Janes, Dylan Delikta, Josephine Arsenault, Luka Carroll, Declan Seviour, George Saad, Xoana Feas Perez, Sarah Griffin, Jintao Liang, Fatemeh Qasemi, Amy Mauger, Chase Moloney, and Joshua Tucker. I am grateful to Xoana for her comments and for transcribing the lectures, and to Dylan and George for their research support.

The musicians who have generously added their efforts to mine in finding new musical forms of philosophical expression: Tania Gill, Chris Banks, Don Scott, Aidan McConnell, Don Kerr, Jean Martin, Nick Fraser, and chief alchemist Julian Pivato who summoned it all into being in the first place.

A group of dear and smart friends officially called the Critical Perspectives in Phenomenology Research Group. Week after week of becoming educated by reading new things with David Ciavatta, Kym Maclaren, Susan Bredlau, Laura McMahon, and Jeff Morrisey, many of which made it into this book, has been such a delight. Your ideas are in this book somewhere, however unregistered; "our perspectives slip into each other."

Others not yet mentioned who have slipped into my constitution: particularly Senem Saner, Mike Sample, Jonathan Weverink, Maliheh Deyhim, John Russon, Karen Robertson, and Patricia Fagan.

Immediate family, including Marcel, whose generosity helps keep the train on the tracks; the other siblings and their kin who continue to make being a family an engaging challenge; and my parents, Elly and Bram, and their absorption of all that intensity all this time, and especially the late-night porch talks. I know where I come from.

And finally, Kristin and the way she carefully nurtures my inhabitation of my own perspective; the unprecedented Michael; Jeff and his ongoing willingness to figure things out with me, including pieces of this book; Kym, with affection for her wisdom and for the generosity of attention that makes it get stretched so thin; and Theodore, as he demands to be called, whose nearness has stretched and expanded my freedom in such rich and unpredictable ways. Let us keep writing!

NOTES

Introduction

1. Feminist theorists, for instance, have asked, is reason "male" (Antony and Witt 1993; Lloyd 1984; Rooney 1994)? Is the description and deployment of reason inevitably exclusionary of things associated with "the feminine"? Decolonial and postcolonial theorists have asked, is the construal of knowledge, and of human becoming and of models of living together, colonial? Has the pinnacle of human development been posited as European, "Western," and modern, through which lens all other forms of social life are perceived as earlier, inferior positions in a historical process (Amin 1989; Fanon 2004; Wynter 2003)?

2. As we will explore later, this is Hegel's critique of the moral stance, which calls for and reveals the significance of the category of "ethicality" or *Sittlichkeit*. See especially the transition in *PS/PG* from Reason in its making and testing of laws to Spirit, and the transition from Morality to Ethical Life in *PR/GPR*. See also Shannon Hoff (2018b).

3. This is the core meaning of Hegel's needlessly controversial observation that "the rational is the actual and the actual is the rational" (*PR* 20/*GPR* 14); see chapter 5 for further discussion.

Chapter One

1. Hegel says, for instance, that in thinking we are not simply single selves confronted by single objects, but our capacity to think makes us a kind of "universal subject," and in our thinking the object becomes similarly universal. He writes that "consciousness as pure insight is not a *single* self which could be confronted by the object which would likewise have *its own* self.... The certainty of itself is the universal subject, and its knowing concept is the essence of all actuality.... It is the universal self, the self of itself as well as of the object" (*PS* §583/*PG* 317).

2. Here I am engaging with the *Phenomenology*'s discussion of "Absolute Freedom and Terror" (*PS* §§582–95/*PG* 316–23), which is Hegel's analysis of the insights of the bourgeois revolution of eighteenth-century France.

3. In the preface to the *Philosophy of Right*, for instance, he mocks those who would think that it belongs to philosophy of the state "to invent and propound *yet another theory*.... If we examine this notion and the activity that is associated with it, we might well

imagine that no state or constitution had ever previously existed or were in existence today, but that we had *now* . . . to start right from the beginning, and that the ethical world had been waiting only for such intellectual constructions, discoveries, and proofs as are *now* available" (*PR* 12/*GPR* 8).

4. Hegel did not himself publish his multiple lecture courses on aesthetics, the philosophy of history and world history, and the history of philosophy, and neither did he publish the Additions (*Zusätze*) to his published texts. While these various sources have different pedigrees, they are gathered from student notes, so scholarly reliance on them is risky. Yet it can nonetheless be desirable, particularly when there are few other avenues of engagement with his incisive and powerful yet sometimes controversial discussions of art, history, and the history of philosophy. For further discussion of the challenges involved in taking up ideas from these kinds of texts, see chapter 3.

5. Simply put, the *Phenomenology* pursues the first question in its first half (Consciousness to Reason) and the second in its second (Spirit to Absolute Knowing).

6. This is my translation of "durch das Prinzip der Besonderung nun, dem alles unterworfen ist, was sich in die reale Objectivität hinaustriebt" (*VA*.III 522).

7. About decision, Hegel writes: "for the universal to reach the point of actually doing something, it must gather itself up into the One of individuality and put a singular consciousness at the head, for the universal will is only an *actual* will in a self that is One" (*PS* §589/*PG* 319).

8. "The government, willing and achieving, starts out from a single point and at the same time wills and accomplishes a determinate order of things and a determinate action. It thereby excludes . . . the remaining individuals from its deed, and . . . , as a result, it constitutes itself as the kind of government which is a determinate will and which is opposed as a result to the universal will. It therefore cannot present itself as anything other than a *faction*" (*PS* §591/*PG* 320).

9. About action, Hegel writes that

> consciousness lets nothing break loose into a shape that would become a freestanding object confronting it . . . consciousness cannot arrive at a positive work, neither to universal works of language nor to those of actuality, nor to the laws and the universal institution of conscious freedom, nor to the deeds and works of willing freedom. The work to which freedom giving itself consciousness can arrive would consist in freedom as the universal substance making itself into an object and a lasting being. . . . Universal freedom, which in this way would have broken itself up into its various parts and by doing so would have made itself into an existing substance, . . . could apportion the plurality of individuals to its different parts. However, the doing and being of personality would thereby find itself restricted to a branch of the whole . . . personality would mean a determinate personality, and it would in truth cease to be universal self-consciousness. (*PS* §588/*PG* 318–19)

10. This is the fundamental thesis of the first of Derrida's two essays in *Rogues* (2005).

11. It is abstract because, as Hegel notes, all the "shapes of consciousness" that precede his discussion of spirit "are abstractions from it"—that is, abstractions from the historical reality of spirit and its existence in the form of a determinate ethical world. Even to philosophically isolate "such moments has spirit itself as its *presupposition* and its *stable existence*, or the isolating only exists in the spirit which is existence" (*PS* §439/*PG* 239), yet nonetheless we are isolating it, rather than describing it in its rich connections to and contextualization in all of the other aspects of that ethical reality.

Chapter Two

1. The focus of this chapter as a whole is "The Independence and Dependence of Self-Consciousness: Mastery and Servitude" (*PS* §§178–96/*PG* 109–16). Here, in the discussion of the struggle to the death, I am focusing particularly on §§185–89/110–12. Hegel's outline of what he calls in §185/110 the "concept of recognition" comes earlier, in §§178–84/109–12, which means that §184/110 brings a conceptual conclusion. How this concept emerges within and is digested by experience is the material of the rest of the section (§§185–96/110–16).

2. See Williams (1997) for an account of how Hegel's conception of recognition was taken up by others such as Sartre.

3. The whole section is *PS* §§166–230/*PG* 103–31; it includes discussions of desire, the struggle to the death, mastery and servitude, and stoicism, skepticism, and the unhappy consciousness.

4. It should be clear from this analysis that those who criticize the idea of recognition in the name of opposition to domination are typically not targeting Hegel, even when they take themselves to be; rather, they are targeting failures of recognition (see Hoff 2014a). Genuine recognition is recognition of the other as a perspective, which means as something that brings its own orientation. Acknowledging the other only if they accept the terms that the "I" or "we" presents is not recognition at all. For discussions of failed recognition, see, for instance, Oliver (2001); Coulthard (2014).

5. See Ciavatta (2009).

6. The German, "*gegenseitig sich anerkennend*," is helpful here. "*Anerkennend*"—"recognizing"—is in the accomplished form: we have been recognized. Some interpretations of Hegel posit recognition as a demand, which is true but only partly; it is always the case that it has always already happened. If we are human, we are human together.

7. One could think here of the conversation that opens the *Republic*: Polemarchus threatening to force Socrates and his companions to stay; Socrates responding by invoking the possibility that they could persuade him to let them go. Indeed, Timothy Brownlee makes this conversation the epigraph of his book on recognition in Hegel (Brownlee 2022; Plato 1968, 327c).

8. I use this term loosely here, with the caveat that the term, as has been made abundantly clear in the phenomenological tradition, is not adequate for capturing the nature of human existence.

9. See also Hoff (2023b).

10. We can also see that the first of these three points is the occasion for the *Phenomenology* as the education of consciousness. How this first point applies to Hegel himself—and what he says about his philosophy's own historicity—is complicated and will be discussed, again, in the next chapter. It has to do with the very possibility of making claims, which is always a universalizing project; philosophy (as we explored in the introduction) is always determinate and transcending, inside and outside, and the historically emergent and situated insight of others has the capacity to build one's own.

11. This is of course only one side; the other is the "I" as "transition from undifferentiated indeterminacy to *differentiation, determination,* and the *positing* of a determinacy as a content and object" (*PR/GPR* §6). There is also the unity of indeterminacy and determination (*PR/GPR* §7).

12. That is not to say that Benjamin simply gets Hegel right. Like others, she takes him to be asserting about self-consciousness that it fundamentally

wants to be absolute... wants to think itself the only one, the whole of the world; it abjures dependency. The I wants to be one and all alone, to negate everything else. It starts out by incorporating everything else, allowing the other to exist only as an object inside itself, in other words, as a mental object... the self only gives up this omnipotence when it realizes its dependency... it does so only out of self-interest. (1980, 152)

While her disagreement with Hegel is not particularly relevant here, it could be helpful generally to challenge these claims: first, that (according to Hegel) the I wants to be absolute, the only one, all alone; second, that it "starts out by incorporating everything else"; and third, that it gives up omnipotence only out of self-interest. Hegel is exploring an aspect of human self-experience—that to be an I is to experience oneself as that to which the world shows itself, and to encounter others is to experience a challenge to that. That is not the whole story, as we find out if we follow through on particularly bad ways of dealing with that challenge. Second, Hegel is not telling a developmental story per se—not asserting that self-consciousness learns all of this in this particular order. A developmental story would have to involve much more detail. Third, self-consciousness does not simply acquiesce out of self-interest. Although (as Hegel regularly observes) satisfaction may be present, this does not fundamentally undermine the integrity of self-consciousness's insight that others are real and have value. The self that might be motivated by self-interest is not even stable because others unpredictably expand it.

13. See Merleau-Ponty's related discussion (1968) of the perceptual faith and the emergence in our experience of a distinction between truth and falsity from which thought borrows and which it can never therefore provide.

14. See de Boer (2003); Harris (1997b); Farneth (2017); Hutchings (2003); Ravven (1988); Russon (2004); Donougho (1989); and Hoff (2007, 2014).

15. Here Nisbet (typically an excellent translator) translates *Einzelheit* as "individuality," which is improper. For a broader account of the philosophical significance of the difference between *Einzelheit* and *Individualität*, and a critique of the problems with long-standing neglect of this distinction in English scholarship on Hegel, see Donougho (2023). I use "single," "singular," or "singularity" to reflect Hegel's use of "*einzelne*" or "*Einzelheit*."

16. In the Addition, Hegel is reported to have said that

women may well be educated, but they are not made for the higher sciences, for philosophy and certain artistic productions which require a universal element. Women may have insights, taste, and delicacy, but they do not possess the ideal. The difference between man and woman is the difference between animal and plant; the animal is closer in character of man, the plant to woman, for the latter is a more peaceful unfolding whose principle is the more indeterminate unity of feeling. When women are in charge of government, the state is in danger, for their actions are based not on the demands of universality but on contingent inclination and opinion. The education of women takes place imperceptibly, as if through the atmosphere of representational thought, more through living than through the acquisition of knowledge, whereas man attains his position only through the attainment of thought and numerous technical exertions. (*PR* §166 Addition)

It does not surprise me to think that Hegel would say this, but H. B. Nisbet does give reasons for taking the Additions with a grain of salt. He notes that they were compiled by Hegel's student Eduard Gans, from lectures Hegel gave on this material after the first edition of the *Philosophy of Right* had appeared. Gans derived them not from Hegel's manuscripts but from the lecture notes of two other students, H. G. Hotho and K. G. von Griesheim, who attended different lectures. Nisbet reports that Gans's extracts are highly selective, combining material from two distinct lecture series and consisting largely of paraphrases (*PR* xxxv).

17. Pippin also approaches ethical life as an extension of recognition and argues that Hegel has a social theory of freedom (2008).

Chapter Three

1. Hegel portrays the reality of ethical life in different ways between the *Phenomenology of Spirit*, on the one hand, and the *Philosophy of Right* and *Encyclopaedia*, on the other (a difference that is worth discussion but that ultimately does not run very deep). Each, however, is a retort to a moral stance. I have analyzed this notion in greater detail elsewhere (e.g., 2014a, 2018, 2023a). For other helpful discussions of the category of ethical life, see Russon (2015); Ciavatta (2009).

2. Harris argues that it is not for Antigone "to accept life as an ethical disposition" (1997b, 219). See particularly pp. 208–30 for a rich discussion of Antigone, Creon, nature, and guilt.

3. *LPWH* 177/*VPW* 218. There have been many attempts to grapple with the issues of racism and coloniality as they are manifest in Hegel's reading of history. Among them, see Bernasconi (1998, 2000, 2003); Brennan (2014); Buchwalter (2009); de Laurentiis (2014); Mascat (2024); McCarney (2000, 2003); Paquette (2003); Parekh (2009); Stone (2017); Serequeberhan (1989); Tibebu (2010); and Zambrana (2016, 2020, 2021). What Hegel is recorded as having said about other cultures is found particularly in his *Lectures on the Philosophy of World History*. Here are some particularly troubling samples of student notes. In speaking of Indigenous cultures, Hegel observes that their subjugation by the Europeans led to their downfall; that especially "in Mexico and Peru" there were "purely natural" cultures that "had to perish as soon as the spirit approached" them; that "America has always shown itself physically and spiritually impotent"; that "culturally inferior nations are gradually eroded through contact with more advanced nations which have gone through a more intensive cultural development" (*LPWH* 163/*VPW* 200–1). These Americans are said to be "like unenlightened children... [;] the weakness of their physique was one of the main reasons why the Negroes were brought to America as a labour force; for the Negroes are far more susceptible to European culture than the Indians" (*LPWH* 165/*VPW* 202). About what he calls "Africa proper," Hegel says that "man has not progressed beyond a merely sensuous existence, and has found it absolutely impossible to develop any further" (*LPWH*, 172/*VPW* 212). "It has no historical interest of its own.... [It is] the land of childhood, removed from the light of self-conscious history and wrapped in the dark mantle of night" (*LPWH* 174/*VPW* 214). "There is no subjectivity, but merely a series of subjects who destroy one another" (*LPWH* 176/*VPW* 216–17). "Their consciousness has not yet reached an awareness of any substantial objectivity—for example, of God or the law—in which the will of man could participate and in which he could become aware of his own being.... The negro is an example of animal man in all his savagery and lawlessness, and if we wish to understand him at all, we must put aside all our European attitudes... nothing consonant with humanity is to be found in his character" (*LPWH* 177/*VPW* 218). In the *Aesthetics*, Hegel writes the following about Indian poetry: "These first, still wildest, attempts of fancy and art we find especially amongst

the ancient Indians. Their chief defect, compatibly with the general nature of this stage, consists in this, that they cannot grasp either the meanings themselves in their clarity, or existing reality in its own proper shape and significance. Therefore the Indians have proven themselves incapable of an historical interpretation of persons and events, because an historical treatment requires *sang-froid* in taking up and understanding the past on its own account in its actual shape with its empirical links, grounds, aims, and causes" (*AE*.I 334–35, *VA*.I 432).

4. Thanks to Jeff Morrisey for his comments in particular on this discussion of freedom and freedom in history, which was a challenging piece of the book to write, and to David Ciavatta for first suggesting that it might need to be written.

5. Themes related to objective spirit are discussed in *PR/GPR* and *PM/E*, sporadically in the *Phenomenology*, and in early work such as *Natural Law* and *System of Ethical Life*. As Hegel notes, "since I have set out this part of philosophy in my *Elements of Right* (Berlin, 1821) I can express myself more briefly than I did on the other parts" (*PM/E* §487R).

6. See Donougho (2023); Rawlinson (2021) for discussion of the term "*der Einzelne*."

7. The I in its abstractness is discussed particularly in "Abstract Right" in *PR/GPR* and *PM/E*. The I in its concrete world is discussed particularly in "Conscience" in the *Phenomenology* (and in the next chapter).

8. Hegel discusses the nature and relations of singularity, particularity, and universality particularly in *SL/WL*.

9. Hegel introduces the idea of a rich rabble in his 1821–22 lectures on the philosophy of right: "This rabble mentality happens as much on the side of affluence ... as on the side of poverty" (*VPR21*, 222). Nisbett also cites the 1819–20 lectures (*PR* 454):

> The rabble disposition also appears where there is wealth. The rich [person] thinks that [s]he can buy anything, because [s]he knows [her]self as the power of the particularity of self-consciousness. Thus wealth can lead to the same mockery and shamelessness that we find in the poor rabble. The disposition of the master over the slave is the same as that of the slave. . . . These two sides, poverty and wealth, thus constitute the corruption of civil society. (*VPR19*, 194–96)

10. For an excellent discussion of the dependence of philosophical thought on history and its accompanying complicity in oppression, see McCumber (2013), particularly chapter 2.

11. Sartre grapples with the consequences of this dual materiality and rationality in the *Critique of Dialectical Reason*; we shall explore this further in chapter 5.

12. For worthwhile intercultural work by Hegelian thinkers, see Fanon (2008); Pinkard (2017), who works particularly through Hegel's reductive orientation to China, India, Persia, and Egypt in "Hegel's False Start: Non-Europeans as Failed Europeans" (50–67); Susan Buck-Morss (2009), who ascertains Haiti's relevance from the point of view of world history; and John Russon (2017), who discerns the development of what are typically labeled modern, Western insights in canonical texts from other cultures and tracks the one-sidedness of the West's own attempts to actualize its principled commitment to individual subjectivity. Von der Luft argues that Hegel makes a mistake in naming his four realms after specific geographical regions, and that the historical regions are flawed illustrations of specific philosophical ideas best understand theologically (1984, 340–41).

13. Allegra de Laurentiis similarly highlights the importance of discerning "the underlying 'authentic' import of Hegel's philosophy of spirit" or "the underlying glue of Hegel's philosophical anthropology, of his philosophy of history and, by extension, his philosophy of right," suggesting that it is not necessarily scholarly responsible to imagine these

to be identical to "the extravagant claims and crude perspectives expressed in the oral Additions and Lectures" and "the philosopher's personal views" (2014, 593–94).

14. As Timothy Brennan observes,

> We come to know by a thinking that coincides with our activity in the world and that constantly modifies itself by engagement with sensuous materiality... the messiness, difficulty, and conflicts of actual life are the medium through which thought achieves its rationality as part of a hard-won effort to make sense of that reality's confusing particularities. In Hegel's words: "The theoretical is essentially contained within the practical" [PR/GPR §4A]. (2014, 92)

15. In an Addition, Hegel distinguishes this kind of colonization from a "second variety" that he observes in history, ascribing it particularly to the cities of ancient Greece, when their populations grew to the extent to which they could no longer provide for them. He describes it as "quite different from the first" and "systematic," "initiated by the state, which is aware of the proper way of carrying it out and regulates it accordingly." In more recent times, he notes, "colonies have not been granted the same rights as the inhabitants of the mother country, and this situation has resulted in wars and eventual independence.... The liberation of the colonies itself proves to be of the greatest advantage to the mother state, just as the emancipation of the servants is of the greatest advantage to the master" (PR/GPR §248).

16. Historian Tom C. McCaskie's 2019 account of Hegel's writing on Africa addresses Hegel's exposure to scholarly sources on non-European cultures. McCaskie argues that, while Hegel's views were more or less consistent with those of his intellectual context, he chose to highlight more prurient and less measured representations of Africa from scholarly (and less than scholarly) texts. He argues that Hegel's use of the texts he consulted to develop a view on Africa was slipshod and selective, that Hegel took problematic sources at face value (176–77), displayed no interest in abolitionist literature (176), actively misread Africanist texts, ignored what did not fit with what he wanted to say (181–86), and displayed an "absolute lack of empirical interest in the materials before his eyes" (185).

17. "La paperson" is a pen name for K. Wayne Yang, a settler in dialogue and collaboration with Indigenous thinkers, particularly Eve Tuck.

18. This self-concealment means that, as Max Liboiron notes, "it is common to introduce Indigenous authors with their nation/affiliation, while settler and white scholars almost always remain unmarked" (2021, 3n10). Liboiron proposes an "imperfect methodological decision... to identify all authors the way they identify themselves," with authors who do "not introduce themselves or their land relations" marked as "unmarked" (3–4n10).

19. For a summary of the final report of the Truth and Reconciliation Commission of Canada on the legacy of Canada's residential schools, see Craft et al. (2015).

20. La paperson follows Tuck, Guess, and Sultan (2014) in using the term "selfsame land."

21. The US government under the leadership of President George W. Bush used Laura Bush to help mobilize enthusiasm for the war against Afghanistan.

Chapter Four

1. Translators and readers of Hegel seem not to have settled yet on a translation for *der Rechtzustand*. I follow Donougho (2023) here in translating it as "legal condition,"

but Harris's (1997b) "condition of right" is also appealing. Miller translates it as "legal status" and Pinkard as "state of legality."

2. Here ethical life and conscience come together. If possibilities are sculpted from the determinate systems we inhabit and from the determinate relations that have shaped us, then we know that individuality and action depend on the world that surrounds them, on its resources and possibilities.

3. Narayan's comparative work on what she calls "death by culture," which brings domestic violence in the US into the conversation, continues to be helpful (1997).

4. Wynter uses the term "adaptive" to describe a certain kind of knowing in contrast with "non-adaptive knowing." See Hoff (2024) for a discussion of the productive points of connection and departure between Wynter and Hegel.

5. "The ethical powers, just like the agents, are differentiated in their domain and their individual appearance. Now if, as dramatic poetry requires, these thus differentiated powers are summoned into appearance as active and are actualized as the specific aim of a human 'pathos' which passes over into action, then their harmony is cancelled and they come on the scene in *opposition* to one another in reciprocal independence" (A.II 1196/VA.III 523).

6. "The substance of ethical life... is an ensemble of *different* relations and powers which only in a situation of inactivity, like that of the blessed gods, accomplish the work of the spirit in the enjoyment of an undisturbed life. But the very nature of this ensemble implies its transfer from its at first purely abstract *ideality* into its actualization in *reality* and its appearance in the mundane sphere" (A.II 1196/VA.III 523).

7. See de Boer (2009), Saner (2025), Pippin (2020), Harris (1983), Buchwalter (2012a, 2015), Houlgate (2016, 2024), and Avineri (1972) for comparable orientations toward Hegel's political relevance today.

Chapter Five

1. Hegel's anthropology is relatively neglected in Hegel scholarship, with some recent exceptions (de Laurentiis 2021; Furlotte 2017; Malabou 2005).

2. Here it seems that the Addition helpfully clarifies a complex philosophical discussion with which it is consistent.

3. The Addition to PM/E §381 reads: "Sensation is just this omnipresence of the unity of the animal in all its members, which immediately communicate every impression to the single whole."

4. Another Addition reads:

> That the externality and multiplicity of matter cannot be overcome by nature is a presupposition which... we have here long since left behind us as invalid. The philosophy of nature teaches us how nature sublates its externality by stages, how matter already refutes the independence of the individual, of the many, by *gravity*, and how this refutation begun by gravity, and still more by simple, indivisible *light*, is completed by animal life, by the sentient creature, since this reveals to us the omnipresence of the one soul at every point of its bodiliness, and so the sublatedness of the asunderness of matter... this sublation is consummated in the substance of *soul*, the soul emerges as the ideality of *everything* material, as *all* immateriality. (PM/E §389A)

Later in the same note Hegel criticizes materialism for portraying "thinking as a result of the material," but nonetheless asserts that we should "recognize in materialism the enthusiastic endeavour to transcend the dualism which assumes two different worlds as equally substantial and true, to sublate this dismemberment of what is originally one."

5. I take this, however, to be a more or less straightforward explication of the meaning of *PM/E* §403:

> We are, as actual individuality, *in ourselves* also a *world* of concrete content with an infinite periphery,—we have within us a countless host of relations and connections which are always within us even if they do not enter into our sensation and representation, and which, no matter how much these relations can alter, even without our knowledge, none the less belong to the concrete content of the human soul; so that the soul, in virtue of the infinite wealth of its content, may be described as the soul of a world, as an *individually* determined *world-soul*.... This counterpart of the soul is not something external to it. On the contrary, the totality of relationships in which the individual human soul stands, constitutes its actual vitality and subjectivity and accordingly has grown together with it just as firmly as, to use an image, the leaves grow with the tree. (§402A)

6. For a rich discussion of this point, see Russon (1997), 65–72.

7. Thanks are due here to my colleague Melanie Coughlin for a helpful orienting discussion of the ideas of "abilities" and "capacities," which led me to distinguish between "capacities" as that which care and the world "aim" at, and "abilities" as accomplished by the support of this development of capacities—or, in short, by fit.

8. For discussion of the way the built world is built for typical male bodies, see Criado Perez (2019).

9. The other essays in Buchwalter (2015) also mostly describe and defend, as I would (and to some extent do), a Hegel at odds with capitalism.

10. For the discussion of scarcity, see especially Sartre (2004), Book I, chapter 3: "Matter as Totalized Totality: A First Encounter with Necessity."

11. Where Sartre uses the term "practico-inert" (such as at 2004, 67, 71), he tends not to explain it, and where he explains it, he tends not to use the term (see 2004, 122–25, 150–65).

12. There he says that in modern states, citizens have only a limited share in the universal business, and the corporation gives the ethical person a universal activity in addition to their private end (*PR/GPR* §255A).

13. As I write this in early 2025, the Trump administration, against the rule of law, is dismantling key governmental institutions and departments. The effective disappearance of large swaths of government may have the effect of revealing to some Americans as if for the first time that government actually does something and what it does.

14. For a more detailed discussion of the constitution, see Siep (2004).

15. Brudner (2021) offers a helpful portrayal of Hegel's proposal for how the parts of the whole are unified so as to ensure the rule of law: "The sovereign is neither a monarch nor a Parliament, but the totality composed of monarch, civil service, elected Parliament, and an independent body of constitutional experts, where each organ plays a role in sustaining Law's sovereignty."

16. See Hegel's account of the singularity of decision in the *Phenomenology*'s discussion of the French Revolution. See also Brudner (2021):

> The subjectivity of ultimate decision is that of a single person. Hence it is institutionally expressed in a way truest to its nature if it is expressed through one per-

son. This person is a monarch rather than an elected or appointed President because the transcendence of a will that is nothing but Law's will requires that it be independent of any partisan will, even of a majority, and succession by birth guarantees that independence. Notice, however, that the monarch's decision presupposes the other two moments of Law's idea; he or she doesn't just will a personal preference in a perfunctory or capricious way. The decision is a *conclusion*, albeit a discretionary one, resulting from the application of a universal to a particular. In other words, the decision, while ungrounded, is not unprincipled.

REFERENCES

Work by G. W. F. Hegel

A   *Aesthetics: Lectures on Fine Art.* 2 vols. Translated by T. M. Knox. Oxford: Clarendon Press, 1975.

E   *Enzyklopädie der philosophischen Wissenschaften.* Vol. 6 of *Hauptwerke in sechs Bänden.* Hamburg: Felix Meiner, 2018.

EL   *Encyclopedia of the Philosophical Sciences in Basic Outline, Part I: Science of Logic.* Translated by Klaus Brinkmann and Daniel O. Dahlstrom. Cambridge: Cambridge University Press, 2010.

GPR   *Grundlinien der Philosophie des Rechts.* Vol. 5 of *Hauptwerke in sechs Bänden.* Hamburg: Felix Meiner, 2018.

LHP   *Introduction to the Lectures on the History of Philosophy.* Translated by T. M. Knox and A. V. Miller. Oxford: Clarendon Press, 1985.

LPWH   *Lectures on the Philosophy of World History.* Translated by H. B. Nisbet. Cambridge: Cambridge University Press, 1975.

PG   *Die Phänomenologie des Geistes.* Vol. 2 of *Hauptwerke in sechs Bänden.* Hamburg: Felix Meiner, 2018.

PH   *Philosophy of History.* Translated by J. Sibree. New York: Dover, 1956.

PM   *Philosophy of Mind.* Translated by W. Wallace, A. V. Miller, and Michael Inwood. Oxford: Oxford University Press, 2007.

PR   *Elements of the Philosophy of Right.* Translated by H. B. Nisbet. Cambridge: Cambridge University Press, 1991.

PS   *The Phenomenology of Spirit.* Translated by Terry Pinkard. Cambridge: Cambridge University Press, 2018.

SL   *The Science of Logic.* Translated by George di Giovanni. Cambridge: Cambridge University Press, 2010.

VA   *Vorlesungen über die Ästhetik.* Vols. 13–15 of *Werke.* Edited by Eva Moldenhauer and Karl Markus Michel. Frankfurt am Main: Suhrkamp, 1970.

VPG   *Vorlesungen über die Philosophie der Geschichte.* Vol. 12 of *Werke.* Edited by Eva Moldenhauer and Karl Markus Michel. Frankfurt am Main: Suhrkamp, 1970.
VPR19 *Philosophie des Rechts: Die Vorlesung von 1819/1820.* Edited by Dieter Henrich. Frankfurt am Main: Suhrkamp, 1983.
VPR21 *Die Philosophie des Rechts: Die Vorlesung von 1821/22.* Edition and commentary by Hansgeorg Hoppe. Frankfurt am Main: Suhrkamp, 2005.
VPW   *Vorlesungen über die Philosophie der Weltgeschichte.* Edited by Johannes Hoffmeister. Hamburg: Felix Meiner, 1994.
WH   *Lectures on the Philosophy of World History (1822/23).* Edited and translated by Robert F. Brown and Peter C. Hodgson. New York: Oxford, 2011.
WL   *Wissenschaft der Logik.* Vols. 3–4 of *Hauptwerke in sechs Bänden.* Hamburg: Felix Meiner, 2018.

Works by Others

Abu-Lughod, Lila. 2002. "Do Muslim Women Really Need Saving? Anthropological Reflections on Cultural Relativism and Its Others." *American Anthropologist* 104 (3): 783–90.

Abu-Lughod, Lila. 2013. *Do Muslim Women Need Saving?* Cambridge, MA: Harvard University Press.

Achebe, Chinua. 1994. *Things Fall Apart.* New York: Penguin.

Adorno, Theodor W. 1973. *Negative Dialectics.* Translated by E. B. Ashton. London: Routledge.

Ahmed, Sara. 2007. "The Phenomenology of Whiteness." *Feminist Theory* 8 (2): 149–68.

Alcoff, Linda Martín. 2006. *Visible Identities: Race, Gender, and the Self.* Oxford: Oxford University Press.

Alcoff, Linda Martín. 2007. "Mignolo's Epistemology of Coloniality." *The New Centennial Review* 7 (3): 79–101.

Alfred, Taiaiake. 2005. *Wasáse: Indigenous Pathways of Actions and Freedom.* Peterborough: Broadview Press.

Allen, S. D. 2005. "Using Perceptual Maps to Communicate Concepts of Sustainable Forest Management." *The Forestry Chronicle* 81, no. 3 (May/June): 381–86.

Al-Saji, Alia. 2014. "A Phenomenology of Hesitation: Interrupting Racializing Habits of Seeing." In *Living Alterities: Phenomenology, Embodiment, and Race,* edited by Emily S. Lee, 133–72. Albany, NY: SUNY Press.

Al-Saji, Alia. 2022. "Fanon, the Dismembered Past, and a Phenomenology of Racialized Time." In *Fanon, Phenomenology and Psychology,* edited by Leswin Laubscher, Derek Hook, and Miraj Desai, 177–93. New York: Routledge.

Amin, Samir. 1989. *Eurocentrism.* Translated by Russell Moore. New York: Monthly Review Press.

Antony, Louise M., and Charlotte Witt, eds. 1993. *A Mind of One's Own: Feminist Essays on Reason and Objectivity.* Boulder, CO: Westview Press.

Arendt, Hannah. 1998. *The Human Condition.* Chicago: University of Chicago Press.

REFERENCES

Armstrong, Jeannette. 2018. "A Single Strand: The Nsyilxcin Speaking People's Tmixw Knowledge as a Model for Sustaining a Life-Force Place." In *Traditional Ecological Knowledge Learning from Indigenous Practices for Environmental Sustainability*, edited by M. K. Nelson and D. Shilling, 95–108. Cambridge: Cambridge University Press.

Atleo, Clifford, and Jonathan Boron. 2022. "Land Is Life: Indigenous Relationships to Territory and Navigating Settler Colonial Property Regimes in Canada." *Land*, vol. 11, 609.

Avineri, Shlomo. 1972. *Hegel's Theory of the Modern State*. Cambridge: Cambridge University Press.

Baldwin, James. 1963. *The Fire Next Time*. London: Michael Joseph.

Benjamin, Jessica. 1980. "The Bonds of Love: Rational Violence and Erotic Domination." *Feminist Studies* 6, no. 1 (Spring): 144–74.

Benjamin, Jessica. 1988. *The Bonds of Love: Psychoanalysis, Feminism, and the Problem of Domination*. London: Virago.

Benjamin, Jessica. 1995. *Like Subjects, Love Objects: Essays on Recognition and Sexual Difference*. New Haven, CT: Yale University Press.

Benjamin, Jessica. 2017. *Beyond Doer and Done To: Recognition Theory, Intersubjectivity, and the Third*. London: Taylor and Francis Group.

Bernasconi, Robert. 1998. "Hegel at the Court of the Ashanti." In *Hegel After Derrida*, edited by Stuart Barnett, 41–63. London: Routledge.

Bernasconi, Robert. 2000. "With What Must the Philosophy of World History Begin? On the Racial Basis of Hegel's Eurocentrism." *Nineteenth Century Contexts* 22 (2): 171–201.

Bernasconi, Robert. 2003. "Hegel's Racism: A Reply to McCarney." *Radical Philosophy* 119 (May/June): 35–37.

Bonhoeffer, Dietrich. 1995. *Ethics*. Translated by Neville Horton Smith. New York: Touchstone.

Brennan, Timothy. 2014. *Borrowed Light: Vico, Hegel, and the Colonies*. Stanford, CA: Stanford University Press.

Brownlee, Timothy L. 2022. *Recognition and the Self in Hegel's Phenomenology of Spirit*. Cambridge: Cambridge University Press.

Brudner, Alan. 2021. "Hegel on the Rule of Law and Democracy." https://www.law.utoronto.ca/blog/faculty/hegel-rule-law-and-democracy. Accessed March 2025.

Buchwalter, Andrew. 2009. "Is Hegel's Philosophy of History Eurocentric?" In *Hegel and History*, edited by Will Dudley, 87–110. Albany, NY: SUNY Press.

Buchwalter, Andrew. 2012a. *Dialectics, Politics, and the Contemporary Value of Hegel's Practical Philosophy*. New York: Routledge.

Buchwalter, Andrew, ed. 2012b. *Hegel and Global Justice*. Dordrecht: Springer.

Buchwalter, Andrew, ed. 2015. *Hegel and Capitalism*. Albany, NY: SUNY Press.

Buck-Morss, Susan. 2009. *Hegel, Haiti, and Universal History*. Pittsburgh: Pittsburgh University Press.

Butler, Judith. 1993. "Endangered/Endangering: Schematic Racism and White Paranoia." In *Reading Rodney King: Reading Urban Uprising*, edited by Robert Gooding-Williams, 49–68. New York: Routledge.

Butler, Judith. 2021. "Why Read Hegel Now?" *Crisis and Critique* 8 (2): 41–55.

Canguilhem, Georges. 1991. *The Normal and the Pathological*. Translated by Carolyn R. Fawcett. New York: Zone Books.

Ciavatta, David. 2009. *Spirit, the Family, and the Unconscious in Hegel's Philosophy*. Albany, NY: SUNY Press.

Clare, Eli. 2017. *Brilliant Imperfection: Grappling with Cure*. Durham, NC: Duke University Press.

Coulthard, Glen Sean. 2014. *Red Skin, White Masks: Rejecting the Colonial Politics of Recognition*. Minneapolis: University of Minnesota Press.

Craft, Aimée, Phil Fontaine, and the Truth and Reconciliation Commission of Canada. 2015. *A Knock on the Door: The Essential History of Residential Schools from the Truth and Reconciliation Commission of Canada*. Winnipeg: University of Manitoba Press.

de Beauvoir, Simone. 1976. *The Ethics of Ambiguity*. Translated by Bernard Frechtman. New York: Citadel Press.

de Beauvoir, Simone. 2009. *The Second Sex*. Translated by Constance Borde and Sheila Malovany-Chevallier. New York: Vintage.

de Boer, Karin. 2003. "Hegel's Antigone and the Dialectics of Sexual Difference." *Philosophy Today: SPEP Supplement*, 140–46.

de Boer, Karin. 2009. "Hegel's Account of the Present: An Open-Ended History." In *Hegel and History*, edited by Will Dudley, 51–67. Albany, NY: SUNY Press.

de Laurentiis, Allegra. 2014. "Race in Hegel: Text and Context." In *Philosophie nach Kant*, edited by Mario Egger, 591–624. Berlin: De Gruyter.

de Laurentiis, Allegra. 2021. *Hegel's Anthropology: Life, Psyche, and Second Nature*. Evanston, IL: Northwestern University Press.

Derrida, Jacques. 2005. *Rogues: Two Essays on Reason*. Translated by Pascale-Anne Brault and Michael Naas. Stanford, CA: Stanford University Press.

D'Hondt, Jacques. 1988. *Hegel in His Time (Berlin, 1818–1831)*. Translated by John Burbidge. Peterborough: Broadview Press.

Donougho, Martin. 1989. "The Woman in White: On the Reception of Hegel's Antigone." *The Owl of Minerva* 21, no. 1 (Fall): 65–89.

Donougho, Martin. 2023. *Hegel's "Individuality": Beyond Category*. Cham: Palgrave Macmillan.

Erdrich, Louise. 2016. *LaRose*. New York: Harper.

Estes, Nick. 2019. *Our History is the Future*. London: Verso.

Fanon, Frantz. 2004. *The Wretched of the Earth*. Translated by Richard Philcox. New York: Grove Press.

Fanon, Frantz. 2008. *Black Skin, White Masks*. Translated by Richard Philcox. New York: Grove Press.

Farneth, Molly. 2017. *Hegel's Social Ethics: Religion, Conflict, and Rituals of Reconciliation*. Princeton, NJ: Princeton University Press.

Fichte, Johann Gottlieb. 2000. *Foundations of Natural Right*. Translated by Michael Baur. Cambridge: Cambridge University Press.

Forbes, Jack D. 2008. *Columbus and Other Cannibals: The Wétiko Disease of Exploitation, Imperialism, and Terrorism*. New York: Seven Stories Press.

Garland-Thomson, Rosemarie. 2011. "Misfits: A Feminist Materialist Disability Concept." *Hypatia* 26 (3): 591–609.

Gilmore, Ruth Wilson. 2017. "Abolition Geography and the Problem of Innocence." In *Futures of Black Radicalism*, edited by Gaye Theresa Johnson and Alex Lubin. New York: Verso.

Gordon, Lewis R. 1995. *Bad Faith and Anti-Black Racism*. New York: Humanity Books.

Gramsci, Antonio. 2005. *Selections from the Prison Notebooks*. Edited and translated by Quintin Hoare and Geoffrey Nowell Smith. London: Lawrence and Wishart Ltd.

Habib, M. A. R. 2017. *Hegel and Empire: From Postcolonialism to Globalism*. Cham: Palgrave MacMillan.

Haraway, Donna Jeanne. 1991. *Simians, Cyborgs, and Women: The Reinvention of Nature*. New York: Routledge.

Harris, H. S. 1983. "The Social Ideal of Hegel's Economic Theory." In *Hegel's Philosophy of Action*, edited by Lawrence S. Stepelevich and David Lamb. Atlantic Highlands, NJ: Humanities Press.

Harris, H. S. 1997a. *Hegel's Ladder I: The Pilgrimage of Reason*. Indianapolis: Hackett.

Harris, H. S. 1997b. *Hegel's Ladder II: The Odyssey of Spirit*. Indianapolis: Hackett.

Hartman, Saidiya. 1997. *Scenes of Subjection: Terror, Slavery, and Self-Making in Nineteenth-Century America*. Oxford: Oxford University Press.

Heidegger, Martin. 1962. *Being and Time*. Translated John Macquarrie and Edward Robinson. New York: Harper & Row.

Heidegger, Martin. 1993. "Origin of the Work of Art." Translated by Albert Hofstadter. In *Basic Writings*, edited by David Farrell Krell, 139–212. New York: HarperCollins.

Hendren, Sara. 2020. *What Can a Body Do? How We Meet the Built World*. New York: Riverhead Books.

Hoff, Shannon. 2007. "Restoring Antigone to Ethical Life: Nature and Sexual Difference in Hegel's Phenomenology of Spirit." *The Owl of Minerva* 38: 77–99.

Hoff, Shannon. 2014a. *The Laws of the Spirit: A Hegelian Theory of Justice*. Albany, NY: SUNY Press.

Hoff, Shannon. 2014b. "Rights and Worlds: On the Political Significance of Belonging." *Philosophical Forum* 45 (4): 355–73.

Hoff, Shannon. 2018a. "Hegel and the Possibility of Intercultural Criticism." In *Hegel and Canada: Unity of Opposites?*, edited by Neil G. Robertson and Susan M. Dodd, 342–67. Toronto: University of Toronto Press.

Hoff, Shannon. 2018b. "The Right and the Righteous: Hegel on Confession, Forgiveness, and the Necessary Imperfection of Political Action." In *Phenomenology and Forgiveness*, edited by Marguerite La Caze, 3–23. London: Rowman and Littlefield International.

Hoff, Shannon. 2023a. "Ethical Life and the Feminist Critic." In *Handbook on German Idealism and Feminist Philosophy*, edited by Susanne Lettow and Tuija Pulkkinen, 293–308. London: Palgrave Macmillan.

Hoff, Shannon. 2023b. "The 'Civilization of the Universal': The Intersectional, Decolonial, and Phenomenological Revision of Philosophy." *Puncta* 6 (1): 19–42.

Hoff, Shannon. 2023c. "A Phenomenological Account of the Conditions of Transnational Feminism." *Symposium* 27 (2): 66–82.

Hoff, Shannon. 2024. "Hegel and Wynter on the Problem of Human Self-Cognition." *Revue Internationale de Philosophie* 309, no. 3 (2024): 71–90. DOI: https://doi.org/10.3917/rip.309.0071; URL: https://shs.cairn.info/journal-revue-internationale-de-philosophie-2024-3-page-71?lang=en.

Hoff, Shannon. 2025. "White Gaze as a Concept in Phenomenology." In *Encyclopedia of Phenomenology*, edited by Nicholas de Warren and Ted Toadvine. Cham: Springer.

Houlgate, Stephen. 2016. "Right and Trust in Hegel's *Philosophy of Right*." *Hegel Bulletin* 37 (1): 104–16.

Houlgate, Stephen. 2024. "A Hegelian Life: Dialogue with Stephen Houlgate." By Johannes A. Niederhauser. https://www.youtube.com/watch?v=Dw_p-jbSHWM. Accessed March 2025.

Hutchings, Kimberly. 2003. *Hegel and Feminist Philosophy*. Cambridge: Polity.

Johnston, Adrian. 2021. "Capitalism's Implants: A Hegelian Theory of Failed Revolutions." *Crisis and Critique* 8 (2): 123–81.

la paperson. 2017. *A Third University Is Possible*. Minneapolis: University of Minnesota Press.

Lévi-Strauss, Claude. 1952. *Race and History*. Paris: UNESCO.

Liboiron, Max. 2021. *Pollution Is Colonialism*. Durham, NC: Duke University Press.

Lloyd, Genevieve. 1984. *The Man of Reason: "Male" and "Female" in Western Philosophy*. London: Routledge.

Mahmood, Saba. 2001. "Feminist Theory, Embodiment, and the Docile Agent: Some Reflections on the Egyptian Islamic Revival." *Cultural Anthropology* 16, no. 2 (May): 202–36.

Mahmood, Saba. 2005. *Politics of Piety: The Islamic Revival and the Feminist Subject*. Princeton, NJ: Princeton University Press.

Malabou, Catherine. 2005. *The Future of Hegel: Plasticity, Temporality and Dialectic*. Translated by Lisabeth During. New York: Routledge.

Marx, Karl. 1994. *Selected Writings*. Edited by Lawrence H. Simon. Indianapolis: Hackett.

Mascat, Jamila M. H. 2024. "Hegel, Colonialism and Postcolonial Hegelianism." *Hegel Bulletin* 45 (1): 120–43.

McCarney, Joseph. 2000. *Hegel on History*. New York: Routledge.

McCarney, Joseph. 2003. "Hegel's Racism? A Response to Bernasconi." *Radical Philosophy* 119: 32–35.

McCaskie, Tom C. 2019. "Exiled from History: Africa in Hegel's Academic Practice." *History in Africa* 46: 165–94.

McCumber, John. 2013. *On Philosophy: Notes from a Crisis*. Stanford, CA: Stanford University Press.

Mehta, Uday Singh. 1999. *Liberalism and Empire: A Study in Nineteenth-Century British Liberal Thought*. Chicago: University of Chicago Press.

Merleau-Ponty, Maurice. 1964. *Signs*. Translated by Richard C. McCleary. Evanston, IL: Northwestern University Press.

Merleau-Ponty, Maurice. 1968. *The Visible and the Invisible*. Translated by Alphonso Lingis. Evanston, IL: Northwestern University Press.

Merleau-Ponty, Maurice. 1969. *Humanism and Terror: An Essay on the Communist Problem*. Translated by John O'Neill. Boston: Beacon Press.

Merleau-Ponty, Maurice. 2012. *Phenomenology of Perception*. Translated by Donald Landes. New York: Routledge.

Mignolo, Walter D. 2007. "Delinking: The Rhetoric of Modernity, the Logic of Coloniality and the Grammar of De-coloniality." *Cultural Studies* 21 (2–3): 449–514.

Mills, Charles W. 2014. "Materializing Race." In *Living Alterities: Phenomenology, Embodiment, and Race*, edited by Emily S. Lee, 19–41. Albany, NY: SUNY Press.

Mills, Charles W. 2017. *Black Rights, White Wrongs: The Critique of Racial Liberalism*. Oxford: Oxford University Press.

Moland, Lydia L. 2011. *Hegel on Political Identity: Patriotism, Nationality, Cosmopolitanism*. Evanston, IL: Northwestern University Press.

Morris, David. 2006. "The Open Figure of Experience and Mind." *Dialogue* 45 (2): 315–26.
Mowad, Nicholas. 2019. *Meaning and Embodiment: Human Corporeity in Hegel's Anthropology*. Albany, NY: SUNY Press.
Narayan, Uma. 2019. "Sisterhood and 'Doing Good': Asymmetries of Western Feminist Location, Access, and Orbits of Concern." *Feminist Philosophy Quarterly* 5, no. 2, Article 7.
Nelson, Maggie. 2021. *On Freedom: Four Songs of Care and Constraint*. Minneapolis: Graywolf Press.
NoiseCat, Julian Brave. 2017. "The Western Idea of Private Property Is Flawed. Indigenous Peoples Have It Right." *The Guardian*, March 27.
Oliver, Kelly. 2001. *Witnessing: Beyond Recognition*. Minneapolis: University of Minnesota Press.
Paquette, Gabriel. 2003. "Hegel's Analysis of Colonialism and Its Roots in Scottish Political Economy." *Clio* 32 (4): 415–33.
Parekh, Serena. 2009. "Hegel's New World: History, Freedom, and Race." In *Hegel and History*, edited by William Dudley, 111–31. Albany, NY: SUNY Press.
Perez, Caroline Criado. 2019. *Invisible Women: Data Bias in a World Designed for Men*. New York: Abrams Press.
Pinkard, Terry. 1991. "The Successor to Metaphysics: Absolute Idea and Absolute Spirit." *The Monist* 74 (3): 295–328.
Pinkard, Terry. 2017. *Does History Make Sense? Hegel on the Historical Shapes of Justice*. Cambridge, MA: Harvard University Press.
Pinkard, Terry. 2021. "Should Hegelian Political Philosophy Jettison the Absolute? Hegel's Political Philosophy Two-Hundred Years Later." *Crisis and Critique* 8 (2): 307–27.
Pippin, Robert B. 2008. *Hegel's Practical Philosophy: Rational Agency as Ethical Life*. Cambridge: Cambridge University Press.
Pippin, Robert B. 2020. "Capitalism at Dusk: Hegel and the Irrationality of the Modern Economy." *The Point Magazine* 22 (April). https://thepointmag.com/politics/capitalism-at-dusk/. Accessed March 2025.
Plato. 1968. *The Republic of Plato*. Translated by Allan Bloom. New York: Basic Books.
Plato. 2012. *Apology*. In *A Plato Reader: Eight Essential Dialogues*, edited by C. D. C. Reeve, 21–46. Indianapolis: Hackett.
Quijano, Anibal. 2000. "Coloniality of Power, Eurocentrism, and Latin America." Translated by Michael Ennis. *Nepantla: Views from South* 1 (3): 533–80.
Rankine, Claudia, and Beth Loffreda. 2015. "On Whiteness and the Racial Imaginary." *Literary Hub*, April. Retrieved from https://lithub.com/on-whiteness-and-the-racial-imaginary/. Accessed March 2025.
Ravven, Heidi Miriam. 1988. "Has Hegel Anything to Say to Feminists?" *The Owl of Minerva* 19, no. 2 (Spring): 149–68.
Rawlinson, Mary. 2021. *The Betrayal of Substance: Death, Literature, and Sexual Difference in Hegel's* Phenomenology of Spirit. New York: Columbia University Press.
Rooney, Phyllis. 1994. "Recent Work in Feminist Discussions of Reason." *American Philosophical Quarterly* 31 (1): 1–21.
Rubin, Gayle. 1975. "The Traffic in Women: Notes on the 'Political Economy' of Sex." In *Toward an Anthropology of Women*, edited by Rayna R. Reiter. New York: Monthly Review Press.
Russon, John. 1997. *The Self and Its Body in Hegel's* Phenomenology of Spirit. Toronto: University of Toronto Press.

Russon, John. 2004. *Reading Hegel's Phenomenology*. Bloomington: Indiana University Press.

Russon, John. 2016. *Infinite Phenomenology: The Lessons of Hegel's Science of Experience*. Evanston, IL: Northwestern University Press.

Russon, John. 2017. *Sites of Exposure: Art, Politics, and the Nature of Experience*. Bloomington: Indiana University Press.

Russon, John. 2020. *Adult Life: Aging, Responsibility, and the Pursuit of Happiness*. Albany, NY: SUNY Press.

Saner, Senem. 2025. "Embedded Agency: A Critique of Negative Liberty and Free Markets." *Philosophy & Social Criticism* 51 (1): 98–131.

Sartre, Jean-Paul. 2004. *Critique of Dialectical Reason, Volume 1*. Translated by Alan Sheridan-Smith. London: Verso.

Sartre, Jean-Paul. 2018. *Being and Nothingness*. Translated by Sarah Richmond. New York: Routledge.

Serequeberhan, Tsenay. 1989. "The Idea of Colonialism in Hegel's *Philosophy of Right*." *International Philosophical Quarterly* 29 (3): 301–18.

Siep, Ludwig. 2004. "Constitution, Fundamental Rights, and Social Welfare in Hegel's *Philosophy of Right*." In *Hegel on Ethics and Politics*, edited by Robert B. Pippin and Otfried Höffe, 268–90. Translated by Nicholas Walker. Cambridge: Cambridge University Press.

Siep, Ludwig. 2021. "A 'Transformative' Reading of Hegel's *Philosophy of Right*?" *Crisis and Critique* 8 (2): 368–91.

Simms, Eva M. 2008. *The Child in the World*. Detroit: Wayne State University Press.

Simpson, Audra. 2014. *Mohawk Interruptus: Political Life Across the Borders of Settler States*. Durham, NC: Duke University Press.

Simpson, Leanne Betasamosake. 2020. *Noopiming: The Cure for White Ladies*. Toronto: House of Anansi Press.

Sophocles. *Antigone*. 1991. Translated by David Grene. Chicago: University of Chicago Press.

Spivak, Gayatri Chakravorty. 1999. *A Critique of Postcolonial Reason: Toward a History of the Vanishing Present*. Cambridge, MA: Harvard University Press.

Stone, Alison. 2017. "Hegel and Colonialism." *Hegel Bulletin* 41 (2): 247–70.

Stone, Alison. 2018. *Nature, Ethics and Gender in German Romanticism and Idealism*. London: Rowman & Littlefield.

Styres, Sandra, and Dawn Zinga. 2013. "The Community-First Land-Centered Theoretical Framework: Bringing a 'Good Mind' to Indigenous Education Research?" *Canadian Journal of Education* 36 (2): 284–313.

Tibebu, Teshale. 2010. *Hegel and the Third World: The Making of Eurocentrism in World History*. Syracuse, NY: Syracuse University Press.

Tuck, Eve, Allison Guess, and Hannah Sultan. 2014. "Not Nowhere: Collaborating on Selfsame Land." *Decolonization: Indigeneity, Education, and Society*, June, 1–11.

Tuck, Eve, and K. Wayne Yang. 2012. "Decolonization Is Not a Metaphor." *Decolonization: Indigeneity, Education & Society* 1 (1): 1–40.

von der Luft, Eric. 1984. "The Theological Significance of Hegel's Four World-Historical Realms." *Auslegung* 11 (1): 340–57.

Williams, Robert R. 1997. *Hegel's Ethics of Recognition*. Berkeley: University of California Press.

Wynter, Sylvia. 2003. "Unsettling the Coloniality of Being/Power/Truth/Freedom:

Towards the Human, After Man, Its Overrepresentation—An Argument." *The New Centennial Review* 3, no. 3 (Fall): 257–337.

Young, Iris Marion. 1980. "Throwing Like a Girl: A Phenomenology of Feminine Body Comportment, Motility, and Spatiality." *Human Studies* 3 (2): 137–56.

Young, Iris Marion. 1990. *Justice and the Politics of Difference*. Princeton, NJ: Princeton University Press.

Zambrana, Rocío. 2016. "Hegel, History, and Race." In *The Oxford Handbook of Philosophy and Race*, edited by Naomi Zack, 251–60. Oxford: Oxford University Press.

Zambrana, Rocío. 2020. "Bad Habits: Idleness and Race in Hegel." *Hegel Bulletin* 42 (1): 1–18.

Zambrana, Rocío. 2021. "Hegelian History Interrupted." *Crisis and Critique* 8 (2): 411–31.

INDEX

ableism, 5, 6, 16, 25, 57, 189, 191, 196, 198, 223
abnormality, 149, 191, 194
abstraction, 8, 10–18, 22, 24, 25, 73, 76, 77, 111, 129, 134, 146, 157, 172, 186, 197, 202, 230n11
Abu-Lughod, Lila, 13, 129, 132, 135–36, 162–63
accommodation, 12, 16, 39, 53, 74, 76, 82, 121, 132, 190–98, 214
accountability, 127, 154, 157, 160
Achebe, Chinua, 106
action, 14, 21–23, 27, 36, 42, 49, 52, 60, 80–81, 85, 99, 110, 113, 117, 121–23, 126, 128, 130–34, 141–42, 175–76, 180–81, 186, 189, 195, 198–201, 204–6, 208–9, 211–12, 216, 230nn8–9, 232n16, 236n2, 236n5; in *Antigone*, 80–81, 85; and conscience, 143–65; in dramatic poetry, 169–71; free, 8, 80, 97, 100, 184, 198, 200, 209, 222
activity, 20, 43, 48, 68, 96–99, 120, 133, 160, 175, 177, 182, 198–99, 201–8, 216–17, 220, 221, 223, 235n14, 236n6, 237n12; free, 16–17, 19, 97, 112–16, 124, 183, 208
actors, 147–51, 159, 164, 170, 200
actual, the, 6, 23–24, 69, 73, 110, 145–47, 151, 155–56, 175, 187–89, 208–11, 214–15, 221, 229n3 (intro.), 230n7, 235n14, 237n5
actuality, 17, 21–22, 24, 38, 78, 90, 96, 102–3, 107, 117, 143, 147–48, 152, 155, 165, 169, 171–72, 184, 188, 193, 211–12, 216–17, 221, 229n1 (chap. 1), 230n9
actualization, 18, 72, 95, 108, 111, 155–56, 189, 217, 236n6
adaptation, 132–33, 194–95, 202
"adaptive knowing," 167, 236n4 (chap. 4)
Additions (*Zusätze*) (Hegel), 69, 93, 177, 179, 208, 230n4, 232n16, 235n13, 235n15, 236nn2–4 (chap. 5)
affect, 50, 89
affirmation, 29, 31, 33, 36–37, 40–41, 46–47, 58–60, 64–67, 72, 80, 86, 98–99, 117, 132, 160, 182, 207
Africa, 6, 91, 106, 163, 233n3, 235n16
agency, 37–38, 52, 64, 68, 86, 89, 99, 120–22, 130–35, 155–60, 163–64, 170–71, 182, 184, 186, 190–91, 196, 198–99, 201, 216, 218, 223, 236n5
Ahmed, Sara, 53–54
Alcoff, Linda Martín, 5, 53
Alfred, Taiaiake, 56
alibis, false, 14, 152–56
alienation, 13, 14, 62, 105, 114, 119, 123, 125–29, 135, 141, 153–54, 192, 205, 223–24
Allen, S. Denise, 124
Al-Saji, Alia, 54, 162
Amin, Samir, 56
answerability, 10, 14–15, 37, 59, 116, 119, 139, 145–50, 156–62, 165–71, 190, 196, 204, 218–19, 223
"Anthropology" (Hegel), 10, 174, 177–80, 193, 234n13, 236n1

Antigone, 70, 80–86, 97, 103, 119, 233n2
antiracism, 4, 104
Antony, Louise M., 229n1 (intro.)
Apology (Plato), 42–43, 122
arbitrariness, 20, 22, 99, 101–3, 125, 136, 219–21
Arendt, Hannah, 171
Armstrong, Jeannette, 124
art, 139, 142, 152, 164–73, 187–88, 212
Asia, 6, 90, 106
Atleo, Clifford, 124
attachment, 3, 13, 25, 86–87, 134, 151, 156–57, 159
authority, 9, 20, 22, 28, 32–38, 43, 83, 85, 89, 101, 103, 123, 128, 146, 164, 168, 206
autonomy, 21, 23–24, 88, 125, 130, 136
Avineri, Shlomo, 236n7

babies, 58–60, 76, 186
Baldwin, James, 47
Beauvoir, Simone de, 24, 75, 148, 185, 192, 193, 210
behavior, 12, 52–53, 61, 74–78, 84, 119, 149, 184, 186, 195
being-in-the-world, 48, 54–56, 106, 128, 174
belonging, 14, 25, 40, 54, 80, 106, 113, 116–17, 122–25, 127, 129–38, 208, 223–24
Benjamin, Jessica, 12, 42, 56–67, 231n12
Bernasconi, Robert, 7, 233n3
Blackness, 50, 55, 121, 123, 127–28, 153–54
body, the, 3, 10, 16, 34–38, 40, 46–58, 70, 92, 120, 125, 127, 153, 172, 174–82, 236n4 (chap. 5)
body schema, 47–52
Bonhoeffer, Dietrich, 154
Boron, Jonathan, 124
Brennan, Timothy, 106–7, 233n3, 235n14
Brownlee, Timothy, 231n7
Brudner, Alan, 219, 237nn15–16
Buchwalter, Andrew, 106–7, 111, 198, 206–7, 233n3, 236n7, 237n9
Buck-Morss, Susan, 234n12
Butler, Judith, 53, 181, 209

Canguilhem, Georges, 16, 189, 194–96
capitalism, 4–6, 16–17, 25, 57, 95, 116, 132, 138, 153, 198, 208–9, 223, 237n9
care, 23, 39, 47, 70–71, 74–76, 82–83, 96, 98–100, 130, 138, 144–45, 157, 160, 177, 187, 191, 195–96, 206, 208, 222, 237n7; for dependents, 40, 56–67, 121, 190, 194, 212; for the "we," 80, 112, 218–19, 221
caregivers, 12, 40, 57–66, 74–76
certainty, 29, 36–37, 142, 229n1 (chap. 1)
children, 32, 34, 40, 56–67, 74–75, 82, 88, 126, 163, 190, 205, 233n3
China, 92, 198, 234n12
Ciavatta, David, 231n5, 233n1, 234n4
civil society, 6, 10, 80, 111–17, 197–209, 213, 216–21, 234n9
Clare, Eli, 195
clothing, 36, 134, 158
collaboration, 95, 99, 113, 120, 182–83, 193, 202
colonialism, 1, 4–6, 13, 20, 25, 55–57, 72–73, 79–80, 86–87, 89, 95, 104, 106–11, 115–39, 150–62, 223, 229n1 (intro.), 233n3, 235n15
communication, 14–15, 25, 41, 45, 53, 60, 74, 85, 89–90, 96, 105, 109, 139, 146, 149–53, 158–64, 168, 190–93, 214, 217, 223–24
concept, 29, 33, 36, 69, 152, 229n1 (chap. 1)
concreteness, 2, 5–6, 11–13, 17, 21–22, 25–26, 45, 47, 69, 72, 76–78, 89, 100–101, 108, 110–12, 116–17, 129, 134, 142–44, 151–55, 164, 168–69, 173–75, 179, 187, 197, 212–18, 224, 234n7, 237n5
conscience, 9, 10, 14, 17, 44, 71, 85, 133, 139–73, 175, 210, 215, 223, 234n7, 236n2 (chap. 4)
consciousness, 76, 85, 105, 111, 143, 164, 168, 174–75, 178–79, 202, 212, 229n1 (chap. 1), 230n5, 230n7, 231n10, 233n3; in the French Revolution, 230n7, 230n9; independent, 37; inessential, 36; and life, 34, 181–82; negation of, 31; pure, 24, 181, 183; servile, 37, 182; in the shape of thinghood, 38–39, 181; shapes of, 73, 76–77, 139, 230n11; unhappy, 231n3
constitution, 21, 78, 108, 142, 152, 154, 168, 199–201, 209–21, 230n3, 237nn14–15
contingency, 44, 75, 88, 97, 103, 113–15, 133, 166, 168, 186–87, 204–9, 212–14, 221, 232n16
corporations, 102, 113–16, 201, 205–8, 217, 219–21, 237n12

INDEX

Coulthard, Glen Sean, 13, 119, 124, 231n4
counterfinality, 8, 17, 197–201, 204–8, 221–22
coupling. *See* pairing
Creon, 81, 83, 85–86, 233n2
Criado Perez, Caroline, 237n8
culture, 9, 12, 45, 51–54, 77–79, 86, 88–93, 101, 104–11, 118, 135–37, 141–42, 162–69, 172, 223, 233n3, 234n12, 235n16, 236n3 (chap. 4)
customs, 9, 12, 15, 53, 76, 89, 103, 109, 122, 131

de Beauvoir, Simone. *See* Beauvoir, Simone de
de Boer, Karin, 109, 232n14, 236n7
de Laurentiis, Allegra, 233n3, 234n13, 236n1
death, 31, 34, 38, 67, 81, 125–26, 162, 181, 236n3 (chap. 4); absolute freedom and, 24; in *Antigone*, 81, 83–84; fear of, 38, 181; struggle to the, 10, 27–33, 39, 125, 180–81, 231n1, 231n3
decision, 22–23, 68, 75, 77, 86, 146, 202, 219, 230n7, 237–38n16
decolonial thought, 56, 80, 104, 109, 119, 229n1 (intro.)
delinking, 56
democracy, 80, 118, 130, 138, 154, 163, 211, 220
dependence: in civil society, 102, 114–16, 202–8; material, 48, 123, 156, 181, 187, 196, 198; on others, 11, 24, 26, 46, 47, 50–51, 56–58, 61, 76, 223; of self-consciousness, 36–43, 47, 73, 76, 231n1
Derrida, Jacques, 230n10
desire, 30–32, 46, 58–59, 62, 66, 72, 82, 102, 114, 128, 130, 134, 175, 186, 231n3; and the master, 35–37, 62, 181; for recognition, 114, 207; and the servant, 37, 181–82
determinacy, 17, 20, 44, 56, 76, 90; of conscientious action, 143–51, 154–62, 166–68; and ethical life, 13–14, 76, 78, 89–90, 121, 133–39; freedom and, 187, 210–11; and the French Revolution, 10, 22, 24–25; and law, 211–15, 218–19, 231n11; and nature, 69, 177, 179; transcendence of, 46
development, 31–32, 75, 77, 133, 149, 190–91, 197, 206, 212, 229n1 (intro.), 237n7; childhood, 40–42, 56–66; history and, 90–92, 105, 233n3; and servitude, 38, 48, 182
D'Hondt, Jacques, 201, 219
dialectic, 48–49, 53, 115–16, 172, 224
dialogue. *See* communication
difference, 23–25, 33, 89, 127, 134, 137, 158–59, 169, 185, 211; sexual, 68–71, 85, 232n16
dignity, 20, 101–3, 113–14, 117, 129, 146, 151, 153, 155–57, 207
disability, 6, 189–97
domination, 3–6, 9, 13, 20, 25, 72, 89–90, 132–34, 149, 160, 220, 223–24, 231n4; and mastery and servitude, 33–40
Donougho, Martin, 232nn14–15, 234n6, 235n1
dramatic poetry, 169–72, 236n5
dualism, 152, 174, 179, 196, 237n4
duty, 114, 144–48, 156, 210

East, the, 90, 92, 106
economy, 6, 8, 16, 25, 174, 176, 199–200, 203; capitalist, 138–39, 198; and civil society, 112–13, 116, 205–7; and inequality, 124, 127, 209
education, 32, 38, 92, 96, 109, 111, 129, 177, 189, 205–7, 213–14, 220–21, 231n10, 232n16
Egypt, 97, 104, 234n12; Egyptian women, 133–34
empowerment, 36, 38, 56, 80, 94, 103, 107, 119, 135, 149, 164, 191, 195, 213, 217
Encyclopaedia of the Philosophical Sciences (Hegel), 6, 10, 165, 174, 177–80, 183, 233n1
epidermal racial schema, 47–51
equality, 9, 20, 23–24, 37, 138, 151–56, 211, 215, 219. *See also* inequality
erotic relations, 12, 56, 61–67
estates, 102, 116, 206–9, 220–21
Estes, Nick, 124
ethical life, 9–10, 12–13, 15, 17, 26, 45, 68–69, 72–141, 150, 155, 159, 162–73, 175, 206, 209–10, 215, 229n2 (intro.), 233n17 (chap. 2), 233n1 (chap. 3), 236n2 (chap. 4); Greek, 5, 67, 79, 80–87, 236n6
Eurocentrism, 54, 106–7

Europe, 14, 90–91, 101, 107, 114, 125, 130, 152–53, 160, 229n1 (intro.), 233n3, 234n12
evil, 68, 147, 218
exclusion, 1–2, 6–7, 11–12, 22–23, 25, 64, 111, 118, 137
executive, the, 218–20
exploitation, 53, 61, 65, 102, 125, 127, 136–37, 153–54, 160, 204, 209
expression, 44, 60, 74, 97, 99, 134–35, 165–71, 182, 187

facticity, 113, 143, 165
familiarity, 3, 54, 87–89, 129, 137–38, 167
family, 32, 76, 112, 216, 218, 221; in civil society, 114–16, 205–8, 213; in the *Phenomenology*, 68, 81–85; in the *Philosophy of Right*, 69–72
Fanon, Frantz, 12, 14, 42–43, 45–57, 67, 91, 150–60, 217, 229n1 (intro.)
farming, 199–200
fear, 162, 218; of death, 38, 181
feminine, 7, 66, 68, 229n1 (intro.)
feminism, 68–71, 80, 118, 129–32, 136, 158, 162–63, 229n1 (intro.)
figure-ground relationship, 53–56, 87
finitude, 12, 38–39, 84–85, 96–97, 101–3, 109, 145–50, 165–73, 175, 183, 186–87, 223
"first accusations," 43–45, 122
fit, 16, 33, 53, 62, 99, 188–96, 237n7
flourishing, 63, 116, 118, 161, 198, 213
Forbes, Jack, 125
freedom, 8, 13, 15, 20, 24, 37, 70, 94–111, 128, 133, 154, 163, 182–85, 224; absolute, 14, 23–24, 229n2 (chap. 1); and being at home, 16, 91, 110, 184, 187, 191, 224; and civil society, 112–17, 206–9, 221; and ethical life, 13, 24, 69, 80, 82, 91, 94–104, 112, 124, 131–36, 155–60, 190, 201, 224; and history, 71–72, 79–80, 87, 92, 94–111, 214–17, 221; individual, 6, 71, 80, 86, 95, 98–99, 103, 108–13, 117, 121, 131–34, 136, 151, 153, 156, 158, 174, 188, 191, 209–10, 212–13, 221; and law, 211–12, 219; and necessity, 15–17, 97–100, 184–85, 193, 222; and objectivity, 15, 113, 126, 156, 183–85, 187–94, 210–18, 221, 223; and others, 9, 24, 40, 57, 59, 62–63, 67, 72, 92, 98, 109–10, 118, 124, 126, 133, 156, 160, 184, 186, 189, 201, 210, 214, 216–18, 221; universal, 23–24, 230n9; and whiteness, 45, 128, 152
French Revolution, 9–17, 20–25, 107, 125, 139, 141, 172, 211, 215, 229n2 (chap. 1), 237n16
Freud, Sigmund, 5
future, the, 149, 160, 165, 194, 210, 212, 224

Garland-Thomson, Rosemarie, 16, 189–90, 195
gender, 1, 6, 7, 25, 61, 63, 66–72
"Germanic" realm, 79, 91, 100, 101, 108
Gilmore, Ruth Wilson, 124
God, 81, 84, 88, 101, 103, 233n3
gods, 81, 83–85, 89, 119, 236n6
good, the, 14, 117, 133, 144–49, 154–59, 162
Gordon, Lewis R., 47
government, 23, 68, 115–16, 126, 154, 173, 189, 197–98, 201, 204, 208–14, 217–22, 230n8, 232n16, 235n21, 237n13
Gramsci, Antonio, 88
Greece, 79, 106, 118
"Greek" realm, 79, 108
growth, 37–38, 133, 163, 237n5
Guess, Allison, 235n20

habit, 3, 22, 43, 45, 48, 53, 61, 74–77, 128, 130, 159, 178–80, 207
Haraway, Donna, 120
hard heart, 148
Harris, H. S., 31, 209, 232n14, 233n2, 236n1 (chap. 4), 236n7
Hartman, Saidiya, 89
health, 57, 124, 194–96, 212, 214
Heidegger, Martin, 43, 48, 49, 174
Hendren, Sara, 195
Herzog, Lisa, 207
heterosexism, 63–64, 67, 196
heterosexuality, 69, 192
historical-racial schema, 47, 49–50
history, 2–4, 16, 21, 24–25, 30, 72, 77–79, 88, 90–91, 93–111, 116, 118, 125, 139, 141–42, 144, 155, 161, 164, 168, 176, 184, 194, 210, 213–15, 230n4, 233n3, 234n10, 234n13, 235n15; and conscience, 14; and freedom, 71–72, 79–80, 87, 94–111, 214–17, 221; of philosophy, 5, 7–8, 21, 88, 230n4; and whiteness, 53–54, 91;

INDEX 253

world, 15, 87, 90, 93, 107, 110, 112, 165, 169, 172, 230n4, 233n3, 234n12
Hoff, Shannon, 109, 131, 135, 150, 229n2 (intro.), 231n4, 231n9, 232n14, 236n4 (chap. 4)
home, 22, 38, 40, 52, 57, 71, 84, 96, 98, 100, 102, 109, 123, 130, 132, 135, 137, 157, 164, 171–72, 183, 191, 196, 211, 217; and freedom, 16, 91, 110, 184, 187, 191, 224
Houlgate, Stephen, 4, 211, 213, 236n7
humanity, universal, 10, 12, 25, 91, 137
Hutchings, Kimberly, 232n14

"I that is we" and "we that is I," 119, 141
ideal (as in "ideality"), 15–16, 175, 178–80, 196, 232n16
ideal (as in "standard"), 14, 17–18, 22–23, 25, 111, 152–57, 161–62, 215, 224; liberal, 14, 152–56
idealism, 175
ideology, 75, 163
independence, 20, 102, 110, 117, 120–21, 124, 160, 164, 191, 196, 204, 210, 216, 235n15, 236n5 (chap. 4), 236n4 (chap. 5), 237–38n16; and dependence of self-consciousness, 11, 34–42, 56–62, 73, 76, 181, 223, 231n1
indeterminacy, 46, 147, 185, 215, 231n11
India, 92, 158, 233–34n3, 234n12
indifference, 68, 123; stance of, 137–39
Indigenous communities, 6, 106, 120–21, 123–24, 127, 233n3
Indigenous erasure, 122–27
Indigenous thought, 56, 80, 109, 119–28, 235nn17–18
individual, the: in "Anthropology," 178–79, 236n4 (chap. 5); in civil society, 6, 113–16, 201–9; and colonialism, 154–56, 157, 160; and conscience, 148–51, 157–60; and ethical life, 14, 45, 68, 70, 120–23, 128–39, 155, 170, 202, 210, 236n2 (chap. 4); and the French Revolution, 9, 11, 13, 23–24, 230nn7–9; modern, 4, 9–11, 14, 71, 95, 99, 110, 129–30, 150, 153, 171, 204; and normality, 194–95; single (*einzelne*), 24, 116, 232n15; and the state, 210, 213–14, 216, 220
individual action, 99, 113, 148, 159–61, 170, 198–99, 200–203, 209

individual freedom, 6, 71, 80, 86, 95, 98–99, 103, 108–13, 117, 121, 131–34, 136, 151, 153, 156, 158, 174, 188, 191, 209–10, 212–13, 221
individual interest, 130, 198–99, 204–5
individual rights, 89, 130–31, 138, 151
individual subjectivity, 86, 95, 99, 103, 108–11, 116–18, 205, 234n12
individualism, 121–22, 127, 135, 150, 153–54, 160, 207
individuality, 11–13, 64, 67–68, 237n5
inequality, 23, 138, 163, 200; economic, 116, 124, 208–9
injustice, 2, 4, 109, 138, 215
institutions, 9, 23–24, 30, 76–77, 80, 88, 99–102, 108, 126, 130, 138, 150, 177, 185, 187, 189; of modern ethical life, 17, 68–70, 102, 113, 116–19, 173, 197–98, 205–6, 208–9, 213–16, 219, 221; of settler colonialism, 121, 122, 128
interaction, 41, 44, 53, 64, 67, 82, 88–89, 95, 98, 100, 127, 147, 162, 186–89, 201, 216–18, 222; with caregivers, 61, 72, 75–76; erotic, 56, 63, 66–67; intercultural, 13, 109, 139, 161, 165, 169; with materiality, 48, 52, 94, 174, 182, 194, 199
interdependence, 24, 37, 57, 61, 81, 119, 124, 160, 187–88, 196, 209, 218, 223–24
interpretation, 28, 52, 63, 75, 77, 80, 85, 105, 128, 133, 135, 149, 162, 167, 172
intertwining, 39, 42, 47–48, 90, 96, 119, 123, 180, 223

Johnston, Adrian, 219
judge, the, 147–50, 155, 164
judgment, 38, 61, 75, 77, 106, 118, 130, 146–50, 158–61
juridical space, 122–23, 127
justice, 1, 8, 95, 100, 110–11, 157, 166, 205, 217

killing, 23, 31–33, 127, 162
kinship, 72, 115
knowledge, 48–49, 69, 81–82, 88, 91, 113, 119, 122, 145, 155, 162, 206, 213, 229n1 (intro.), 232n16

la paperson, 13, 119–28, 235n17, 235n20
labor, 16, 24, 36, 69, 95, 100–101, 104, 116, 127, 176–77, 184, 198, 201–4, 208–9, 212,

labor (*continued*)
    220–21; division of, 113, 115–16, 203–4; exploitation of, 65, 136, 153; in Fanon, 153, 156–57; in Greek ethical life, 81, 83, 85, 119; in Indigenous thought, 119, 121–28, 235n18, 235n20; of the servant, 10, 36–37, 48, 180–83; of third self, 50–51, 56–57; women's, 61, 63–65, 67, 71–73, 153, 196
land, 198–200
language, 7, 42, 53, 74, 83, 90, 96, 159, 230n9
law, 23, 46, 100, 102, 111, 122, 126, 172, 205, 210–11, 217–20, 233n3, 237n13, 237n15; and conscience, 145, 147–48, 159
Lectures on Aesthetics (Hegel), 10, 92, 97, 100, 104, 165, 230n4, 233n3
legal condition (*Rechtzustand*), 141, 235n1
legislature, 116, 208–9, 218–20
Lévi-Strauss, Claude, 91–92, 106
liberal ideals, 11, 14, 17, 131, 138, 150–53, 156–61, 215
liberalism, 4, 14, 151–55, 160, 162
Liboiron, Max, 124, 235n18
Lloyd, Genevieve, 229n1 (intro.)
Locke, John, 1, 7, 88, 174
Loffreda, Beth, 152
look, the, 47, 185, 193
love, 40, 46, 57, 71, 96, 145, 175, 186, 191
luxury, 114, 116, 204, 207–8

machines, 16, 92, 160, 202–4
Mahmood, Saba, 13, 129, 131–36
Malabou, Catherine, 236n1 (chap. 5)
Marx, Karl, 14, 92, 152, 174
Mascat, Jamila M. H., 233n3
masculine, 7, 66, 198
master, 10, 33, 35–38, 47–48, 62, 180–82, 234n9, 235n15
materiality, 38–40, 52, 96, 120, 127, 172, 174, 180; and body, 175–82, 190, 196, 203; and determinacy, 25, 115, 144, 176, 197, 215, 235n14; and freedom, 15–17, 38, 94, 105–6, 113, 126, 134, 156, 174, 183–94, 200, 210–18, 221, 223; and meaning, 15, 53, 78, 90, 119, 124, 153, 168, 175, 178–80, 190, 194, 196, 199; and the practico-inert, 198–205, 234n11; as objective spirit, 10–11, 183–89, 223; organization of, 15–17, 98, 128, 172, 176, 183, 189; as shared, 105, 199–200; and thinking, 2, 78, 105, 117, 134, 152, 164, 175
McCarney, Joseph, 233n3
McCaskie, Tom C., 235n16
McCumber, John, 234n10
meaning: of action, 27, 57, 148, 150, 156–57, 161, 164, 170, 200, 208; and determinacy, 14, 21, 46, 56, 89–91, 103, 108, 110, 158–59, 166–69, 172, 184; and history, 53, 55, 172; and materiality, 15, 53, 78, 90, 119, 124, 153, 168, 175–76, 178–80, 187, 190, 192–94, 196, 199; and others, 24, 33, 35, 39, 49, 59–60, 96–98, 101–6, 116–17, 127, 129, 131, 133–35, 148–50, 158, 164, 167, 172, 186, 192, 216–17; pursuit of, 46, 56, 98, 101–3, 165, 186; and the self, 28, 41, 46, 133
mediation, 36, 52, 103, 117, 178, 181, 184, 186, 202, 206, 215
Mehta, Uday Singh, 129
membership: in civil society, 114–15; in corporations, 113–14, 206–8, 209; in family, 82, 205; in the legislature, 116, 208, 220; in worlds, 55, 82, 86, 99, 106, 112, 123, 130, 135, 141, 170, 209, 213–14, 216
men, 63–65, 69, 192
Merleau-Ponty, Maurice, 150–52, 155–57, 160, 168, 174, 193, 221, 232n13
Middle East, the, 80
Mignolo, Walter, 56
Mills, Charles W., 17
misfitting, 16, 189, 194
misrecognition, 45–56
modern world, 10, 18, 20, 25, 54, 68, 80, 86, 91–92, 102, 107–10, 121, 125, 130, 138, 151, 161, 204, 212, 221, 229n1 (intro.), 234n12, 237n12
Moland, Lydia, 102, 114
monarchs, 22, 218–20, 237n15, 238n16
moral action, 147–48
moral self-consciousness, 116–17
moral situations, 144–45, 149
moral stance, 112, 116–18, 214, 229n2 (intro.), 233n1
moral subjectivity, 117, 164
moral vanity, 146

morality, 3, 9, 21, 78, 87, 112, 141–42, 145, 168, 212, 229n2 (intro.)
Morris, David, 134
mother-other, 56–67
mystification, 9, 152–53

Narayan, Uma, 162, 236n3 (chap. 4)
nature, 38, 46, 68, 70, 81, 85–86, 89, 102, 104, 125–27, 138, 178–79, 181, 183–84, 186, 192, 199, 210–11, 233n2, 236n4 (chap. 5)
necessity, 48, 68, 69, 115, 168, 187, 237n10; and contingency, 168, 187; of determinacy, 139, 149, 150, 210; and freedom, 15–17, 97–100, 183–85, 193, 221–22
needs, 35–36, 46, 82, 97, 109, 113–15, 117, 138, 142, 167, 183, 186, 189, 201–4, 209, 215, 218, 220
negativity, 39, 172, 218
Nelson, Maggie, 152, 155
NoiseCat, Julian Brave, 124–25, 127, 153
nonhumans, 25, 119, 123–24, 153
non-sense, 77–78, 87–88
non-transparency, 24–25, 76, 84, 86–87, 89, 122, 158, 172
normality, 149, 191, 194–95
normativity, 107, 122, 131–32; grounded, 13, 119, 120–21
norms, 1, 9, 11, 17–18, 32, 41, 52, 54, 63, 122–23, 131–32, 134, 137–39, 142, 160, 191–92, 194–95, 197
North America, 80, 118, 121, 123

objective actuality, 41, 143–44, 172
objective freedom, 101, 107, 131
objective reality, 41, 101, 117
objective spirit, 9–11, 15, 17, 97–98, 102, 116–17, 172, 174–221, 234n5
objectivity, 22, 37, 43, 69, 77, 97–99, 101, 103, 138, 168, 170–71, 183–85, 193–94, 205, 223, 233n3
Oliver, Kelly, 231n4
one-sidedness, 4, 8, 11, 16, 22, 43, 79–80, 85–86, 89, 94–95, 103–4, 107–9, 111, 119, 133–34, 138, 155, 159, 161, 166, 168, 234n12
oppression, 5, 11–12, 17, 25, 90, 94–95, 101, 108, 136–37, 139, 154, 224, 234n10

organization: and freedom, 115, 187, 212, 217; of materiality, 15–17, 98, 128, 133, 172, 176, 183, 189; self-, 109, 115, 201; social, 4, 17, 22, 68, 99, 120, 173; of space, 120, 123, 128, 176; and the state, 211–12, 218, 220; of the struggle, 154
"Oriental" realm, 79, 91, 108
other, the, 29–36, 41–42, 46–47, 50, 57–58, 62–63, 65–67, 109, 149, 159, 168, 231n4, 232n12
otherness, 35, 46, 57–67, 72, 92

pairing: of body and world, 48, 52, 126, 177, 197; of individual and world, 11, 16, 40, 42, 74, 97, 157, 161, 176–77, 184, 192–96; as method, 6, 8, 11; with objects, 126, 157, 189, 193
palimpsests, 50, 105
Paquette, Gabriel, 233n3
Parekh, Serena, 233n3
parents, 34, 40, 57–58, 76, 82, 88, 167
parochialism, 129, 131–32, 134
particularity, 12, 17, 42, 53–55, 61, 74, 79, 95, 98–99, 103, 116, 122, 133, 142, 164, 167, 172, 179, 183, 193, 202, 207–10, 213, 218–20, 234nn8–9, 238n16
partridgeberry jam, 36
perception, 28, 40, 45, 77, 87, 90, 144–45, 197, 224; racist, 12, 42–45, 49–55, 127, 223; sexist, 6, 71; white, 50, 52–55
perspective: of the child, 58–59, 64–65; of conscience, 144–45, 148–49, 156; of the I, 26, 31, 39, 112, 166–67, 180–81, 184–86, 204–5, 221; of the other, 26–42, 45–47, 49–50, 53, 58–59, 72; suppression of, 12, 47, 51, 55, 72; of the whole, 200–201, 204, 217–22
phenomenology, 18, 71, 155, 231n8
philosophy, 1–9, 14–15, 44, 77, 79, 87–92, 96–97, 110, 118, 129, 139, 155, 164–65, 167–72, 175, 216, 231n10, 232n16
Pinkard, Terry, 100, 110, 221, 234n12, 236n1 (chap. 4)
Pippin, Robert, 208, 233n17, 236n7
place, 3, 15, 54, 58, 119, 124, 135, 176, 184–85, 187, 191, 216
Plato, 1, 43, 88, 122, 231n7; *Apology*, 42–43, 122; *The Republic*, 88, 201, 231n7

pleasure, 60–61, 65–66, 114, 132, 204
police, 115–16, 205–6, 208, 217, 219
pornography, 56, 66
porosity, 32, 41–42, 44–45, 50–51, 86–87
poverty, 6, 113–15, 205–9, 221, 234n9
practico-inert, 17, 204–5, 237n11
principles, 21–22, 36, 68, 71–72, 78–80, 86, 90, 95–96, 100–102, 105, 107–11, 118–21, 129–31, 134, 137–40, 142, 148–52, 154–70, 223, 232n16
property, 68, 122, 123–24, 126–28, 131, 172, 191, 209, 212
purity, 144, 146–47, 161, 180

rabbles, 102, 114–16, 234n9
race, 6, 25, 47, 53, 121–22, 127, 160
racialization, 45, 47, 49–55, 128
racism, 6–7, 12, 25, 42–57, 72–73, 121, 127, 162–63, 223, 233n3
Rankine, Claudia, 152
rationality, 9–10, 17, 21, 22, 24–25, 55, 69, 76–78, 100, 102, 105, 121, 125, 164, 168, 187, 211, 213, 215, 218, 234n11, 235n14
Ravven, Heidi Miriam, 232n14
Rawlinson, Mary, 70–71, 234n6
reality, 8, 18–19, 21–22, 28, 31–33, 37–38, 40–41, 43, 46–47, 58–62, 64, 67–68, 74, 90, 107, 119–20, 140, 143, 155, 161, 165, 168, 170–72, 177, 182, 186, 208, 213, 223–24
reason, 1, 22, 24, 55, 76–77, 80, 88, 106, 110, 229nn1–2 (intro.), 230n5, 234n11
recognition, 9–10, 17, 27–73, 110, 128, 131, 172–73, 175, 180, 185, 209, 217, 231nn1–2, 231nn6–7; dependence on, 26, 36, 61, 76, 187, 223; desire for, 114, 207; of determinacy, 137, 150; failures of, 12, 42, 45, 231n4; free, 41–42, 57, 61; of human as such, 137; of individuality, 112–14, 116–17, 206–8, 213, 221; and law, 211, 219; of the mother, 60; mutual, 4; norm of, 11; relations of, 14, 40, 43, 61; social reality of, 12, 71, 73, 76, 233n17. *See also* misrecognition
regulations, 15, 176–77, 184, 186, 189, 212–15, 221
relations, 4, 11, 12–18, 25, 35–36, 40, 42–43, 45, 50, 56–57, 60–63, 65–67, 69, 72–73, 87–88, 90, 108, 116–17, 119, 124, 127–28, 130–33, 143–44, 150–52, 154, 156, 158, 160, 165, 180, 183, 189, 192, 198, 223–24, 235n18, 236n2 (chap. 4), 237n5; between master and servant, 10, 33, 180
relativism, 134, 163
religion, 14–15, 92, 96–97, 102, 139, 164–65, 167–69, 171–72, 212
Republic, The (Plato), 88, 201, 231n7
resistance, 5, 30, 131–33, 158, 160
responsibility, 23, 66, 81–82, 86, 116, 137, 143–45, 156–57, 161–62, 191, 204; of civil society, 205–8
rights, 22, 89, 115, 122, 126, 130, 131, 138, 151–52, 156, 160, 163, 205, 214, 235n15
"Roman" realm, 79, 108
Roman world, 14, 91, 100, 118
Rooney, Phyllis, 229n1 (intro.)
Rubin, Gayle, 5
Russon, John, 105, 137–38, 167, 232n14, 233n1, 234n12, 237n6

sadism, 65–66
Saito, Kohei, 206
Saner, Senem, 184
Sartre, Jean-Paul, 185, 197–204, 231n2, 234n11, 237nn10–11
satisfaction, 37, 40, 59, 66, 102, 114, 134, 166, 181–83, 202, 207, 232n12; of need, 115, 174, 187, 201–2, 204, 220
science, 102, 122, 138; philosophical, 188, 221
Scientific Revolution, 138–39
scyborgs, 119–20
self-consciousness, 21, 29, 31, 33, 46, 51, 57, 76, 78–79, 90, 101, 183, 196, 231n12, 234n9; independence and dependence of, 39, 56, 73, 76, 231–32n12; and life, 31, 125; moral, 117; and others, 44–47; pure, 31, 39, 47, 49, 181; and recognition, 39, 43–47, 61, 136; and the servant, 38–39; and thinghood, 36, 47, 49, 181; and the universal, 68–69, 230n9
self-interest, 14, 101, 103, 114, 116, 136, 147, 196, 205, 207, 218, 232n12
self-understanding, 96–97, 102, 105, 126, 128, 172
sensation, 177–79, 236n3 (chap. 5), 237n5

Serequeberhan, Tsenay, 233n3
servant, 10, 33, 35–39, 47–48, 177, 180–83, 189
servitude, 33–34, 37–38, 180–82, 231n1, 231n3
"settler, native, slave" triad, 121, 126–28
settler colonialism, 13, 118–28
settler technologies, 13, 120–28
settlers, 106, 119–28, 235nn17–18
sexism, 5, 12, 25, 57, 63–72, 76, 95, 153, 196, 223
sexual difference, 68–70, 87
sexuality and sexual relations, 6, 56, 61, 65–67, 122
Siep, Ludwig, 93, 237n14
Simms, Eva M., 58
Simpson, Audra, 56
singularity, 69, 98–99, 103, 234n8, 237n16
slavery, 121, 126–27, 152–53, 160, 234n9
society, 76, 113, 152, 154, 156, 159, 208; civil (*see* civil society); and family, 69, 81–82; Greek, 68, 71
Socrates, 42–43, 122, 201, 215, 231n7
solidarity, 125, 148, 154–55, 159, 160, 200, 204, 208
Sophocles, 80, 83–84
soul, 46, 56, 80, 171, 236n4 (chap. 5), 237n5; and body, 174, 177–80, 193, 236n4 (chap. 5); feeling, 177–79; natural, 177
soul-body, 177–79, 193
space, 2, 15–16, 45, 51–53, 76, 91, 96–97, 112, 120, 126, 135, 174–76, 184–85, 187, 189, 195, 197, 212, 215; in settler colonialism, 122–24, 127–28; white, 53–54
specificity, 10, 13, 15, 24, 42–43, 61, 98, 103, 110, 145–46, 148, 158, 164, 167, 187, 195, 211
spirit, 21, 71, 73, 76–78, 101, 105, 139, 141, 148, 155, 159, 166, 172, 202, 213, 229n2 (intro.), 230n5, 230n11, 233n3, 236n6; absolute, 10, 14–15, 96–97, 102, 104–5, 164–73, 175, 217; objective, 9–11, 15, 17, 97–98, 102, 116–17, 172, 174–221, 234n5
spirituality, 69, 92, 115, 124, 135, 152, 165, 169, 172, 233n3
Spivak, Gayatri Chakravorty, 151
state, 10, 17, 68–70, 85, 102, 112–13, 116, 126, 152, 154, 163, 186, 197, 201–2, 204–20; settler and, 122, 126–27, 130
Stone, Alison, 233n3
stories, 46, 50, 106, 169–70, 172
struggle, 34, 55, 69, 101, 110, 154; to the death, 10, 27–32, 34, 36, 39, 125, 180, 231n1, 231n3
Styres, Sandra, 124
subjectivity: absence of, 233n3; and decision, 237–38n16; and freedom, 86, 95, 99, 101, 103, 108, 112, 116, 210, 214; of government, 212, 214, 221; modern, 20, 87, 107–10, 154, 161, 165, 171, 234n12; moral, 116–17; and objectivity, 99, 185, 193; self-destruction of, 116, 118–20, 125, 157, 171; support of, 111, 117, 151, 157, 201, 205, 237n5
subordination, 13, 34, 37, 54, 90, 119, 132–34, 182, 189, 192
Sultan, Hannah, 235n20
symbolization, 60, 65–66

technologies, 8, 89, 92, 105, 111, 113, 138, 192, 203; settler, 13, 120–28
ternary relations, 73, 224
Terror, the, 23, 229n2 (chap. 1)
things, 16, 49–51, 80, 97–99, 112, 122, 124–26, 157, 166, 174, 176–77, 180–84, 186–89, 191–94, 221; and master and servant, 31, 35–36, 38–41, 48
thinking, 3–4, 8, 11, 19–22, 25, 33, 44, 52, 70, 75–80, 83, 86, 88–90, 97, 105–8, 129, 141, 152, 165–66, 199–201, 208–11, 214–16
Thompson, Michael J., 198
Tibebu, Teshale, 233n3
time, 37, 53–54, 72, 76, 78, 91–97, 101–13, 117, 119–20, 128, 145, 149, 156, 159, 169, 177, 198, 210–12, 216–17, 224
tmix^w, 124
tools, 33, 38, 57, 60, 83, 87, 89, 126, 142, 181–82, 205
traces, 88, 96, 146–47, 150, 186
traditions, 1–8, 56, 64, 74, 86–87, 89, 91, 104, 111, 126, 131–34, 156, 158, 161, 174
tragedy, 169–70; Greek, 170–71; modern, 170–71
transcendence, 3–4, 15, 46, 55, 79, 83, 95, 108, 167–68, 185, 216, 231n10, 238n16

transformation, 14, 38, 50, 54, 66, 82, 94, 100–101, 105–6, 118, 129, 143, 151, 165–66, 170–72, 181, 185, 195
transparency, 76–77, 164
truth, 3, 6–7, 19, 37, 44–45, 54, 62, 78–79, 87–88, 97, 101, 103–4, 112, 138, 152, 154, 165–71, 214, 224, 232n13; of self-certainty, 29, 36–37
Tuck, Eve, 123, 126–27, 235n17, 235n20

understanding, 53, 76, 100, 107, 155, 178, 188, 212; self-, 96–97, 102, 105, 126, 128, 172; shared, 20, 134
universal, the, 7, 10, 14, 22–25, 68–71, 80, 90, 91, 93, 97, 99–100, 103, 136–37, 145–46, 148, 158–59, 161, 165, 167–68, 170, 178, 188–89, 202, 207–20, 229n1 (chap. 1), 230nn7–9
universal family, 115, 205–6
universal freedom, 23–24, 230n9, 232n16, 237n12, 238n16
universal humanity, 7, 10, 25, 137–38
universal spirit, 165, 169
universal thought, 22, 23, 25, 229n1 (chap. 1)
universalism, 150, 215

value, 10, 37, 39, 51, 55, 72, 74, 80, 90–92, 99, 108–9, 112, 114, 119, 122–24, 130–36, 144–45, 153, 159, 165, 170, 198, 209, 211, 232n12
valuing, 20, 30–31, 40, 64, 103
violence, 34, 72, 137, 163, 236n3 (chap. 4); colonial, 13, 72, 79, 126–27, 135, 152–54, 158–59, 161; non-, 154

virtues, 100, 106, 136
von der Luft, Eric, 101, 234n12
vulnerability, 2, 11, 30, 34, 38, 41–42, 45, 47, 50, 57, 63, 67, 84, 86, 115, 117, 148, 153, 185, 196, 203, 205–8, 217, 221

wealth, 6, 16, 114–16, 121, 136, 153, 163, 204, 207–8, 221, 234n9
West, the, 3, 5, 13, 53, 63, 86, 90–92, 107, 109, 111, 119, 129–31, 135, 141, 150, 161–62, 234n12; and colonialism, 20, 87, 89–90, 103, 136, 150–51, 153, 158, 162–63, 229n1 (intro.)
whiteness, 6, 7, 45–56, 63, 91, 95, 123, 126, 128, 152, 235n18
will, 46, 126, 174, 181, 183–85, 188–89, 211, 233n3; rational, 188, 211–12
Williams, Robert R., 231n2
wisdom, 9, 68, 84–85, 103
Witt, Charlotte, 229n1 (intro.)
women, 5, 56–57, 61, 63–65, 67–71, 132–36, 163, 192, 232n16
Wood, Allen, 100, 188
work. *See* labor
worship, 134, 147, 171
Wynter, Sylvia, 167, 229n1 (intro.), 236n4 (chap. 4)

Yang, K. Wayne, 123, 126, 235n17
Young, Iris Marion, 196

Zambrana, Rocío, 7, 233n3
Zinga, Dawn, 124

Printed and bound by CPI Group (UK) Ltd, Croydon, CR0 4YY
08/04/2026

14857418-0003